Comment on a controversial and startling book:

FROM THE NORTH

"Dr. Otto Eisenschiml is the author of seven previous books on the Civil War. Most of them have been both provocative and important. This present volume is no exception...most stimulating to student of the Civil War. Many of his evaluations will be severely criticized but no reader is likely to label this a dull book"
Boston Herald

"Otto Eisenschiml is back at the craft at which he is master. The author has style, is never dull and, we suspect, is often right"
The New York Times

FROM THE SOUTH

"Provocative and informing, so radically different from the text books that blood pressures will rise in many quarters...food for thought —if we keep our tempers in check"
Birmingham News

"Rich in material...Shocking, highly controversial...Will cause furious debates everywhere. It will not be ignored"
Montgomery Journal

By OTTO EISENSCHIML

Why the Civil War?
Why Was Lincoln Murdered?
The Story of Shiloh
The Celebrated Case of Fitz John Porter
(editor)   *Vermont General*
(with E. B. Long)   *As Luck Would Have It*
(with Ralph Newman)   *The American Iliad*

Charter Books represent a new venture in publishing. They offer at paperback prices a set of modern masterworks, printed on high quality paper with sewn bindings in hardback size and format.

THE HIDDEN FACE OF THE CIVIL WAR

OTTO EISENSCHIML

Charter Books

CHARTER BOOKS
Published by
THE BOBBS-MERRILL COMPANY, INC.
A subsidiary of HOWARD W. SAMS & CO., INC.
Publishers   Indianapolis and New York

Distributed by the Macfadden-Bartell Corp., Inc.,
205 East 42nd Street, New York 17, New York

*

Unless you are interested in the truth about the Civil War, do not read this book. It may shock you.

Unfortunately, our knowledge of the greatest war fought on American soil rests on shaky foundations, because some of the very people who helped chart its course also helped to pollute the sources from which its history must be written. They have distorted important events, suppressed others. General William Tecumseh Sherman in his Memoirs *remarked cynically that "the truth is not always palatable, and should not always be told."[1] General George Gordon Meade, the victor of Gettysburg, was still more outspoken, when he declared, "I don't believe the truth will ever be known, and I have great contempt for History."[2]*

Nor can the statesmen of the Lincoln era be trusted. One may read in the biography of Senator Zachariah Chandler of Michigan that "the secret history of these days . . . concealing many startling revelations, has yet been sparingly written; it is doubtful if the veil will ever be more than slightly lifted." His colleague, Senator Benjamin F. Wade of Ohio who, like Chandler, was an influential member of the Committee on the Conduct of the War and possessed much inside information, admitted to a reporter that "If I tell the whole truth, I shall blast too many reputations."[3] An Ohio Congressman named Albert Gallatin Riddle, who was close to the War Department, asserted brazenly that "the secret history of the Provost Marshall General's office . . . never can be written, perhaps never should be."[4]

Another obstacle to the dissemination of historical truth was pointed out by Donn Piatt, a contemporary Northern soldier, diplomat and author. "History ... as a pleasant fiction," he observed, "is more acceptable than a naked fact, and ... the historian shapes his ware ... to suit the customers."[5] This caustic comment was made more than seventy years ago. It could just as well be made today.

Abraham Lincoln was strongly opposed to these devious practices, and looked with scorn at all those who shunned truthful reporting. "History is not history, unless it is the truth," he wrote to his law partner William Herndon in 1856. I have tried to compose this book in conformity with Lincoln's doctrine. If you, too, conform to it, you are invited to read it. Before you do so, however, I suggest that you shed all preconceived opinions, and let yourself be guided solely by the evidence, as it will evolve through the unbiased judgment of the test tube.

*

THE argument has been advanced that only professional soldiers are qualified to criticize military operations. This argument may apply to technical details, but the over-all policies of big business—and war is big business—are not determined by technicians; they are determined by those who see the picture as a whole. It was a French statesman who coined the maxim that "war is much too important to be left to generals." In the Civil War, as in all modern wars, much of the successful over-all planning originated in the minds of men who had received no military training at all. In the Second World War even this writer, who never served in the armed forces, was able to submit a modest idea, which was immediately accepted by the then Under Secretary of War Robert Patterson, in a personal interview.

In writing this critical study, I have tried, so far as it is humanly possible, to observe the strictest impartiality; I have avoided second-guessing and restricted my criticisms to what could have been foreseen at the time. I have shunned the citations of latter-day "authorities," because usually an equal number holding the opposite view could be cited in rebuttal.

The book does not cover the entire Civil War, but only some of its outstanding facets. In many instances I have disliked what I found; but, while I agree with Sherman that the truth is not always palatable, I disagree emphatically with his dictum that it should not be told.

OTTO EISENSCHIML

Contents

*

Contents

LIST OF MAPS

BOOK

I

NORTHERN
OVER-ALL STRATEGY

CHAPTER

➤➤➤ 1 ◄◄◄

THE BLOCKADE AND
FOREIGN DIPLOMACY

"CIVIL WAR BURST upon the United States with about the suddenness of the meteor's glare," a contemporary observer wrote in
the flowery style of his day.[1] In more prosaic terms he might have
said that the outbreak of the war found both North and South
mentally unprepared for what was in store for them. Few had believed the conflict inevitable, and almost no one believed that, if it
should come, it would drag on for four years; the majority
expected it to last no longer than two or three months. General
Winfield Scott, head of the United States Army and veteran
of two wars, even thought that, despite Lincoln's call to arms,
peace could be restored in short order without much, if any, actual
fighting.

Lincoln was one of the few who did not share the prevailing
optimism,[2] and prudently gave consideration to the possibility of a
prolonged struggle. Acting on this assumption, he decided that the
situation required all-embracing long-range planning. This in-

cluded a great many subjects and would take time; nevertheless, one important measure could be instigated at once, and that was a sealing up of the Confederate ports. Without delay, only four days after calling out the militia, he declared a blockade in effect. It was the first basic step, also the most important single one taken by the North during the entire war. It contributed more to the downfall of the seceded states than Robert E. Lee's defeat at Gettysburg, Sherman's march to the sea, or any other notable event on land. The Union could afford to lose battles or campaigns, but so long as the blockade was rigidly enforced, the South was bound to lose in the end. Depriving the enemy of the wherewithals to fight was the surest road to peace. Measured by any yardstick, the blockade takes first place among the factors which led to the collapse of the Confederacy.

In whose mind the idea of the blockade originated is uncertain, but the closing of Confederate harbors was discussed by the Cabinet as early as April 15, the day after the surrender of Fort Sumter. Strangely enough, no record of this all-important meeting is known to exist, but it may be assumed that Edward Bates, Lincoln's Attorney General, broached the subject, as is shown by an entry in his diary on that day:

April 15. Memo: of E Bates in Cabinet[.]
Now that we are at open war, it is my opinion . . . that the Southern ports, at least from Charleston to New Orleans, ought to be closed at once. . . .[3]

To close a multitude of harbors and inlets with the scant means then on hand seemed nothing short of farcical, and quite understandably was laughed at in the South. The United States fleet at that time consisted of 90 ships, of which only 42 were in commission, and nearly all of these were in foreign ports. In January 1861 the only warship on the Atlantic coast was the steam frigate *Brooklyn,* and she, having just reached home after a three-year cruise, was badly in want of repairs. Matters had not changed greatly by April. Quick augmentation of the fleet therefore was imperative, not only to make the measure effective, but also to prove that it was not a paper blockade which, according to international law, need not be respected by other countries. Lincoln was aware of the urgency, and ordered the commandants of all navy yards to hurry the purchase and equipment of suitable vessels, while warships in foreign ports were hastily recalled.

How clearly Lincoln realized the necessity for speed is shown by a private memorandum he wrote for himself on July 23, 1861, two days after the Northern defeat at Bull Run. At a moment when generals were confused and civilians panicky, the President calmly put on paper nine steps that he thought should be taken. Significantly, the first on his list was that the blockade "be pushed forward with all possible despatch."[4]

As might have been expected, the blockade did not hit its full stride immediately, and for a year or so did not materially hamper Southern ocean trade. Cotton, tobacco and naval stores passed out freely through the thin line of Federal ships. Over the return route rifles, gunpowder and other war impedimenta from Europe reached Confederate ports in substantial quantities. Gradually, however, the noose tightened. By July 1861 the blockading fleet already consisted of 42 steamers, by December the number had doubled,[5] and as a result, fear of capture had reduced the number of Confederate ships in transatlantic service from 6,000 to about 1,000.[6] At the end of the war no less than 600 Federal warships would bar the way to incoming or outgoing blockade-runners,[7] and only one out of two of these would escape the watchful Union fleet.[8] In this manner, the Confederacy was being paralyzed through slow starvation, both in the literal and the broader sense of the word.

Despite prophetic warnings by his legal adviser Bates, and by Gideon Welles, the Secretary of the Navy, Lincoln did not close the Southern ports, as both had recommended, but ordered them blockaded. Bates protested vigorously, and explained the difference between blockading and closing. "Blockade," he wrote later, "*is an act of war,* which a nation *cannot* commit against itself. . . . The President . . . had the power . . . *to close the ports.* In that case anyone trying to . . . bring in goods can be punished only as a smuggler. But the attempt to break [the] blockade works a forfeiture of ships and cargo . . . and . . . imperils our relations with neutrals."[9]

Welles's arguments complemented those of his colleague. A year and a half afterward he declared that "there ought to have never been a blockade. . . . I had taken that view at the commencement, but had been overruled." He then pointed out that much more was involved than the irritation of neutrals. "We had placed ourselves in a wrong position at the beginning, made the Rebels belligerents, given them nationality—an error and anomaly."[10] Welles and Bates were right: the President had seriously blundered in not heeding the counsel of the two members of his Cabinet who were well informed on international law. England and France also knew the rules and, since they were not averse to see the United States being split in two, must have been amazed by Lincoln's ill-considered action. Before Charles Francis Adams, the newly appointed minister to the Court of St. James, set foot on British soil, England had conceded to the Confederacy the status of a belligerent, thus giving it important rights, to which otherwise it would not have been entitled. True, Lord John Russell, England's Foreign Secretary, had only proclaimed England's neutrality, but his meaning was made clear in a letter to Lord Richard Lyons, the British Ambassador to the United States, in which he explained that the South must be recognized as a belligerent.[11] Closing the Southern ports would have fully served the purpose Lincoln had in view; but in that case marked advantages would have accrued to the North. The Confederate States would have been considered in a state of rebellion, their privateers been declared pirates, and as such denied the use of neutral ports for coaling and repairs. Without these facilities they could not have successfully operated, Northern victory would have come much sooner, and the United States would have been spared many diplomatic difficulties and severe material damage, both during the war and afterward.

Before the harmful consequences of the President's injudiciousness became apparent, its backwash swept him into a sea of trouble. His proclamation had declared the blockade to be "in pursuance of the law of nations." By this was meant the Declaration of Paris, which the United States had not signed. In an attempt to correct this inconsistency, Lincoln's Secretary of State, William Henry Seward, informed Lord Lyons that the government had changed its mind and now had decided to become a party to the agreement. This turnabout only aggravated matters. A belated signing of the Declaration, Lyons explained, would signify recognition of the seceded states as an independent nation; furthermore, it would bind only the North, while the Confederacy would still be free to issue letters of marque to privateers.[12]

Lincoln and Seward were in a dilemma. The application for membership was on its way and could not be recalled. This did not worry Seward, who knew many devious ways to avoid being cornered. On this occasion he got out of his predicament by a clever stratagem. To all outward appearances he remained anxious to sign the Declaration, but assigned the details to his foreign ministers, to whom he gave secret instructions to dawdle.[13] They did, and the issue died from malnutrition. As to the anomalous blockade order, he depended on Lincoln to talk himself out of it, knowing that the President was a genius in the use of words. In his message to Congress on July 4, 1861, Lincoln undertook this unpleasant duty. "A proclamation was issued for closing the ports," he said, ". . . by proceedings in the nature of a blockade." It was a clumsy retraction, but to explain the inexplicable was a task which overtaxed even the President's ingenuity.

The price which the country eventually had to pay for Lincoln's mistake was the virtual loss of its entire merchant marine. This development was brought about by an act of the Confederate President, which led to catastrophic consequences. On April 17, 1861, two days after Lincoln's call for troops, Jefferson Davis invited applications for letters of marque, which granted the owners of suitable vessels the right of privateering. "Soon a small fleet . . . hovered on the coast of the Northern States," he wrote gleefully, "capturing and destroying their vessels, and filling the enemy with consternation."[14]

The initial success of privateering did not long continue, and it never became a big factor in the war, partly because not enough ships were available, and partly because prizes could not be taken into neutral harbors. Another handicap was that important home ports soon fell into enemy hands. Soon, however, the Confederate maritime offensive was taken out of amateurish hands and entrusted to professional talent, whereupon it became a real menace. The man selected to take over its direction was a former sea captain named James Dunwody Bulloch. His task was to go abroad and replace privateers with powerful warships which he was to buy or have built to order. The first of these vessels, the *Sumter,* was commissioned in the spring of 1861, and was followed in 1862 by the *Florida* and *Alabama*. These ships became roving seawolves and a terror to Northern shipping. If their number could have been sufficiently increased, and their armament made superior to that of the blockading vessels, the blockade could have been broken. By the spring of 1863 things looked hopeful for the Confederacy. Bulloch had several rams under construction, both in England and France, and they were almost ready for delivery. Then came the news of Gettysburg and Vicksburg, whereupon the attitude of the two foreign governments changed abruptly. Under one pretext or another they withheld the rams from the Confederacy and sold them to other European powers.[15]

Unfortunately for the North and South alike, by that time irreparable damage had been done to American shipping. Marine insurance rates had been driven to such dizzy heights that only neutral bottoms could be used profitably for ocean transportation. Rather than let American ships rot in dock, they were sold. While in 1860 the American merchant marine had boasted a fleet of ocean-going vessels totaling close to 6,000,000 tons, all that was left of it four years later was a trifle over 1,000,000 tons, and that mostly scrap.[16] In July 1865 Admiral David Dixon Porter sadly admitted to the *New York Herald* that the American merchant marine had almost ceased to exist. Fifty years later Seward's son Frederick William, who had served as Assistant Secretary of State under Lincoln, Johnson and Hayes, mourned the fact that the American merchant marine had not yet recovered from the blow it had suffered during the Civil War.[17]

In order to draw a tight ring around the seceded states it was not enough to close the Atlantic and Gulf seaports, as imports could still come in from Mexico; in addition, the comparatively tranquil, fertile trans-Mississippi territory could furnish abundant provisions to the war-ridden eastern states. The closing of the Mississippi, which would put a stop to this interstate trade, had to be left to the future and, due to shortsightedness of the high command for which Lincoln was not blameless, would not be brought about until July 1863. As to Mexico, Lincoln managed to cripple her European imports on the grounds of "continuous voyage." It was a device contrived by the British during the Napoleonic wars, and stipulated that products carried by neutral ships from one neutral port to another were subject to confiscation, provided it could be shown that their ultimate destination was an enemy country. Lincoln established a precedent by approving the seizure of a British merchant ship on her voyage to Matamoros, followed it up consistently, and so managed to minimize the number of foreign cargoes which reached Mexican ports.

Of course, goods indigenous to Mexico were not affected by the blockade. Copper, lead, saltpeter, powder, cattle, mules and coarse cotton fabrics continued to flow across the Rio Grande, in spite of Northern efforts to stop this traffic by diplomatic means. Most of these goods, though, benefited only the western part of Texas;[18] long distances, bad roads and lack of transports made reshipping to other parts of the Confederacy impracticable, and after the fall of Vicksburg, impossible.

While the sea blockade never became complete, the quantity of imports into the South steadily dwindled, as one of her harbors after another passed into Northern hands. The fall of Wilmington, the last of the lot, in January 1865, sounded the death knell of large-scale blockade-running, and with it that of the Confederacy.

For the part which the blockade played in the course of the war,

Lincoln must be given the lion's share of the credit. He had wasted no time in ordering it, had seen that it was properly executed and had pursued it to the bitter end. The blockade was vital to the victorious outcome of the war. It may well be argued that if the sea lanes had been kept open, the Confederacy would not have been defeated.

To maintain the blockade in continued operation was not solely a matter of sufficient ships and constant vigilance; it also required the adroit handling of foreign diplomacy, a field in which Lincoln was a complete novice. The blockade was not to the liking of some European countries, and was especially obnoxious to England and France, who depended on Southern cotton for their vast textile industries. The danger Lincoln had to guard against was that, when and if the cotton shortage abroad should assume a ruinous aspect, British and French war vessels might reopen traffic with the Confederate ports by armed force. Against their combined fleets the Northern navy would be powerless; nor could Lincoln afford a foreign war while fighting one on domestic soil.

The President therefore was confronted by two major problems. The first and most important was to prevent foreign interference with the blockade, by friendly diplomacy if possible, by bold threats if necessary; the second and no less essential one was how to sow discord between England and France, so as to keep them from acting in unison.

On the surface it looked as if in this diplomatic game the two principal foreign powers held all the high cards; but there was a joker in the deck, and it was in Lincoln's hands. While still President-elect he had been informed of a hint dropped by the

Russian minister to the United States, that his country was willing to aid the Washington government, should it be menaced by England and France.[19] The Czar's promise was not based on friendship, but on self-interest, which made it that much more trustworthy. Russia was yet smarting under its recent defeat in the Crimean war, and now and then threw a greedy glance in the direction of India, the most precious of the British crown jewels. Whenever this happened, the Queen's government trembled. Lincoln recognized the potency of the Czar's offer, and throughout the war made use of it with the skill of a professional poker player.

With Russia to back him up, Lincoln entered the diplomatic arena boldly. Never did his native wit shine to better advantage, nor was it ever employed more profitably. Since he could not match European diplomats in experience, he perplexed them with unorthodox tactics. For this purpose he and his wily Secretary of State assumed sharply divergent roles. Seward was to act the crude, reckless American, who cared not what he said or what language he used; but after his buffoonery had produced the desired effect, the President would step in and pour oil on the troubled waters. Seward played his part to perfection. Before he was warm in his post, he threatened in turn to make war on Spain, France and England, horrifying and bewildering them, but he was always restrained by some invisible strings before he had gone too far.

During the first months of the new Administration an accidental circumstance strengthened the hands of the Lincoln-Seward team. William Russell, a roving correspondent of the *London Times,* was then sojourning in Washington. He proved a godsend to the two American statesmen, who employed him time and again to convey unofficial messages of an explosive character to the British authorities. On March 27, Seward took supper with the English journalist and made the preposterous statement that no foreign power had the right even to mention the Civil War, although it seemed imminent. With crescendo audacity he then declared that if the British government received Confederate emissaries, though only informally, or accepted documents from them, it would risk severance of relations with the United States. But when the flustered Russell returned to his hotel, he found there an invitation to dine with the President on the following night.[20] At the reception and dinner Lincoln was geniality itself, and did not say one word about the subject which had so alarmed his guest the night before.[21]

A week later Russell had another interview with Seward, and was given a different kind of shock treatment. This time he was told at great length how weak the new Administration was, due to treacherous acts of former Cabinet members. One of them had purposely scattered the navy, and another had shipped arms in large lots to the Southern states. On top of all this erosion of Federal striking power, naval and military officers were resigning *en masse,* and forts with their garrisons were being surrendered all over the South. These untoward conditions notwithstanding, Seward cautioned Russell that if Britain were to recognize the Confederate government, the United States was ready to go to war with its motherland.[22] When the Englishman got home he speculated in his diary whether Seward's exotic behavior was a sign of strength, or empty bombast.[23] Secretly he may even have doubted the Secretary's sanity.

On July 4, after his return from a trip through the seceded states, Russell received a shock of a new kind. The United States, he was told, bitterly resented that England had conceded the status of belligerency to the Confederacy. In fact, the Washington government felt so outraged by this unfriendly act that it would not shrink from a war between the two countries, which would "wrap the world in fire," but in which England was sure to get the worst of it.[24]

Seward's outburst left Russell speechless. "I could not but admire the confidence—may I say the coolness?—" he wrote, "of the statesman who . . . spoke so fearlessly of war with a Power which could have blotted out the paper blockade . . . in a few hours, and, in conjunction with the Southern armies, have repeated the occupation and destruction of the Capital."[25]

When the British diplomats received Russell's report, they may have suspected that Seward's bellicose attitude was only a gigantic bluff, but if so, they did not dare call it.

Lincoln and Seward hid the secret of their teamwork so well that they even hoodwinked Henry Brooks Adams, son of the American minister in London. In June 1861 he wrote to his brother that "a dispatch arrived yesterday from Seward, so arrogant . . . and so . . . unparalleled in its demand, that it leaves no doubt in my mind . . . the Washington government means to have war with England. . . ." War with England was the last thing the Washington team wanted, but Lincoln and Seward must have been gratified to note that they were doing their play-acting so convincingly.

On November 8 of that year an unexpected difficulty arose through the unauthorized action of Charles Wilkes, commander of the warship *San Jacinto,* who stopped the British mailboat *Trent* and forcibly removed from her two Confederate emissaries, James M. Mason and John Slidell. This defiance of British sovereignty endangered the efforts of his government to keep the British Cabinet in leash. Excitement in England ran high, and war appeared inevitable. This time Lincoln had luck on his side. Prince

Albert, the royal consort, died just then and left behind him an urgent request to keep the peace. Public feeling changed with surprising rapidity, but not before the Queen had declared an embargo on war materials, including the indispensable saltpeter, of which England possessed a quasi-monopoly. She also dispatched 8,000 soldiers to Canada as a tangible proof that she meant business. Lincoln released the emissaries, but could not resist the temptation to inject some of his quaint humor into the picture. He invited the English soldiers to disembark at Portland, Maine, where they were welcome to make use of American train service. His offer was politely refused, but the pleasantry did no harm and probably helped to ease whatever tension still lingered.

Lincoln played his trump card, the understanding with Russia, only when he found himself in a tight corner, but when he did play it, it always took the trick. In the summer of 1862 Great Britain was beginning to feel the ravages of the long-delayed cotton shortage, and Parliament was debating intervention. Thereupon Lincoln had Seward write a private letter to John Bigelow, the American consul general in Paris, making casual mention of a Russian-American alliance, which in fact did not exist. The contents of this letter were allowed to leak out and, as if in confirmation of the rumors which were making the rounds, the Russian minister in London called on his American *confrère*.[26] Whatever conclusions European diplomats drew from these mysterious doings were sure to make Lincoln chuckle.

To nail down his victory, Lincoln made use of still another card, one which providentially had been slipped into his deck. What he did with it was so extraordinary that it has puzzled some historians to this day.

In the spring of 1862 a horde of "lawless brigands and vagabonds," serving in a Union brigade under a colonel of Russian

birth named John Basil Turchin—his real name was Ivan Vasilie-
vitch Turchininoff—had committed the "most terrible outrages
. . . robberies, rapes, arson and plunderings. . . ." So it was stated
officially by Turchin's superior, General Ormsby M. Mitchel.[27] To
aggravate the offense, the Alabama town of Athens, which the soldiers had sacked, was loyal to the Union cause. The Russian officer was court-martialed, and on August 6, having been found
guilty, was dismissed from the Army; but the verdict was mean-
ingless, for while the charges against the culprit were still pending, Lincoln had promoted him to the rank of brigadier general,
the new rank to date back to July 19.[28]

The President's reason for this amazing act is not too difficult
to guess. Turchin once had served in the Russian army; hence
Lincoln's clemency was certain to be brought to the attention of
the Czarist regime, which should be highly pleased by this am-
icable gesture. Other foreign diplomats probably saw in it an
additional confirmation of the nebulous *entente* between the
Washington and St. Petersburg governments. If so, it was all to the
good.

The situation remained critical, however, and agitation for
British intervention came so near to the boiling point that the
occupant of the White House found it advisable to play another
of his winning cards. He countered the English threat by having
a bill introduced in Congress to legalize privateering on the high
seas. England shuddered, and the motion for intervention was
withdrawn; so was the privateering bill.[29] Once more an American
ace had trumped a British queen.

The President thought of other subtle ways to keep England
from running interference for the South. He had a galaxy of
prominent Northern personages descend on the British Isles to
influence public sentiment. There was Thurlow Weed, owner of

the *Albany Journal,* well versed in European affairs, who acted as Lincoln's all-seeing, all-hearing scout.[30] The famous preacher Henry Ward Beecher orated about human rights and slavery.[31] With him in the front line were the Catholic Archbishop John Joseph Hughes and the Episcopalian Bishop Charles Pettit McIlvaine; the army was represented by General Winfield Scott,[32] high finance by Robert J. Walker, who, under President Polk, had been Secretary of the Treasury.[33] He would warn English investors that any Confederate loans would turn out to be worthless. Other propagandists of lesser caliber, such as a former slave coachman of Jefferson Davis, helped to round out the cast. Heading the players was Mr. Adams, Lincoln's dignified but skillful British minister, an ideal choice for the positon to which he had been appointed. To make the most of this impressive ensemble, two shrewd minds in Washington did the stage directing.

Lincoln and Seward did not for a moment overlook the danger of English-French co-operation, and skillfully played the two nations against each other. On one occasion Lincoln used a very simple trick to give fresh impetus to the mistrust that for centuries had existed between them. In the spring of 1862 the French minister in Washington, Henri Mercier, expressed a desire to visit Richmond, in order to check Seward's assertion that the Confederacy was on the verge of a military collapse. He was encouraged by Seward to do so, provided he would urge the secessionists to come back into the fold, in which case they would not be punished.[34] Mercier left for Richmond, but found the Confederates confident and unwilling to discuss anything but complete independence. Wisely he said very little about a peaceful surrender, and after his return to Washington so reported to Seward.[35]

Lincoln's Secretary of State now was ready to gather the fruits of his sly intrigue. He published an account of Mercier's trip in the

New York Times, in which he made the Frenchman appear as an agent of the Washington government, who had been sent south to convince the Confederates that further resistance was futile. That this was contrary to the truth did not bother Seward, for the article was sure to accomplish what he had in mind. The British diplomats would consider this tale a crude ruse, and deduce that what Mercier really had done was to steal a march on them by negotiating a commercial treaty with the Confederacy. As a result the rift between the two European powers widened,[36] much to the delight of the Washington schemers, who now made ready for their next coup. Inasmuch as England had been given something to worry about, it should be France's turn next. To please the United States, England had withdrawn her forces from Mexico, which owed money to the two European countries, and Lincoln seized the opportunity to show his displeasure at France's reluctance to do likewise. He made it plain that he did not approve of foreign troops south of the Rio Grande. His balancing act proved a success, for both powers vied with each other to get back into Lincoln's good graces. Outsiders were at a loss to explain why the British and French so frequently came close to harmony, but never quite achieved it.

Aside from driving a wedge between England and France, Lincoln tried to split them internally. To the spinning industry of Great Britain he held out the bait of early cotton shipments, and to her starving working classes he painted the war as a crusade against slavery. This picture was drawn strictly for foreign eyes, for it was flatly contradictory to his avowal at home that he had neither the power nor the inclination to interfere with slavery. There was danger in working both sides of the street, but Lincoln had seen to it that all his emissaries to Europe, official and unofficial, were known abolitionists. It was like winking an eye at the

English people to look over this selection and invite them to take his official statements on slavery with a grain of salt.

The French Emperor, who feared that the growing unemployment in his country would lead to revolution, was given a promise that the hunger of his people would be alleviated, and was persuaded that bread was more important to him than cotton. Spain, being the weakest of the trio, was treated more roughly, and some affronts of Japan, which also showed signs of aggressiveness, were ignored. What made Lincoln's tasks difficult was the recurring defeats of the Union armies. Diplomats are wont to incline toward the winning side, and so far the Confederates seemed to have had the upper hand. Some smashing victories of his generals would have saved Lincoln many a struggle in his foreign relations.

A dangerous crisis arose in the summer of 1863. Its cause was England's apparent disinclination to stop the building of Confederate cruisers. At this juncture, as if by a strange coincidence, the Russian fleet left its home waters to pay American ports a visit, which, so the Russian minister explained, had "no unfriendly purpose."[37] This time Russia's moral support was not needed, however, because the twin victories of Gettysburg and Vicksburg had come in the nick of time. All foreign governments understood their significance and formed in line to assure Washington of their devout sympathies.

England's intervention need no longer be feared for another reason. The British isles were basking in the sunshine of ever-mounting prosperity. Both American governments were spending money lavishly on all kinds of war implements. Munitions plants were humming, and cotton mills were turning out undreamed-of quantities of cloth for American soldiers. The shipbuilding industry flourished; before the war ended, 400 steamers and 800 sailing vessels would have been built to carry necessities and luxuries across the ocean. The profits of the blockade-runners ran into fantastic figures[38] and found their way into wide circles. The entire British population was profiting by this hothouse prosperity and dreaded the day when peace would return to America.

During the last two years of the war Lincoln rode high, wide and handsome on the international highway, because the days of his diplomatic troubles were over. Ably assisted by Seward, he could point to his work with justifiable pride. He had shielded the Northern armies from foreign intervention, had kept the ocean traffic lanes open for his side, while obstructing them for his opponents and, all in all, had made another valuable contribution to victory.

MILITARY PLANNING

WITH the blockade successfully launched and his foreign diplomacy firmly outlined, Lincoln gave his full attention to overall plans for the war on land. Curiously, he failed to show the same deftness and foresight in this field that he had displayed in the others. His first recorded ideas on the subject were almost puerile. On April 25, 1861, John Milton Hay, his junior secretary, wrote in his dairy that his chief proposed to punish Charleston for having taken Fort Sumter by force, thereby inaugurating Civil War: "I intend . . . to fill Fortress Monroe with men and stores, . . . provide for the entire safety of the Capital, . . . and then go down to Charleston and pay her for the little debt we are owing her."[1]

Considering the few ships and trained soldiers ready for this debt-paying expedition, it would have received a reception too hot for comfort, and probably would have returned badly crippled, if at all. Could it be that Lincoln was joking? Maybe he was. But he was in dead earnest when, a short time after the battle of Bull Run, he wrote a memorandum for himself as to what his next moves should be. Aside from the blockade, which already was in its initial stages, he contemplated seizing Manassas Junction or a near-by point on the Alexandria and Orange Railroad. The town of Strasburg also was to be occupied, for the Shenandoah Valley, in which it was located, was the path leading to Washington's back door. The lines to these places and to Harper's Ferry were to be kept open.

This done, Lincoln was considering a simultaneous movement from Cairo on Memphis, and from Cincinnati on East Tennessee,[2] while General John Charles Frémont, commanding in the West, was to push his operations as quickly as possible, giving special attention to Missouri.[3]

The seizure of Manassas Junction as an outpost was a commendable precautionary measure against an enemy attack by rail, as was that of Strasburg against attack via the Shenandoah Valley, although in less than a year Stonewall Jackson was to teach Lincoln the painful lesson that Winchester, which lay closer to the capital, would have been preferable.

No fault can be found with the President's instructions to Frémont, for Missouri was an important state, both militarily and politically; but the joint movements which he suggested were likely to fail this early in the war. A campaign from Cairo to Memphis certainly was premature, and that from Cincinnati to East Tennessee impracticable besides. The eastern part of that state, loyal to the Union cause and deserving of support for that reason, had poor roads, few towns, and for lack of food could not sustain large bodies of troops. The lateral railroad, which crossed it, could be broken at other, more accessible points.

Greater merit is due to the President's plans to use Northern superiority in manpower for simultaneous attacks on several fronts, thereby nullifying the advantage of the enemy's interior and therefore shorter lines of communications. He evidently had not forgotten that the Confederates had won the battle of Bull Run by these means. Theoretically Lincoln had logic on his side, but simultaneous movements called for well-trained troops and experienced generals, neither of whom had as yet been developed. Even three years later, when Ulysses Simpson Grant in his great spring campaign of 1864 put the President's idea into practice, he was not so successful as he had hoped, because Benjamin Franklin Butler and Franz Sigel, two of the commanding generals, bungled their assignments.

In 1861 the only man in the country who ever had commanded a sizable army was General Winfield Scott. The North looked to him for the grand strategy of the land war about to be fought.

What General Scott had in mind became known as the "Anaconda Plan." It depended mainly on a nonaggressive encirclement of the South for the purpose of subduing her by economic pressure. Lincoln had already ordered the blockade of the Confederate ports, and Scott based his calculations on its successful operation. "In connection with such blockade," he declared, "we propose a powerful movement down the Mississippi to the ocean, . . . and the capture of Forts Jackson and St. Philip" [which protected New Orleans]; "the object being to clear out and keep open this great line of communication, . . . so as to envelop the insurgent States and bring them to terms with less bloodshed than by any other plan."[4] Possession of the Mississippi was to be made secure by strongly garrisoned posts at Columbus in Kentucky, Memphis, Vicksburg, New Orleans and other suitable places.[5]

Scott foresaw one serious obstacle to his project. The masses

33

were impatient and clamored for action. They would oppose the plan, because it could not be executed until 80,000 men had been fully trained. In addition, some forty steam transports and from twelve to twenty gunboats had to be outfitted and commissioned.[6] With the exception of this unavoidable drawback the Anaconda Plan had considerable merit, although it was more of a humane and political than of a military nature and would be slow to mature. The North had no river fleet, and with both banks of the Mississippi in Confederate hands, mobile shore batteries and sharpshooters could have destroyed any venturesome Union vessels or killed their crews. Eighteen months later the Confederate General Richard Taylor reported that these conditions had not changed much, that light Federal gunboats were helpless against his field guns, and that even heavily armored ironclads, which had not been fully developed in 1861, were threatened by his riflemen, protected as they were by the timber and levees along the Southern streams.[7] So long as river transportation was uncertain, Federal posts on its shores stood in danger of being cut off and their garrisons made prisoners. Even after the Mississippi had passed into Union hands from Cairo to New Orleans, and the Confederacy had been weakened by severe losses, complete domination of the great river was not immediately achieved. In December 1863 General Sherman complained that the "Rebels" still threatened navigation on the Mississippi, and received permission from Grant to prevent further molestation by striking at the Confederates from the east, while General Nathaniel Prentiss Banks would assail them from the opposite side.[8] What was difficult to accomplish late in 1863 would have been impossible two and a half years earlier.

Humanely, the Anaconda Plan promised an almost bloodless conflict, for it entailed no invasion of the seceded states. They in turn had neither the incentive nor the strength to wage an aggressive war. Politically, Scott's plan was nearly ideal, for it allowed time for overheated tempers to cool, and so opened the possibility for a peaceful re-establishment of the Union.

Scott elucidated his ideas to the President in blunt words: "If you will maintain a strict blockade on the sea-coast, . . . and send a force down the Mississippi strong enough to open and keep it free . . . to its mouth, you will thus cut off the luxuries to which the people are accustomed; and when they feel this pressure, not having been exasperated by attacks made on them, . . . the Union spirit will assert itself, . . . and I will guarantee that in one year from this time all difficulties will be settled. But if you invade the South . . . I will guarantee that at the end of a year you will be further from a settlement than you are now."[9]

In making these predictions the aging general showed good sense, spiced with the curious supposition that, inasmuch as the luxury-loving planters had led the secession movement, they could best be induced to reverse themselves by being disturbed in their easy and luxurious living. With strange prescience of the ordeals which George Brinton McClellan, his successor, was to undergo by following his principles, he wrote that "it is more glorious to win a sure success, without a single reverse, by waiting until our . . . preparations are perfected, than to plunge into the midst of dangers, . . . intending by . . . courage and energy to rise above them."[10]

Scott was right in apprehending that his proposal would carry scant popular appeal. People were not satisfied with anything but a quick victory, which to them meant the capture of the enemy capital, as it has meant to people in all wars before and since. This was something they could understand, something they thought spelled the end. They would not learn until much later that the defeat of the Confederate Army, not the occupation of Richmond, was the real target. Over Scott's strenuous objections Lincoln bowed to political expediency and ordered an immediate offensive. On the day when a Union army marched to the field of Bull Run, the Anaconda plan died. It was never revived in its original form.

Two days before Lincoln issued his blockade edict, Attorney General Bates had submitted to the Cabinet his thoughts on the conduct of the war. Aside from closing the ports from Charleston to New Orleans, he recommended that the mouth of the Mississippi be guarded against ingress and egress, the junction point of the Mississippi and the Ohio be occupied, and such key points as Fort Monroe, Harper's Ferry and the Gosport navy yard be made secure.

Like Scott, Bates was convinced that the South could not exist without importing various necessities and exporting her principal products, and that therefore the closing of her ports was the cheapest and surest method of smothering her into submission.[11] "Others," he admitted, "may think it wiser and better to . . . enforce the laws at the point of the bayonet. . . . If that opinion [should] prevail . . . the Government ought to take and hold . . . New Orleans." This city, he believed, could be occupied without a serious struggle by 8,000 to 10,000 "hardy and bold" river boatmen coming down from Cairo in secrecy.[12]

A year later he complained bitterly that the principle of encirclement, which he and Scott had championed, had not been adopted. "If, at the beginning we had seised [seized] the great River," he wrote, ". . . fortified a few strong points, and . . . patrolled its whole length, we might have restored the Union without destroying the Country . . . spared rivers of blood, and great heaps of ashes."[13]

General McClellan, who was to replace General Scott on November 1, favored a different procedure. He agreed with Lincoln that fighting should not necessarily be avoided, but believed that a mere show of superior power might persuade the Confederacy to submit without bloodshed. "We have . . . to display such an overwhelming strength as will convince . . . our antagonists . . . of the utter impossibility of resistance,"[14] he suggested in a memorandum to the President on August 2, 1861.

If this threat should not serve its purpose, he intended to concentrate his main military effort in Virginia. So soon as it was clear that Kentucky would remain loyal, he would use her roads for a drive into East Tennessee, to assist the Unionists in that territory, and seize the railroad from Memphis to the east, then use the western part of Virginia as a springboard for a march on Richmond. For these campaigns McClellan asked for an army of 273,000 men, with enough reserves to replace losses. He further wanted a powerful naval force to transport, protect and convey troops along the enemy's coastline. Occupation of Charleston, Savannah, Montgomery, Pensacola, Mobile and New Orleans was another part of his program. McClellan likewise advocated a movement down the Mississippi to push the Confederates out of Missouri, and an invasion of western Texas, where he believed Union sentiment was predominent. On top of all this he hoped to utilize the resources of the Pacific "if at all practicable," and even hinted at a possible alliance with Mexico.

In contrast to these overambitious schemes he compressed his maxim of greatly superior military strength into a single question: "Shall we crush the rebellion at one blow, terminate the war in one campaign, or shall we leave it as a legacy for our descendants?" The following year, after having gained some fighting experience, McClellan reduced his grandiose ideas to more modest proportions, but added a sound principle. "The national forces," he argued in a letter which he handed to the visiting President at Harrison's Landing on July 7, 1862, "should not be dispersed in expeditions, posts of occupation, and numerous armies, but should be mainly collected into masses and brought to bear upon the armies of the Confederate States. Those armies thoroughly defeated, the political structure which they supported would soon cease to exist."[15]

If Lincoln had followed this advice, instead of waiting till its wisdom had been brought home to him by the bitter method of trial and error, the war would have been over much sooner.

The most laudable feature of McClellan's program was his emphasis on a war machine of overpowering strength. In other ways it was similar to the Anaconda Plan in proposing a movement down the Mississippi, but differed from it by making the occupation of Virginia its primary object, while Scott wanted to undertake his main action in the Mississippi Valley. The two plans were alike in their insistence on lengthy and thorough preparations. The reason why neither was given a fair test was that Lincoln did not dare take the time needed for their perfection. He had to choose between correct military reasoning and politics. He chose politics.

A well-worked out over-all strategy calls for boldness, foresight and original thinking. Northern strategy rarely measured up to these requirements, and its sponsors were guilty of many shocking blunders. The one which stands out as especially glaring is that the country's capital, so obviously located in a faulty place, was allowed to remain the seat of the government to the very end.

As a war capital Washington was an absurdity. Surrounded by

secessionist territory, wide-open to attack from all sides, it had to be protected by a long string of forts and many miles of rifle pits. Even so, the Potomac offered easy access to an enemy fleet. The inhabitants were largely Southern in sentiment, making it a favorite center for Confederate spy activities. Whole armies had to be immobilized for its protection, campaigns had to be shaped, reshaped, reorganized and disorganized, in order to hold a dangerously exposed city of no military value. It was as if a chess player deliberately kept his king in front of his pawns in order to impose a handicap on himself.

Removal of the nation's capital to Philadelphia or some other Northern city should have been ordered on the day Lincoln issued his call for troops. True, this would have involved some risk of losing prestige, but the risk could have been turned into a political advantage, if the President had publicly announced what he wrote privately to the prominent Maryland lawyer Reverdy Johnson, that it was fear of an attack by Virginia which had prompted him to call out the militia.[16] A few additional words, phrased in his inimitable, beautiful language, to the effect that the change in capitals was being undertaken in order to avert the perils of an armed clash, would have evoked sympathetic understanding at home and abroad.

The idea of moving the capital in times of war was not new. In 1683 the Austrian government had fled from Vienna, and had returned with an untarnished reputation after the besieging Turks had departed. The evacuation of Moscow in 1812 had left Russia triumphant. But there was no need to go outside the United States to find a precedent. Washington had been put to the torch by the British in 1814, yet the standing of the American government had in no way been permanently impaired. General Joseph K. F. Mansfield showed better sense than his superiors by viewing its possible loss with equanimity. "These things happen . . . ," he told the correspondent of the London *Times,* who called on him after the Northern defeat at Bull Run. "If the capital should fall into the hands of the rebels, the United States will be no more destroyed than they were when you burned it."[17]

McClellan thought along similar lines. On September 11, 1862, when he was on the move to repel Lee's invasion of Maryland, he urged Henry Wager Halleck, the general-in-chief, to send him two army corps from the defenders of the capital, inasmuch as it now seemed certain that Lee had withdrawn almost his entire army to the vicinity of Frederick. "Even if Washington should be taken," he added, ". . . this would not, in my judgment, bear comparison with the ruin and disaster which would follow a signal defeat of this army."[18]

Halleck indignantly refused McClellan's request, stating that the capture of Washington "will throw us back six months, if it should not destroy us." But indirectly he admitted that the capital was a strategic handicap. The troops could not be spared, he explained, because nearly all new arrivals had to guard the railroads leading to the north. [19] The obvious conclusion, which he did not draw. was that if the government had been moved out of the fighting zone, these troops could have been used for combat rather than for guard duty.

Transferring the seat of the government would not only have released large numbers of troops, but would have given the Union generals a free hand for offensive operations. Moreover, it would have been a body blow to some military aspirations of the South. Without Washington as a lure, the Shenandoah Valley, which her military leaders used as a sally port with such outstanding success, would have become a dead-end street. Yet in spite of the desirability, not to say urgency, of giving up Washington as a capital, the idea seems never to have been discussed. The shibboleth that its location was sacrosanct was generally accepted, and even received the approval of Lincoln's astute Advocate General, who wrote in his diary that "the Seat of Government, of course must be protected, cost what it may."[20] He did not say why.

All through the war the Northern generals were tied to a rope, one end of which was fastened to Washington. At the beginning, when McClellan undertook the first Northern offensive, he had to provide a garrison of 35,000 men for the safety of the capital. The question arose whether troops some distance away should be considered part of the garrison. The dispute was decided against him, and he had to split off another 40,000 men for what Lincoln considered adequate protection. Thus the germ of failure was implanted into the Peninsular campaign even before it started.

A few months later, while McClellan was battling Lee at Antietam, 70,000 Union soldiers were idling in the capital, and were kept idling even after Lee had recrossed into Virginia. The idea that this was an ideal time to use these troops in the field was so plain that it could scarcely have escaped notice, but apparently few men fretted about it. Before the battle of Antietam General Mansfield had suggested that 65,000 men should be kept in Washington, to hold it if McClellan were defeated, but "to improve victory, if . . . successful."[21] In other words, these troops were to be sent into the field as soon as any danger for the capital had passed. General Samuel Peter Heintzelman, who was then commanding the defenses of Washington, entertained the same idea. After Lee's retreat he asked the War Department to let him lead 60,000 of his troops out of the capital and close in on the battered and vastly outnumbered Confederate troops.[22] He would have found an enemy army which, according to the Confederate Colonel Henry Kyd Douglas, had been "depleted by battles, weakened by privation, broken down by marching, and ruined by straggling."[23] Its number of effectives five days after the battle totaled some 35,000 men, and Heintzelman's 60,000 fresh troops, possibly strengthened by detachments from McClellan's army, could have overwhelmed it. Neither Mansfield nor Heintzelman was a military genius, but they realized, as everyone else must have done who had kept his head, that an immediate Confederate offensive was out of the question, and that Washington was as safe as if it had been on another continent. Even if Heintzelman had been defeated, there was little to be lost, for he had the forts of the capital at his back, and McClellan's only slightly weakened army within reach. Nevertheless, Secretary of War Edwin McMasters Stanton turned down his proposal, presumably with the blessing of Lincoln who, due to an almost pathological fear for the safety of Washington, allowed this exceptional opportunity to fade away.

Lincoln never was able to shake off his dread of an attack on the capital. After McClellan's dismissal, Generals Ambrose Everett Burnside and Joseph Hooker received the President's nod of approval for their ventures, because they kept Washington covered while taking their beatings. General George Gordon Meade followed the same cautious course, although a few months after his hollow victory at Gettysburg he boldly stalked out to beard the enemy in his lair. But the hurry in which he rushed back, when Lee shook his fist at Washington, was as amusing as it was humiliating. When someone asked Lincoln one day what his immense army was doing, he replied with unconscious humor that he could not learn what his general was doing with it, except defending the capital.[24] He complained about the "imbecility" and "inefficiency" of his generals,[25] but apparently it never occurred to him that so long as the capital had to be protected, "cost what it may," they were as helpless to move aggressively as if they had been fenced up in a corral.

Only once did Lincoln seem to glimpse that something was wrong with his policy. When, after the battle of Gaines's Mill, McClellan painted a black picture of the situation, Lincoln wired him, "if you have had a drawn battle or a repulse, it is the price we have to pay for the enemy not being in Washington. We protected Washington and the enemy concentrated on you."[26] Had a vague suspicion arisen in his mind that excessive safeguarding of Washington had doomed McClellan's campaign?

Whatever arguments could have been put forth against moving the Northern capital were refuted by the war itself. After John Pope's defeat at Second Bull Run in August 1862, it was feared that Lee might follow the disorganized Union army into Washington, and hasty preparations were made to evacuate the city. Vessels were kept under steam to carry members of the government out of the danger zone. Abandoning the capital under the threat of enemy invasion presented a far greater risk to prestige than a voluntary evacuation earlier, but the matter attracted only passing attention and did no diplomatic damage. The incident, though, left no doubt that the North had sacrificed incalculable military advantages for a mirage which, when closely approached, was shown to contain no substance.

AMATEUR STRATEGISTS, TOO, SUBMITTED PLANS

PLANS FOR bringing the Confederacy to her knees were hatched not only by professional soldiers, but by amateurs as well. Perhaps the most capable of them was a college president and doctor of divinity by the name of Asa Mahan. Born in Vermont and 61 years old at the outbreak of the war, a graduate of Hamilton College and Andover Theological Seminary, he had been a passionate student of warfare all his life. In 1835 he had been elected president of Oberlin College and at the time of the Civil War was president of Adrian College in Adrian, Michigan.

Mahan was a man of great ability and a pronounced individualist. He had accepted the presidency of Oberlin under the condition that no color distinction be allowed among the students, and that women should receive the same degrees as men. Both these innovations were revolutionary at that time. His individualism sometimes bordered on fanaticism and, in connection with his domineering personality and dictatorial ways, did not make him popular either with his colleagues or with the trustees of his college. He was respected, but not liked. Nevertheless, all his contemporaries agreed that "there never was any doubt about [his] high moral principles, his sincerity, his devotion to truth."[1]

Mahan was a prolific writer, and his position enabled him to make himself heard in the highest quarters. He was in frequent touch with Secretary of the Treasury Salmon Portland Chase, Senators Charles Sumner, Zachariah Chandler, Benjamin Franklin Wade, Henry Wilson and Preston King and with Generals Irvin McDowell, Hooker, William Starke Rosecrans and Burnside. Once he was invited to present his views to the President in person, and when, after many disappointments, his advice finally was taken, he claimed that it prevented a threatening disaster and made victory certain. After the war he moved to England, where he put his views and experiences pertaining to the Civil War into a book which was published in 1877. In his "Preface and Introduction" the author declared that honest criticism is no respecter of persons, and that those who conduct public enterprises should invite it. While it was intended mainly for Americans, he commended the work to all friends of truth, who wished to understand important events as they really had happened. He hoped that his readers would study his analysis of generals and their conduct of the war in the same spirit of impartiality in which he had written it.

The book, titled *A Critical History of the Late American War,* was published by A. S. Barnes and Company of New York, Chicago and New Orleans, and can by no means be called a literary masterpiece. It is badly organized, always militant, often repetitious. Yet one must admire his reasoning power and the courage with which he trod on delicate toes. If his suggestions had been followed, the war might have taken a sharply different course, and one more favorable to the Northern side. There can be no doubt that Mahan had many brilliant ideas, but he could be wrong too, and often was misinformed. He was highly critical of the Anaconda Plan. "No plan conceived is more utterly defective," he stated vehemently. "One of the best known principles of weakness in war is operation on a widely extended line."[2] Inasmuch as Scott's plan did not call for an invasion, but for a holding operation, Mahan's comment is not quite to the point. Lincoln's proposal to advance half a million men simultaneously on a line some 1500 miles long he considered fatuous.[3] Even if the attackers were successful, two thirds of their forces would be required to guard communications and garrison the conquered territory.[4]

Mahan's chief objection to Lincoln's plan rested on the assumption that offensives were to be undertaken at every point of a 1500-mile line. This was not the case, because the number of invasion routes was limited. As to the troops required to guard communications, this was an evil which could not be entirely avoided, but the excessive number of places which were garrisoned and over-garrisoned, did warrant Mahan's censure. In the fall of 1864, for instance, Nashville was garrisoned by some 8,000 to 10,000 troops and several thousand cavalry, Chattanooga and Murfreesboro each by 5,000, Decatur, Florence and Huntsville each by 4,000. Besides these troops, more were scattered through the adjoining territory— one brigade with 2,500, and another with 1,200 men. Thus a total of 45,000[5] men, enough to form a mobile army of considerable strength, was kept on noncombatant duty in a comparatively small area.

Mahan's criticism applies with full force to the course which

McClellan also had opposed in his letter to Lincoln—the waste of troops on such side enterprises as the capture of fortified places or cities in the interior, and on fringe campaigns in North Carolina, Florida, Texas, Arkansas or the Red River Valley. What Mahan recommended instead was, as McClellan had done, to concentrate all troops into two armies, one in the east and one in the west. He believed that 500,000 men could win a complete victory within six months after they had taken the field.[6] Like McClellan he was convinced that this method would automatically bring about the surrender of the whole South, outlying districts, interior cities, seaports and all.

The president of Adrian College, while usually correct in principle, sometimes ignored some factors of importance. He argued that the climate of the Confederate states would permit campaigning during the entire year, and was outraged that the Confederates were allowed to rest in the winter months, giving them an opportunity to repair their damages, while the Union armies were weakened by disease, dissipation and desertion. No rest, winter or summer, was Mahan's dictum.[7] Among others he cited Napoleon's winter campaigns to drive home his point. What he overlooked was the difference between European roads and those in the South which, with few exceptions, turned to quagmire in the winter whenever thaws set in. Burnside's sad experience in January 1863, when his whole army literally became stuck in the Virginia mud, demonstrated forcefully that winter campaigning in America was a foolhardy undertaking.

Mahan had many prejudices, McClellan being one of his pet victims, and sometimes he chose methods of criticism which were questionable. But he made up his defects by displaying, on the whole, astounding good judgment on strategy and tactics. Most of his suggestions were not second guesses; he had submitted them

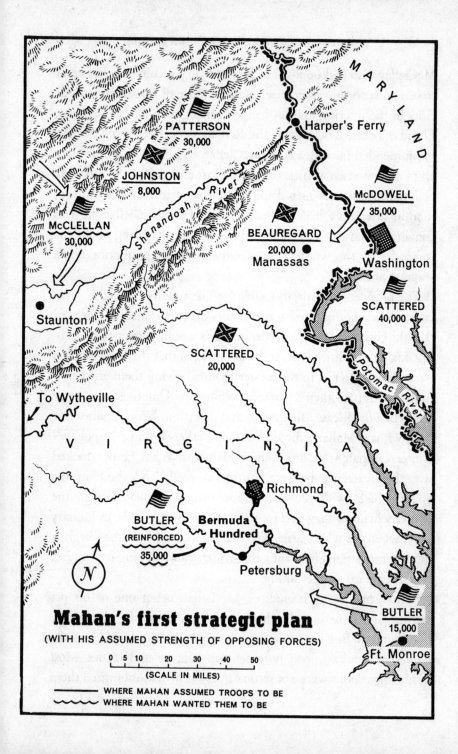

MARYLAND

PATTERSON
30,000

Harper's Ferry

JOHNSTON
8,000

Shenandoah River

McDOWELL
35,000

McCLELLAN
30,000

BEAUREGARD
20,000
Manassas

Washington

SCATTERED
40,000

Staunton

SCATTERED
20,000

Potomac River

To Wytheville

V I R G I N I A

Richmond

BUTLER
(REINFORCED)

Bermuda
Hundred

35,000

Petersburg

N

BUTLER
15,000

Mahan's first strategic plan

(WITH HIS ASSUMED STRENGTH OF OPPOSING FORCES)

Ft. Monroe

0 5 10   20   30   40   50

(SCALE IN MILES)

——————— WHERE MAHAN ASSUMED TROOPS TO BE
∼∼∼∼∼∼∼ WHERE MAHAN WANTED THEM TO BE

in writing before the foreshadowed events—to Lincoln, to Chase, to senators, high officers and newspapers.[8] He also was in the habit of expressing them orally to his students and to leading minds at his college.[9]

Mahan claimed that the first battle of Bull Run had been unnecessary, because the Confederate General Pierre G. T. Beauregard could have been forced into an early surrender. As of July 4, 1861, Secretary of War Simon Cameron had reported to Congress that the United States had 310,000 men under arms.[10] Deducting the 90-days men, whose service was about to expire, this left some 230,000 men for active campaigning, of whom 150,000 were in the east. On July 15, so Mahan asserted, Patterson with 30,000 men was moving up the Shenandoah Valley,[11] while McDowell had 35,000 men ready to march on Manassas; 40,000 more were stationed around Washington and various other places; Butler at Fort Monroe commanded 15,000 troops.[12] By the middle of July McClellan had been able to report that he had "completely annihilated the enemy in western Virginia," thereby releasing approximately 30,000 men for other fields.[13]

Against these imposing Federal forces the Confederates had 20,000 men under Beauregard at Manassas and 8,000 under Joseph E. Johnston in the Valley. About 20,000 additional troops were scattered throughout the Old Dominion state.[14]

These figures on man power, although based on the current information available to Mahan, were grossly inaccurate. Patterson, for instance, had only 16,000 men,[15] and McClellan about 20,000[16]. Moreover, of the men under arms only a small portion had received sufficient training. Yet Mahan's proposed strategy is not without interest. He suggested strengthening Butler at Fort Monroe with 20,000 men. These troops were to be moved to Bermuda Hundred, a tongue of land between the James and Appomattox rivers, while McClellan would march to Staunton, and Patterson would occupy a position in the lower Shenandoah Valley. The result, Mahan prophesied, would be that Richmond, being still unfortified, would fall to Butler, and his presence there would prevent reinforcements being sent to Beauregard and Johnston; it also rendered a retreat of the Confederates into North Carolina impossible. Beauregard and Johnston at Manassas, being completely isolated, would have to surrender. Following this victory, the Carolina seaports would be cut off, and this would mean the end of all resistance in the eastern theater of war. [17]

This was Mahan's first idea for a victorious campaign and showed good promise; the proposed occupation of Bermuda Hundred is especially interesting in view of the part it was to play later in the war. But the execution of the plan would have met with obstacles which he had not taken into account. McClellan, thinking along similar lines, had intended to cut the railroad from Memphis to Lynchburg at Wytheville instead of Staunton, but had been rebuffed by Scott.[18] Butler's march to Richmond would have been opposed by Benjamin Huger and "Prince" John Bankhead Magruder,[19] with the outcome uncertain. Yet sending a strong force to Bermuda Hundred involved a risk small in proportion to the possible results. Butler would have been under the protection of the fleet and, even though remaining on the defensive, posed a greater threat there than at Fort Monroe, and would have pinned down strong enemy forces. McClellan would have been far from his base, but could retreat into the mountains if necessary and, in combination with Patterson, might become a decisive factor against Johnston. And if Butler were successful, complete victory might be achieved even with raw troops. After all, the soldiers they would meet were just as inexperienced, and their armament was worse. At any rate, the strategic lesson to be gained by following

Mahan's plan might have been well worth its price, regardless of results.

The Federal disaster at First Bull Run rightfully was blamed on popular pressure; this was no reason, Mahan commented very disgustedly, why from then on intelligent civilians were to have nothing to say about the conduct of the war, and why "military imbecility" was to have its unobstructed way.[20] The frowns of the generals did not deter him from speaking his mind. McClellan, strongly opposed to Lincoln's desire to march on Richmond by a land route, had shipped his army by sea to Fort Monroe, on the tip of the Virginia peninsula, and was proceeding from there toward the Confederate capital. Mahan sharply condemned him, because the approach to Richmond from Fort Monroe was the only direction which left all of the city's communications undisturbed.[21] He also was severe in his implied censure of Lincoln for detaching part of McDowell's corps from McClellan's army in order to help capture Stonewall Jackson, who was then making history in the Shenandoah Valley, because this brought all segments of the Federal forces demonstrably out of supporting distance from one another: McClellan was slowly working his way toward Richmond, John Ellis Wool's garrison was idling at Fort Monroe, McDowell's remaining troops were at Fredericksburg, Banks's and McDowell's detached forces in the Shenandoah Valley, Frémont's in western Virginia, while a sixth segment in Washington under James Samuel Wadsworth was doing nothing at all. A unity of action was thus prevented, and any of the forces could be successfully attacked by stronger numbers.[22] Due to this mismanagement, he estimated that fully 100,000 troops were directly or indirectly defending the capital and western Virginia,

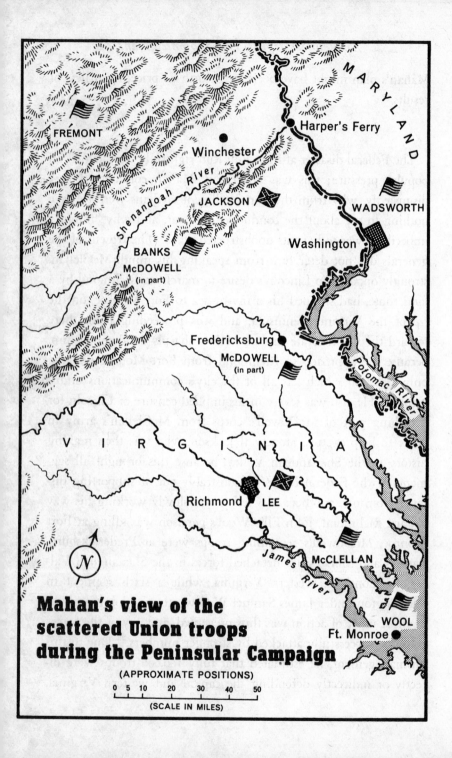

FRÉMONT

MARYLAND

Harper's Ferry

Winchester

Shenandoah River

JACKSON

WADSWORTH

BANKS

Washington

McDOWELL
(in part)

Fredericksburg

McDOWELL
(in part)

Potomac River

V I R G I N I A

Richmond

LEE

McCLELLAN

James River

WOOL

Ft. Monroe

N

Mahan's view of the scattered Union troops during the Peninsular Campaign

(APPROXIMATE POSITIONS)

0 5 10   20   30   40   50

(SCALE IN MILES)

instead of co-operating with McClellan's offensive.[23] A council of Confederate generals, Mahan scoffed, could not have devised a better plan to sweeten their dreams.[24] Had McDowell, as he wished to do, been allowed to throw his corps on Richmond while Stonewall Jackson was at Winchester, too far down the Valley to join Lee against the McClellan-McDowell attack, Lee would have been in great peril. Mahan had been told by McDowell in a personal interview that his army had been especially trained for rapid marches, and that he had been ready and anxious to fall on Lee's flank from the north, while McClellan attacked from the east, when he received the order to stop the movement and send part of his corps to entrap Jackson. It was, he said, "a crushing blow to us all."[25]

By 1862 the amateur critic had learned a great deal, and his comments now showed that his strategic sense had ripened. Yet up to the end of that year he tried in vain to make Lincoln or the War Department listen to his suggestions, although he was constantly in contact with several senators and members of the Committee on the Conduct of the War.[26] But most of these men were Radicals, then still a small but powerful minority of the Republican party, who were bent on prolonging the war until heavy sacrifices would enrage the voting public, and they could gain control of the government. They were polite to Mahan, but not inclined to back his advice.

A letter Senator Sumner wrote to him in the latter part of 1862 was remarkably frank in this respect, its concluding sentence hinting plainly at the reason why victory was not yet welcome. "I have, from the beginning, been profoundly impressed with your views," the Massachusetts senator declared with tongue in cheek.

"A Government more quick and positive than ours would have adopted them early, and the war would have been ended long since." Then his tongue resumed its natural position, and he revealed his real thoughts, contradictory though they were to his avowed hope for an early peace. "Perhaps, however, these delays and disasters may result in consequences which you and I value more than we do any present victories and advantages."[27]

Mahan was not in agreement with this Radical point of view. As the year 1862 came to its close, he became impatient and decided to visit Washington, in order to lay his ideas before Lincoln in person. The moment was propitious. The debacle of Fredericksburg was fresh in the public mind, and official Washington was weltering in despair. Chase introduced the visitor to Secretary of War Stanton, and Mahan somewhat tactlessly began reading his analysis of past military errors, when the Secretary interrupted him, saying that he wanted only to know the answer to the question, "What now?"[28] Mahan thereupon unfolded a plan which he insisted would put an end to the war.[29] Lee was then lying at Fredricksburg with about 80,000 men, confronted by Burnside, 120,000 strong, while other Union troops were stationed at Fort Monroe. Mahan, returning to his first plan, proposed to bring this force up to 80,000, transport it to Bermuda Hundred, and seize Lee's communications south of the James. As soon as Lee became cognizant of this threat, he would retreat. Anticipating this move, Burnside would cross the Rappahannock above Fredricksburg and press the enemy with all energy, compelling Lee to fall back into Richmond.

The two armies thus would encircle Lee and leave him the choice of fighting against a force two or three times as strong as his own, or face starvation in Richmond. Should a portion of his army escape into North Carolina, a fleet was to be held in readiness to move troops to Hilton Head, South Carolina, which was in

Federal hands. From there they would march inland and intercept the retreating enemy. Caught among these three forces the Confederates would be crushed, the Carolina and Georgia seaports would be flanked, and the eastern war would be over.[30]

This plan was submitted to General Rosecrans, who endorsed it vigorously, as did other Union officers.[31] The men needed were available. According to Mahan, who cited a report of the Secretary of War to Congress, the Army of the United States had then in the field 800,000 men, fully armed and equipped.[32] Whether or not these figures were correct, it appeared to Mahan that 60,000 men could easily have been spared for this enterprise, especially since the Army of the Potomac alone had about 80,000 men doing only garrison duty.

When Stanton had this plan explained to him, he became irritated, although he did not deny the availability of the troops. "Where is your general," he exclaimed, "to carry it out?" Mahan stood his ground. He had not come to Washington to furnish generals, he said, but to submit a plan to win the war. Stanton kept repeating his request for a general, and with that the interview came to an end.[33]

The college president spent half of the following day with Senators Wade and Wilson, and the evening with Lincoln, who listened to his caller with great interest and asked that he reduce his recommendations to writing. This done, a second conference took place, at which the President again lent an attentive ear, and then addressed the senators. "Gentlemen," he said, "I am in earnest in what I am about to say to you. If you . . . advise it, I will adopt this plan, and appoint a new commander-in-chief to carry it out."[34] The man he was going to name, he indicated, would be McDowell, who had endorsed the plan in writing. His choice met with unanimous approval.[35]

It seemed to Mahan that at last he had won out; but soon he learned of an ominous fact—Stanton and Halleck, the general-in-chief, had closeted themselves with Lincoln during the entire next day, to the exclusion of all visitors.[36]

At the meeting which followed, and which Mahan attended, the additional endorsement by General McDowell was handed to Lincoln,[37] but those present noticed that a great change had come over him. He admitted that Mahan's plan was the best he had heard of, but that it could not be executed because of the utter impossibility of concentrating the needed forces at Fort Monroe in time to make them useful. He had been told that the railroads would be hard pressed to transport as few as 10,000 men to Fort Monroe in four weeks.

Mahan protested angrily. He quoted the superintendent of the Pennsylvania Central, who a few days before had assured the Committee on the Conduct of the War that he could convey not merely 10,000 but 50,000 men with all their equipment to Fort Monroe, and not in four weeks, but in four days. Members of that committee confirmed the statement.[38] Nevertheless, the President adhered to his conviction, "the one fixed in his mind by Stanton and Halleck," as Mahan assumed.[39] Finally he declared that he felt bound by his pledge to Wade and Wilson, but had no confidence in the practicability of the project. In these circumstances the senators declined to hold the President to his promise.[40] This seemed to sound the end of Mahan's plan, but one of the senators went to see Burnside at Falmouth and was able to add his endorsement and that of his corps commanders to those given by Rosecrans and McDowell. Unfortunately, Burnside had a plan of his own, which he desired to try out first. He did, was dismissed, and Mahan's proposal was pigeonholed.

There was an epilogue to this chapter. Several months later,

Mahan recorded, a major general of the Army of the Potomac reported that Halleck had been heard to say, "It would never do to have a civilian plan our campaigns."[41] Mahan was still a novice in political intrigue, and believed that petty jealousy was the sole reason why he had failed.

Significantly, the movement Mahan had so passionately recommended was exactly what Lee stood in fear of at that time. He apprehended that strong Union forces would be sent south of the James to undertake an attack on the Weldon Railway, the main southern supply line for his army, and was fully aware of the disastrous consequences which were bound to follow.[42] General Gustavus W. Smith, who was in command at Richmond, also was fearful of a Federal advance on the south side of the James.[43] His uneasiness was intensified by a raid of 10,000 Federal troops, who had issued from New Bern and destroyed part of the Weldon Railway, threatening an attack on the capital from the south.[44] Uneasiness had penetrated even the lower echelons of the army. When, in the middle of January 1863, the 15th Alabama was ordered to take position three miles south of Richmond, on the Petersburg road, its colonel interpreted the move as a precaution to protect the capital against an attack from that direction.[45]

The paper which the sage of Adrian College had brought to Washington contained more than suggestions for immediate action; it gave also a summary of the fundamental fallacies in the past conduct of the war. This reference to past errors, which Stanton had so impatiently turned aside, were set forth in detail in Mahan's memorandum.[46] He looked askance at the tendency of the Northern armies to strike at Confederate places instead of at their armies, but injudiciously, cited Corinth as an example to demonstrate the faultiness of this kind of warfare.[47] He should have realized that this little town in northern Mississippi was the junction of two vital railroads, and in Federal possession proved a serious obstacle to Southern generalship. On the other hand, he was right in deploring the scattering of Union forces beyond supporting distance of each other. He might also have pointed out that if the dispersed troops of Banks, Frémont and McDowell and most of the Washington garrison had united and attacked Lee from the west, while McClellan was pressing him from the east, Jackson would never have ventured forth on his famous Valley campaign, in which he marched more than 250 miles, won battle after battle and captured 4,000 men, besides guns, wagons and immense military supplies.

Another fault Mahan found with Northern strategy, and to which he returned time and again, was the waste of efforts on the borders of the Confederacy, where the victories gained and the places conquered were of no practical value.

One of the most striking of Mahan's criticisms was aimed at moving troops into enemy territory on single lines.[48] Instead he urged pincer movements, although this expression was then not in use. The one from Bermuda Hundred which he repeatedly urged was a case in point.

In the remainder of Mahan's paper he ridiculed the idea of keeping whole armies in the environs of Washington for purely defensive purposes against "fancied attacks," and referred to similar conditions prevailing in the west. This state of affairs, he claimed, did not prevent raids, but invited them. "It is only when armies are lying still that raids occur," he explained. "Whenever they are striking . . . at the enemy . . . raids are impossible."[49]

Hooker took command of the Union forces early in 1863, and is said to have declared himself ready to execute Mahan's plan to seize Lee's communications.[50] He sent Burnside's corps to Fort Monroe, from where it was to proceed in its projected movement south of the James. But on March 26, 1863, about a month before Hooker started on his Chancellorsville campaign, Burnside was appointed commander of the Department of Ohio, and ordered to take his corps with him. The reason given was that a plan for an enemy invasion into Kentucky had been reported. The invasion turned out to be an unimportant foraging raid by General John Pegram,[51] whom the Union General Quincy Adams Gillmore, at the head of only 1,200 men, forced to retreat into Tennessee.[52] Yet Burnside's corps was not returned to Fort Monroe; it was taken from him and sent to Vicksburg.[53] If it had been united with the troops at Fort Monroe and other parts of the Peninsula, (who, according to Mahan's estimate, totalled 60,000 men), and then marched out from Bermuda Hundred in April 1863, Lee might have had to fight on two fronts; or with Richmond in danger from both sides, he might have left his position on the Rappahannock and moved south. In this case, having Hooker's army at his flank at Chancellorsville, he would have been at the same disadvantage which would bedevil Grant a year later on his march through the Wilderness, when his flank was exposed to an enemy standing in wait for him. To project the speculation still further, Mahan could have claimed that, so long as large Northern forces were stationed at Bermuda Hundred, Lee would hardly have dared to undertake the Gettysburg campaign.

When Mahan heard of Burnside's removal to Ohio, he became furious. "In view of the palpable facts of the case," he roared, "but one motive can be assigned for this order, a deliberate intent to defeat, or rather prevent, this great movement upon General Lee's communications. . . . I challenge the world to assign any motive for it but that under consideration. . . . The great invasion of

Kentucky . . . to repel which he [Burnside] and his corps were professedly taken from their proper sphere, [was] repelled by a few hundred cavalry and infantry then in the interior of the State."[54] An unsophisticated college president was beginning to lose his naïveté, and shuddered at what he was discovering and suspecting. Had the two senators who had sponsored his meeting with Lincoln been sincere? Or had they known all along that Stanton would kill any plan that might end the war quickly? Could it be that by inviting Mahan to Washington, they had done so to discourage and silence him? While he did not put these thoughts into his book, they must have passed through his mind, as he wondered what was behind the "deliberate intent to prevent" a military movement which had been endorsed by leading generals, and which Lincoln himself had called the best that had yet come to his attention.

Perhaps Mahan's suspicions would have been strengthened had he known that Wade was deep in the confidence of Stanton and that, as his apologist agreed, "differences of aim and opinion [between them] were exceedingly rare."[55]

While Mahan found much that was wrong in the east, he also looked at Grant's Vicksburg campaign with a skeptical eye. Even the fall of the city left him cold, because in his opinion by then the opening of the Mississippi had ceased to be of great moment, as intercourse between the eastern and western states of the Confederacy had virtually ceased.[56] This assertion, bold as it must have seemed at the time, subsequently was verified by Confederate reports. One Colonel Thomas Lowndes Snead wrote that as early as the spring of 1862, northern Arkansas thought itself abandoned, that many of her men were enlisting in the Federal Army, and that neither citizens nor soldiers did anything to help or encourage the eastern Confederacy during the winter of 1863–64 or in the following spring.[57] This argument applied to other western districts with even stronger force. Snead even accused General Edmund Kirby-Smith of having tried to organize "a sort of independent Trans-Mississippi republic."[58] General Taylor, who was then campaigning in that section, was equally suspicious, but less outspoken. He observed that Kirby-Smith "displayed much ardor in the establishment of bureaus, and on a scale proportioned rather to the extent of his territory than to the smallness of his force. His staff surpassed in numbers that of Van Moltke during the war with France. . . ."[59]

Whatever plans Kirby-Smith may have entertained, however, the underlying estrangement grew in intensity. In the summer of 1864, when Jefferson Davis asked General Taylor what help might be expected from Trans-Mississippi, the reply was "none"; that far from desiring to send more men to the east, their leaders clamored for the return of those already there. "Certain senators and representatives," Taylor added ominously, ". . . talked . . . about setting up a government west of the Mississippi, uniting with Maximilian and calling on Napoleon for assistance."[60] At any rate, from May 18, 1864, to the close of the war, eleven months later, not a shot was fired in the Trans-Mississippi Department.[61]

Mahan foretold that if Lee's Northern invasion in 1863 were turned back, the victory would not be exploited. At the beginning of the Gettysburg campaign he had written to Chase that "no important reinforcements will be called up from Fort Monroe or anywhere else; nor will any plan be devised to capture the army of General Lee. All that will be done . . . will be to . . . drive [it] back . . . just as we drive out a herd of unruly cattle who have broken into our grain field; and while General Lee shall escape with all his plunder, his expulsion will be proclaimed as one of the great events of the war."[62] No crystal gazer could have made a more accurate prophecy.

After the surrender of Vicksburg and Port Hudson, Mahan wrote a letter to the *New York Times,* in which he suggested that Grant's army join that of Rosecrans to crush Braxton Bragg, who was heading a Confederate army in Tennessee, or else be used in the east against Lee. "I will venture a prediction, however," he added, "as to what will occur. . . . All our vast armies will now remain in comparative idleness . . . until the opening of the campaign next spring."[63]

Mahan's suggestion again went unheeded, and Bragg beat Rosecrans, while Grant's army, broken up and scattered, was far from the scene of action. So far as the eastern zone was concerned, the amateur's prediction of events to come likewise proved true, for George G. Meade, afraid to tarnish the newly acquired prestige he had earned by beating the Confederates at Gettysburg, could not be coaxed into engaging Lee in another battle. In the west it proved only partially true, for something had to be done to lift the siege of Chattanooga. Nevertheless, after the victory of Missionary Ridge, hostilities on a large scale were suspended until the next spring, as he had foretold, although much might have been accomplished in a few days, if Grant had not called a halt after his smashing victory.

The Adrian College critic was distressed to see that his comparison with the strayed cattle continued to hold true. Victorious commanders always seemed satisfied with having driven the enemy from his position instead of following through. Just as Grant had stopped fighting after the battle of Missionary Ridge, Meade had let Lee escape. James Longstreet's corps, after its bloody repulse at

Knoxville, was allowed to retire into Virginia, thereby strengthening Lee both in leadership and man power.

One of Mahan's best-founded criticisms concerned the manner in which the attacks on the Sourthern seaports were conducted. These ports, he noted, had been heavily fortified on the sea side, but were vulnerable to an assault by land, yet they were always attacked where they were strongest. In 1861 the North had established a foothold at Hilton Head, near the town of Port Royal on the South Carolina coast, and Mahan estimated that an army of 80,000, if landed there and marched inland, could have captured Savannah, Charleston and Wilmington from the land side in very short order.[64] When Mahan remonstrated with Lincoln on this subject, he received the startling reply that Hilton Head was to be used exclusively as a supply depot for the Navy. The President did not elucidate, and unfortunately his visitor did not press the point.[65] The President's explanation would have been quite illuminating.

The unsuccessful and costly attempts to capture Charleston through frontal attacks by combined army-navy operations bear strong testimony to the validity of Mahan's views. That the city could at one time have been taken without great difficulty from the land side was freely admitted by its defenders after the war. Beauregard told how worried he had been in 1861 that Union land forces might strike at Charleston, and how easily they could have pierced its defenses.[66] And when Lee took over in November of that year, he too was greatly perturbed. He noted with anxiety how readily accessible the vital Charleston-Savannah railroad was by means of numerous rivers, over which the Federal gunboats could gain control, and how little the scattered Confederate force of less than 7,000 could have done to save the hundred-mile railroad between the two Southern ports.[67] As to the coast defenses in that region, Lee was equally pessimistic. In a letter to one of his daughters, dated November 22, '61, he wrote that "they are poor indeed. . . . I hope our enemy will be polite to wait. . . ."[68]

The Federal commander was as polite as Lee could have wished, because "instead of making after his easy capture of Port Royal a rapid movement toward the railroad at Pocotaligo and Charleston by the Edisto, or toward Savannah by way of Hilton Head—in either of which movements he would have met with little or no opposition—[he] contented himself with gathering the harvest of cotton found on Beaufort Island and provided a refuge for . . . fugitive slaves. . . ."[69]

In appreciation of his victories at Vicksburg and Missionary Ridge, Grant was appointed commander-in-chief of all Northern armies on March 8, 1864, and proposed to strike at the Confederacy on several fronts simultaneously, in accordance with Lincoln's long-cherished idea. But Mahan disapproved this dispersion of the Union forces, which were to fight in widely separated territories—Grant in Virginia, Sherman in Georgia, Banks in the Red River Valley, Sigel in the Shenandoah Valley, Butler south of the James, George Crook in West Virginia and Frederick Steele in Arkansas.[70] He was particularly opposed to the Red River campaign, because to send an army into Texas he considered as silly as sending it to Alaska.[71] In this he clearly was right, but the concept had been Lincoln's, not Grant's, and the goal was not a military but a political one, directed against Napoleon III, who was striving to put a puppet monarch on the Mexican throne. As to Sherman, Mahan thought he should have engaged Johnston two months earlier, because, while the Union forces were ready for combat in March, their opponents then were still disorganized and would use the interim to strengthen their army and fortify defensive positions on the road to Atlanta. Furthermore, the coming summer months were sure to be hard on the Northern men and decimate them through sickness.[72] Mahan rightly ridiculed the thought that Lee might send reinforcements to Johnston, or vice versa, since each was facing an enemy vastly superior in numbers and equipment.

Superficially there was something to be said in favor of Mahan's arguments, but he ignored the early spring rains, which might have bogged down Sherman's soldiers as they had bogged down those of Burnside. Other reasons also called for delay. Many enlistments were expiring, and new levies had to be trained. Moreover, large supplies had to be accumulated at Chattanooga, and this required time and a drastic change in railroad transportation. Sherman was right in acting slowly, for a setback at the beginning of the combined drive would have had a bad effect on Northern morale within the armies and out of them. On the other hand, Mahan was delighted that the movement via Bermuda Hundred, which he had favored from the start, was at last going to be given a trial. Burnside was to bring Butler's army up to a strength of 60,000 men, and against such a force Lee's communications south of the James could not be held. Mahan claimed that his plan had been explained to Grant, who had adopted it.[73] But just before the campaign started, Grant changed his mind, and ordered Burnside to join him in the Wilderness campaign, leaving Butler with an army of only 35,000 men to carry out the task singlehanded.

How correctly Mahan had again assessed the situation is proved by the fact that the project which he had urged caused Lee considerable worry. In a dispatch to Davis, dated April 15, 1864,[74] Lee referred to the large number of troops Burnside had gathered at Annapolis, and predicted that if they were intended to take the Confederate army in flank or rear, it would have to retire from the

Rappahannock, in which case "great injury will befall us." Even after Butler's advance from Bermuda Hundred with his small army had been halted, Lee admitted that it "had occasioned me great uneasiness."[75]

Beauregard also had looked anxiously at Burnside's corps and feared that its destination was Petersburg or Weldon, both important railroad points south of Richmond. "On either hypothesis," he wrote, "we should have been prepared to meet the assault in time, and clearly, we were not." As things turned out, he had his hands full even without the presence of Burnside's corps. "Orders came," he recalled, "one hurriedly following the other," [to collect all scattered forces] . . . and to rush them on to protect Richmond."[76] That his small contingent could not have withstood the huge Butler-Burnside combination is as certain as anything can be that did not actually happen.

Lee had grounds to be uneasy, for the movement which Mahan had advocated came close to consummation. In later years Grant told of his plan to throw Burnside's corps, 20,000 strong, on the seacoast south of Norfolk, to operate against Richmond from that direction. "In fact," he wrote, "up to the last moment Burnside and the War Department both thought the Ninth corps was intended for such an expedition." The reason he gave for attaching the corps to his own army instead, was that he wanted to concentrate all the force possible against the Confederate armies he himself would have to meet in the field.[77]

When Mahan learned of Grant's sudden change in dispositions, he became highly indignant, and expressed his feelings so openly that a friend of his, one Judge Barbour, warned him to be more cautious. But Mahan paid no heed, and predicted that the unsupported Butler would fail and be driven back to Bermuda Hundred.[78] Events once more proved Mahan a good prophet. He was

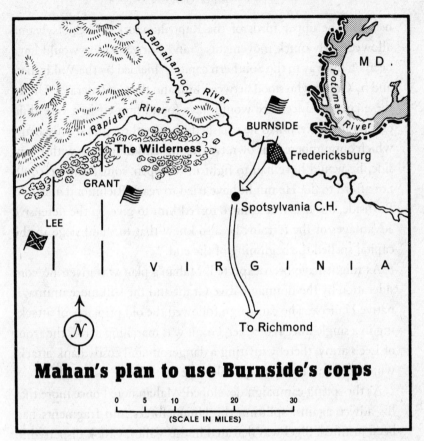

Mahan's plan to use Burnside's corps

not the man, however, to see his plan mutilated without protest. He sent a letter to Washington, to be laid before the President, advising him that under the new arrangements Butler had best be withdrawn, united with Burnside's corps, reinforced with from 10,000 to 20,000 men and stationed at the fords above Fredericksburg. As soon as Grant started to move, Burnside's corps, swelled now to the size of an army, should move directly to Spotsylvania, and from there to Richmond, while Grant would hold Lee in the Wilderness.[79]

Mahan's daring plan had much to recommend it. The roads

between the upper fords of the Rappahannock and Spotsylvania allowed fairly quick movements,[80] and Burnside soon would have been on his way to the Southern capital, shielded by the Wilderness and by Grant, who stood between him and the Confederates. Under these circumstances Lee would have found himself in a very difficult position. Even had he smashed his way through Grant's army, which outnumbered his own two to one, and caught up with Burnside, he would have had to fight in the open, something he could not afford to do. He might have tried to reach Richmond ahead of Burnside, but this would have forced him to give up the defensive advantages of the terrain; he also knew that to stand siege in the capital spelled the beginning of the end.[81]

As might have been expected, Mahan's plan was given no consideration by the unimaginative Grant and the still more unimaginative Halleck. The campaign followed the old principle of attacking in a single line. Worse yet, Grant was marching across the front of Lee's army, thereby inviting a dangerous and costly flank attack, which Lee was not slow to undertake.

As the spring campaign developed, Mahan noted once more that his advice against splitting the Union forces into fragments had been justified. Sigel was defeated in the Valley, Crook dispersed in West Virginia, Butler bottled up at Bermuda Hundred. If all these splinter armies had been united and made to fight either in the Shenandoah Valley or at Bermuda Hundred, much might have been achieved.[82] As it was, the Confederates managed to stage a counteroffensive in the Valley, which carried them to the gates of Washington, restored Southern confidence and brought them badly needed supplies.

Mahan's censure of Sherman's Atlanta campaign was no less severe than the one he bestowed on Grant. What Sherman should have done, in Mahan's opinion, was to divide his effective force, which he estimated at 180,000 men, reserve 70,000 for marching against Johnston, whose army numbered some 53,000, and station 60,000 men under George Henry Thomas at Decatur, Alabama. This would have left about 50,000 men to protect his communications. Thomas then should have marched on Atlanta simultaneously with Sherman's attack on Johnston. The Confederate commander, in danger of losing his base, would have retreated hurriedly, because he could not allow Thomas to beat him to Atlanta. The result of this stratagem would have been the saving of four months' time, and most of the loss in men and material.

Mahan's idea was good, but Sherman needed more than 50,000 men to guard his one-railroad supply line, which stretched all the way to Nashville and had to be defended against such redoubtable cavalry leaders as Nathan Bedford Forrest and Joseph Wheeler. If this line had been broken for any length of time, the invaders would have been in desperate straits. Yet Mahan was right to a certain degree. Considering the comparatively small number of men in Johnston's army,[83] Sherman could easily have detached 30,000 men from his mobile army of 100,000 for the movement from Decatur, the sole purpose of which would have been to make Johnston abandon his carefully prepared defenses between Dalton and Atlanta. So long as Sherman kept as close to the heels of the retiring Confederates as he did during the actual campaign, they would have been unwise to attack either portion of his army, knowing that the other portion might reach their base ahead of them.

Mahan was intensely critical of Sherman's march to the sea. In his judgment Sherman should have followed General John Bell Hood to Nashville and pinned him against that city, which was strongly fortified and held by Thomas. Caught between the two Union armies, each one larger than his own, his destruction would have been a certainty. This accomplished, Sherman should have moved all his men east by rail and augmented Grant's forces.[84] In this way he could have accomplished in a few weeks what took him five months by his march through Georgia and the Carolinas. Undoubtedly the movement would have been less spectacular, but it would have been decidedly more effective.

Strangely, Grant shared Mahan's opinion, in part, if not in toto, for he wired Sherman on November 1, 1864:

Do you think it advisable, now that Hood has gone so far north, to entirely ruin him, before starting on your proposed campaign? . . . If you can see a chance of destroying Hood's army, attend to that first, and make your other work secondary.[85]

Grant hesitated before allowing Sherman to have his way, but finally yielded and thereby committed a serious error. By marching through Georgia Sherman sacrificed valuable time. If he had reinforced Thomas at once with the two corps which he later sent him, then taken the bulk of his army to Grant as soon as he had broken contact with Hood, he would have reached Richmond in early fall when the conditions of the roads still made military operations possible. With such a heavy reinforcement of veteran troops, Grant might have crushed Lee before the advent of winter, and brought the war to an end.

Eventually the time was to come when Mahan would have his reward, when his advice was taken and put into effect. It was late in the conflict, while Sherman was sloshing his way through the Carolinas, and Johnston was ready to make a last stand against him.[86]

This is the way Mahan presented the matter in his recollections.

Johnston's army, he claimed, had been strengthened and "brought into such a state of organization that its commander had no doubt whatever of being fully able to defeat . . . Sherman."[87] But Mahan saw a way to make Sherman secure by drawing on Thomas who, after destroying Hood at Nashville, had a surplus of troops that were engaged merely in local mopping-up operations. On one of these expeditions John M. Schofield and his corps had proceeded as far as Clifton on the Tennessee when, on January 14, 1865, he received a telegram to rush his corps to Annapolis, whence it would be transported to North Carolina.[88] Once there it would free Sherman from all danger.

This change of plan, so Mahan proudly recorded, was due to his own fervent recommendation. He had analyzed the military situation at the turn of the year and come to the conclusion that Lee might some day steal out of the Richmond fortifications, join forces with Johnston and overpower Sherman. Worried about this possibility, Mahan had written to Senator Sumner in feverish excitement. "Never were we in such peril of great national disaster as at this present time. Our army . . . is divided into three parts, . . . Thomas at Nashville, Sherman at Savannah, and Grant at Petersburg, with the enemy in the centre, and ready to concentrate with crushing force upon the portion of our army which shall make the next move,—and that will be made by Sherman. . . . In existing circumstances there is one, but one thing to be done."[89]

Applying clever psychology, Mahan did not disclose what this one thing was, hoping that Sumner would take his letter to Lincoln, and that it would make both men anxious and curious. His hopes were fulfilled, for he promptly received an urgent request from Stanton, who by this time did no longer dare postpone the end: "We wish to know *immediately* . . . what the movement is which, in your judgment, ought to be made." He added the information that Sherman had between 50,000 and 60,000 men under his command.[90]

Mahan now divulged his plan: it meant reinforcing Sherman with enough of Thomas' troops to make him invincible. This idea was immediately adopted in a conference of the President, the Secretary of War and others, with the result that Grant was ordered to have Schofield report to Sherman, who was reinforced by other detachments, bringing the total of his army to about 81,000. Against such an array Johnston had no other choice but to retreat. His surrender would be only a matter of time. For this happy and relatively bloodless ending Mahan took full credit.

Sherman probably had no knowledge of Mahan's existence, let alone his advice, but paid him a fine compliment in later years. "Few military critics," he wrote, "who have treated of the Civil War in America have ever comprehended the importance of the transfer of Schofield from Nashville to co-operate with me in North Carolina."[91] Perhaps these critics had a clearer picture of the situation than Sherman himself, whose army, even before Schofield's arrival, numbered 57,000 men,[92] about twice as many as his opponent.[93]

It is regrettable that Mahan was misinformed about the relative strengths of the two opposing armies, else he would not have proclaimed that, if Sherman had not absorbed Schofield's corps, a terrible battle would have been fought in North Carolina, with an attendant slaughter of 30,000 to 50,000 men; that Sherman "unquestionably" would have been defeated and the war prolonged into 1866.[94] Such an assumption is entirely unwarranted. In the battle of Bentonville, which was his final effort to delay Sherman, Johnston could get no more than 14,000 men together, most of them in tatters, shoeless and badly equipped. He wired Lee that he could only annoy the invading army, not stop it.[95] To say that Johnston "had no doubt whatever of being able to defeat . . . Sherman"[96] is a wild exaggeration. What Johnston himself thought of his prospects he divulged after the war. He had accepted the command, he said, "with full consciousness on my part . . . that we could have no other object, in continuing the war, than to obtain fair terms of peace; for the Southern cause must have appeared hopeless then to all intelligent and dispassionate Southern men."[97] Lee had been equally downhearted. He confided to Senator Louis T. Wigfall that Johnston's command offered "not exactly no hope, but only a faint hope.[98]

The possibility of Lee combining his troops with Johnston's must be ruled out. During the first three months of the year the roads were impassable, and when they hardened enough to allow army movements, Grant began to watch Lee with catlike vigilance, ready to pounce on him the moment he came out of his trenches. He certainly would not have stood idly by while the two leading Confederate generals joined forces; but even had they succeeded, their defeat would have been inevitable, cut off, as they were, from supplies and wedged in between two strong armies. Mahan's suggestions showed his intelligent strategic sense, but his claim that it saved the North from "the perils of a great national disaster" is ridiculous. Mahan should have been satisfied that at last his talents had been acknowledged by the government. Moreover, the quick adoption of his recommendation was an implied apology for his previous ones having been ignored or rejected.

It was not until fairly late in the war that Mahan definitely recognized the real obstacle that had stood in his path all the time. "The men who actually controlled matters in . . . high places," he wrote, ". . . had no desire . . . to bring the war to a speedy termination."[99]

It is fortunate that Mahan, a man whose veracity was never

questioned, even by those who disliked him,[100] had the rare privilege of witnessing from a ringside seat, as it were, one of Stanton's unblushing intrigues. History has been enriched by his account of how the war was deliberately sabotaged by him and the Radicals, and was not brought to a close until hatred of the South had grown sufficiently to let them perpetuate themselves in power by depriving the conquered states of their constitutional privileges.

Another born strategist whose suggestions sprang from high intellect, common sense and deep study was Anna Ella Carroll, a native of Maryland and a woman of many extraordinary talents. Like Mahan she lacked military book knowledge, but relied on clearheaded reasoning to form her opinions. She too stressed that the North should rely on two armies, and considered all others auxiliary. Of the two she considered the one in the west the more important. The Confederates, she contended, could have abandoned all Atlantic states and still maintained their independence. The one possession they could not relinquish was the Mississippi Valley, because if they sustained themselves there, they could connect themselves with France through Texas, and with England through the states of the great Northwest. "With the Mississippi in their possession to the mouth of the Ohio, the presence of the English and French fleets at New Orleans would have brought about that result. . . ." So wrote Miss Carroll in the *North American Review* in 1876.[101]

This analysis of the situation contains much that is sound, and something that is debatable. Miss Carroll paid scant attention to the fact that most of the few war industries which the South possessed were concentrated in the Atlantic states, and that without them the Confederacy would have had to depend almost entirely on imports. England and France, however, the prime sources of supplies with which the South had to reckon, were risky railings to lean on. That these two powers would have openly and actively sided with a combatant of such reduced size against a much more powerful opponent is extremely doubtful. Moreover, England and France might have exacted conditions for their help which would have infringed the sovereignty of the seceded states, thereby jeopardizing the goal for which they were waging war.

Miss Carroll's strategic fame rests mainly on her success in replacing Scott's Anaconda Plan of going down the Mississippi with one that was vastly superior. What she advocated instead was to use the Tennessee River as the principal invasion route. In reality, however, this was only the starting point of her generalship. She wanted to have the Union armies penetrate the South as far as the vital Memphis-Charleston Railroad, secure it, then move troops as far up the Tennessee as Chattanooga. From there it was only a short distance to the headwaters of the Tombigbee, which provided a convenient waterway to Mobile.[102] With Chattanooga in Union hands, she argued, the whole country from the Gulf west to Memphis would drop into the Federal lap.

A by-product of this plan, perhaps even more important than its original aims, was the inevitable fall of the Mississippi River forts, which would be outflanked by a campaign in their rear.[103] In line with this strategy she advised against trying to take Vicksburg by a frontal attack, pointing out that a less costly but equally effective way was to paralyze the city by occupying Jackson, some fifty miles to the east.[104] An evacuation of the river fortress was sure to follow. It has been claimed that Grant's initial plan to take Vicksburg was based on her recommendation, although this is a moot question. At any rate he proved the correctness of Miss Carroll's theory, for when he did take Jackson, he isolated Vicksburg, and Johnston urged its abandonment.

Miss Carroll's role in evolving the strategy which Grant adopted in his Tennessee River campaign had been the subject of bitter controversies. Some of her partisans have accorded her all the credit for the Union victories from Fort Henry to Shiloh, while her critics pointed out that the choice of the Tennessee River was obvious, that anyone looking at the map could see that it flowed north, that the Confederates themselves had advertised the vulnerability of this route by erecting Fort Henry. Lew Wallace was quite outspoken in contesting the credit accorded to Grant for conceiving the campaign, because the idea of attacking via the Tennessee River most likely would occur to many minds. It "must have been discerned by every military student . . . who gave himself to the most cursory examination of the maps,"[105] he declared. Other critics cited a private letter that General Frémont had written to Lincoln on September 8, 1861, almost three months before the day when Miss Carroll presented her plan, in which he outlined one that was apparently similar. Frémont, though, had wished only to occupy Paducah at the mouth of the Cumberland, then move up to Nashville and from there to Memphis, which he intended to attack from the land side. The plan was clumsy, neither far-reaching nor far-sighted, and cannot be considered in the same class with that of Miss Carroll.

Despite all protestations there is no doubt that Miss Carroll was the first on record to bring the Tennessee River route to Lincoln's attention. She also contributed much to its success by her detailed studies of how the enterprise should be executed. It was unquestionably her influence that brought about the transfer of the army from the Mississippi to the Tennessee,[106] thereby prompting Grant's campaign. She considered the detour from Fort Henry to Fort Donelson needless, as by taking the former the Cumberland fort would have been flanked and given up. Her real objective was the Memphis-Charleston Railroad, which was in due time breached at Corinth, with the resultant evacuation of Columbus and Fort Pillow. The fall of Memphis followed. Had her reasoning been followed, the siege of Fort Donelson and the battle of Shiloh might have been avoided. There was one possible flaw in her suggestion, however. If Fort Donelson had been given up without a fight, its garrison would have remained intact, and might have strengthened Johnston enough to hold the railroad which Miss Carroll coveted.

Up to the point of Grant's Vicksburg campaign Miss Carroll's ideas were both faultless and ingenious, but beyond this they became somewhat illusory. She advocated the occupation of Chattanooga, but this city was difficult of access, because at its location the Tennessee was no longer navigable; the city also was too inaccessible by land to be held permanently at that time. From there she outlined a movement to Mobile via the Alabama and Tombigbee rivers in order to cut the Confederacy in two.[107] This project was clearly infeasible, as were similar projects hatched elsewhere. Cutting enemy territory in two was a popular armchair speculation in those days, but the catch phrase never was properly evaluated. "Many an orator in his safe office," Sherman wrote scornfully, "... had proclaimed his purpose to cleave his way to the sea ... but things were not ripe till the Western army had fought ... down to the Atlantic."[108] If a path through enemy territory was to be permanently held, it required a firm base on both ends, and neither existed for the strip from Chattanooga to Mobile in the early part of the war. Chattanooga never did qualify as a supply depot, situated as it was in a district so barren of resources that in 1863 a Union army there almost starved to death; a year later it had to be supplied from Nashville, so it might serve as a secondary supply depot. "A Union army of 31,000 at Chattanooga in July 1862, without supplies," General Don Carlos Buell thought, ". . . might well have been in a worse condition than the stronger army in November '63."[109] On the southern end of the line lay Mobile, which was heavily fortified, and as late as 1864 still proved too hard a nut for Admiral David Glasgow Farragut to crack. While he forced his way into the bay, he did not try to take the city itself. Assuming, however, that both terminals had been occupied and well stocked, how could the strip itself have been made secure? In the fall of 1864, when Sherman marched through Georgia, he cut a wide swath through the state, but did not occupy it, although he failed to encounter the strong resistance which the Confederacy would have offered in 1862.

When Miss Carroll urged the project, it was the strip, not the enemy country, that stood in danger of being cut in two if not into shreds. The plan never became an actuality, and would not have served a worth-while purpose if it had been executed.

Miss Carroll received little thanks for her patriotic services. The Ohio Congressman Riddle, who had stood close to Senator Wade and to his powerful Joint Committee on the Conduct of the War, many years later lifted a corner of the curtain behind which her activities had been purposely hidden. These efforts of concealment notwithstanding, Miss Carroll's role in helping to shape the early course of the war could not be entirely suppressed. After the fall of the Forts Henry and Donelson, Riddle wrote, "We [men in Congress] began to surmise that there must have been a remarkable stroke of genius in the conception of this short, decisive and wonderful campaign, and on inquiry we were surprised that it was not claimed for Halleck [commanding the western armies], Grant [who had conducted the campaign], or Buell [commanding the

Department of Ohio], nor in fact for anybody. There was a world of innocent wondering over this, as the campaign certainly did not manage itself. There was apparent in the record, even to us, a really wonderful brain. Whose was it? ...

"Stanton and even Lincoln were approached, but said 'the public service required secrecy.' . . . Some, among them Wade, knew the truth. All this time there sat daily in the galleries a short, stout, middle-aged maiden lady, intently listening through an ear trumpet to the ineffective talk, which was sure to break out over our resolutions of thanks. This lady *knew* all the time; she was Anna Ella Carroll, the oldest daughter of Governor Thomas King Carroll of Maryland. . . .

"She had made such valuable suggestions to the President, showing such aptitude (genius we should call it in a man) for affairs, and for schemes and plans of campaign, that at the suggestion of Thomas A. Scott, Assistant Secretary of War, the President sent her to St. Louis to advise as to an expedition down the Mississippi. She went, held counsel with the most experienced river pilots, and advised against it. . . . She returned to Washington with the matured plan of the Tennessee campaign. . . . *She was a woman,* and that fact would have discredited all the generals and professionals in the army. . . .

"In 1871 ... committees of both Houses made the strongest reports in her favor, [but] she has ... sunk in[to] neglect."[110]

Riddle remarked sorrowfully that, due to this secrecy, "the world might never know [the truth], and indeed it never has generally known."

Riddle was almost right, for it was not until 1940, when Marjorie Barstow Greenbie published *My Dear Lady,* her first book on this subject, that later generations became acquainted with Miss Carroll's amazing story.[111]

Anna Ella Carroll, unlike Mahan, never concerned herself with the eastern theater of war, and after 1863 employed her gifts in fields unrelated to over-all strategy. She already had established a reputation as a keen debater by preparing a pamphlet on the war powers of the President, in which she had set forth to what extent he must follow the Constitution during an insurrection. Lincoln undoubtedly used many of her persuasive arguments, when in 1862 a Democratic convention in Albany challenged the constitutionality of his edicts,[112] and on other occasions. This pamphlet was followed by others, one of them about emancipation. All of them showed her unusual legal acumen. She also accepted assignments from various government agencies, and undertook some inspection trips at the President's request, to his complete satisfaction. Her patriotism, however, made her spend more money than she could collect, and she became embarrassed by financial difficulties, which increased as time went on. "And now," Riddle pleaded, "it is earnestly hoped that this woman, whose unaided brain changed the fortunes of the war, and whose plans, if followed out, might have ended the rebellion in twelve months, may at least be acknowledged ere the earth closes over her."[113]

Unfortunately, Riddle's pious hope was not fulfilled. Miss Carroll died poor, lonely and half forgotten. She shared with Mahan the regrettable distinction of having been denied the outstanding place in history which was well earned by both.

Of other people who suggested splitting the seceded states in two there was no want. Robert J. Breckinridge, member of a prominent Kentucky family, wished to establish a one-hundred-mile-wide strip of land in East Tennessee.[114] Another idea expressed in high circles was to start the strip at Chattanooga and extend it to Savannah.[115] It suffered from the same shortcomings as all others of this kind.

A North Carolina merchant of Northern birth and Northern sympathies named Edward Kidder tried to resurrect a plan which the British had evolved during the Revolutionary war, and which had contemplated a split starting at Charleston and stretching west for an indefinite length. Its purpose had been to separate the southern colonies from their northern allies. This scheme had not appealed to the British high command, and deservedly received no attention from the Washington authorities.

However, Kidder did propose another strategical move which, though originally conceived as a local enterprise, might have led to such important consequences that it might be classified as grand strategy. By 1864 the city of Wilmington, North Carolina, where he resided, had become the principal port for blockade-runners, and its loss would have been irreparable to the South. To take the town by a naval attack meant running the gauntlet of the mighty Fort Fisher, which guarded it, and of a thirty-mile stretch of battery-studded river banks. Kidder, in harmony with Mahan's recommendation, suggested to sidestep Fort Fisher by taking the city from its land side, and thought 12,000 men sufficient for the purpose. Lincoln was so interested in the idea that he was willing to increase the number to 20,000, and designated General Burnside as the leader of the enterprise, although many generals of greater capacity were available. To worsen matters, the President ordered the training of new levies for the venture,[116] instead of drawing on idle garrisons. When finally all preparations had been completed, Grant was about to start his Wilderness campaign and requisitioned Burnside's corps.

In September of '64, Edward Kidder's plan was revived through the influence of Governor John A. Andrew of Massachusetts, who went to Washington and had it approved again. Kidder was summoned to the capital and had an interview with Grant, who agreed to send the bulk of General Philip H. Sheridan's army from the Shenandoah Valley to North Carolina. But hard luck pursued Kidder and his carefully worked out design. Just at that time Jubal A. Early began offensive operations in the Valley, which made it manifestly injudicious to remove the Union troops from that region. It was then decided to abandon Kidder's plan. Thus the Confederates were left in possession of their prize harbor for almost another year.

One wonders how much the Washington high command might have gained, had it risen above Halleck's narrow-minded view not to let civilians do any planning, but had made greater use of brilliant laymen like Miss Carroll, Dr. Mahan, Kidder and maybe others, whose potentialities were not exploited, and of whom contemporary historians have left only shadowy records or no records at all.

LINCOLN'S GENERALSHIP

Both Lincoln and Jefferson Davis were commanders-in-chief of their respective armies; hence the way in which they met their responsibilities was of great, sometimes of decisive influence on the course of the war.

Lincoln's qualifications for this task were of a mixed character. He had received no military training to speak of, but he possessed an uncommon amount of common sense. His thinking, unencumbered by book rules, was straight and penetrating. Intellectual unorthodoxy, which was one of his outstanding characteristics, had often upset his courtroom opponents,[1] and promised to make him an equally formidable opponent in warfare.

Like many others who lack formal education, however, he was awed by people who held college degrees, especially West Point diplomas. When he entered the White House he considered the opinions of professional soldiers the essence of military wisdom. He probably was impressed by their casual references to flank movements and lines of communications, and by such technical expressions as abatis, chevaux-de-frise, logistics, attacks en echelon and batteries en barbette. But by and by he discovered that, despite this high-toned terminology, strategy and tactics were easy enough to understand. Flanking movements? Why, when a puddle of water made it difficult to enter a house by the front entrance, one used the side door. And when as a child he had had to remove the snow from the path to reach the spring, he had kept his line of communications open. He also may have remembered having seen better strategy in games played by boys on sand lots than the kind he had observed in the early battles of the war. At Bull Run the two generals had tried to outflank each other, with the result that they had walked part way around each other like two wary dogs. Neither accomplished what he had set out to do, because both had learned the same trick from the same teacher. At Pea Ridge one of the two West Point-trained generals walked clear around the other, so that in the end the Confederates, facing south, stood as if they were defending Missouri and Iowa, while the Union troops stood as if defending Arkansas and Louisiana. Each general was sitting on the supply line of the other and, if beaten, had no way to retreat.

Gradually Lincoln's awe of uniforms and epaulets gave way to contempt. He may have agreed with Clausewitz that "an acquaintance with military affairs is not the principal qualification of a director of war—it takes a superior mind." Lincoln's mind certainly was superior to that of most of his generals, and it is not surprising that at one time he played with the idea of taking the field himself, especially since his Attorney General had advised him that as commander-in-chief it was not only his right but his duty to lead the army.[2] He began to study books on strategy and tactics, and felt that he could do at least as well as his generals.

Simon Cameron, Lincoln's first Secretary of War, gave most of his attention to his own welfare and that of his friends, but his successor, Stanton, had very decided views on how to conduct the war and proclaimed them in the *New York Tribune* on February 20, 1862.

"Much has recently been said of military combinations and organizing victory. I hear such phrases with apprehension. . . . Who can organize victory? Who can combine the elements of success on the battlefield? . . . Battles are to be won . . . in the same and only manner that they are won by any people, or in any age, since the days of Joshua—by boldly pursuing and striking the foe."[3]

According to Stanton, winning the war was that simple. At any rate, he believed that the country would be better off if the generals did only what Lincoln and he told them.

Thus it came about that at the end of January 1862, a few days after Stanton had entered on his duties, Lincoln issued his War Order No. 1. He gave McClellan explicit orders, directed him how to carry them out, and specified the date on which he was to "strike the foe." McClellan, who intended to campaign via the Virginia peninsula, submitted a plan of his own, but Lincoln questioned its efficacy and warned him that, once on the peninsula, he would face the same enemy and the same entrenchments he was facing near by.[4] It was a naïve observation, which did little credit to Lincoln's military thinking, for he overlooked the topographical obstacles between Washington and Richmond, the winter weather, the sticky Virginia mud, the advantages of transportation by sea over that by land. Furthermore, he disregarded the fact that by publicly an-

85

nouncing his intended operations he had tipped his hand to the enemy. Where a few months before he had been afraid that he knew nothing about war, he now flattered himself that he knew everything.

Lincoln's and Stanton's generalship soon had occasion to prove itself. McClellan was about to close in on Richmond, when Stonewall Jackson created a diversion by sweeping through the Shenandoah Valley. Then and there he taught the President and Stanton their first practical lesson. They had assumed command of all troops in and around the Valley, and were going to show their generals how to catch Jackson, even instructed them how to go about it. But by stopping the advance of McDowell's corps which was about to join McClellan, and sending part of it into the Valley, they were, so a friendly contemporary critic observed, "swallowing a bait so plain that it might almost be said to be labelled."[5] The consequence was that the wily Confederate played fast and loose with his amateur opponents and, besides scoring one victory after another, attained his main purpose—the disruption of McClellan's campaign.

The two Washington tacticians had fumbled their first attempt at generalship, had fumbled it badly. The claims of their panegyrists, that bad weather had ruined their plans, reflected curiously on the ridicule they had heaped on McClellan, whose frequent complaints about the weather they had met with the quip that rain usually falls on friend and foe alike.

Strategically the attempt to entrap Thomas Jonathan Jackson was a blunder of the first magnitude. Even if everything had gone as planned, it would have been done at the cost of scuttling a possibly decisive campaign, which was nearing its culmination. The fact that Jackson had been detached and was out of supporting distance from Lee, should have prompted a quick attack on Richmond by McDowell's corps, in conjunction with the army of

McClellan, as Mahan had pointed out so convincingly. This would have made a triumphant conclusion of the campaign a near certainty, especially as McDowell, an aggressive fighter who was not under McClellan's command until his corps had joined the main army, might well have attacked on his own responsibility before it was possible to stop him. In that case McClellan would have been forced to lend his support.

Lincoln's discomfiture at the failure of his generalship had a sobering influence on him, at least temporarily. He realized that common sense alone, without some military know-how, was not enough. To correct this deficiency he appointed General Halleck to serve as his adviser. Halleck had distinguished himself by the slowest march ever made by a victorious army, eighteen miles in thirty days. It was his only field command of an army, but he had the reputation of possessing a wealth of theoretical knowledge, and this is what Lincoln was looking for. Together with his own good judgment, he hoped to have formed a winning combination; but the choice he made was the first example of Lincoln's remarkable ineptitude in selecting capable generals. Although he soon saw through Halleck's utter incompetence, he kept him on, perhaps to remind himself how obtuse major generals could be. At least no one has ever offered a better reason.

Measuring other generals by Halleck's low standard, the President thought that perhaps they all needed a refresher course. In the midst of the battle of Fair Oaks he sent McClellan this quaint suggestion: "Stand well on your guard, hold all your ground, or yield only inch by inch and in good order."[6] A schoolmaster was telling a backward pupil to be careful, try to win if he could, but put up a good fight anyway.

The President was talking down to McClellan, and McClellan was talking down to the President. Thus the friction between the two men kept growing. Nevertheless, where common sense alone counted, Lincoln's comments generally were straight to the point, often unanswerable. When, for instance, McClellan excitedly reported that 10,000 men had gone from Richmond to the Valley, and for this reason pleaded for reinforcements, Lincoln replied coolly that the departure of that many Confederates was equal to a like reinforcement to his side.[7] McClellan was left without a rejoinder.

Shortly afterward, though, Lincoln himself received a well-deserved rebuke. General Scott, to whom the President had gone for advice, suggested that he should either return McDowell's corps to McClellan or, if he wanted to strengten the defenses of Washington—which Scott thought well enough protected—draw it closer to the capital. At the conclusion of the conference Lincoln recognized that his generalship left something to be desired.

McClellan had signed his death warrant as an army commander by a letter he had handed to Lincoln at Harrison's Landing, in which he offered him much unwanted advice. The President from then on saw in him a future rival, and became more and more inclined to believe the sly innuendoes which were dinned into his ears. Yet, after the battle of Second Bull Run, he had the moral courage to recall the popular general, despite the threat of a mutiny in his own Cabinet.

But Lincoln's suspicion lingered on, and the interval between the battle of Antietam and the coming fall campaign showed him at his worst. His dispatches to McClellan had an irritating, nagging tone, as if he expected to receive intemperate replies, which would give him a wedge for an open break. On October 25 he sent this sarcastic message to his general, who had reported that many of his horses were on the sick list:

"I have just received your despatch about sore-tongued and fatigued horses. Will you pardon me for asking what the horses of your army have done since the battle of Antietam that fatigues anything?"[8]

If Lincoln expected to receive an angry reaction to his sarcasm he was disappointed. McClellan calmly explained the work the cavalry had done,[9] and then abided by the President's wish to advance on the east side of the Blue Ridge Mountains, where the army shielded Washington. His campaign was proceeding well, and everything appeared harmonious. Appearances, however, were deceiving. Disregarding his own maxim about the danger of swapping horses in midstream, Lincoln chose this inopportune moment to remove the commanding general, although as an experienced lawyer he must have realized the risk involved in changing counsel in the midst of a trial. The military situation presented a perfect parallel.

Welles, who was no admirer of McClellan, was amazed at Lincoln's action. "After [McClellan] commenced to move," he wrote, "I was less prepared to see him displaced, and the announcement came with a shock."[10] It also came as a shock to the Confederates, but their shock was a pleasant one. Lee had split his army into two corps, one under Jackson in the Valley, the other east of the mountains under Longstreet. McClellan proposed to move against Longstreet, sealing off the passes between the two parts of the Confederate army as he went along. "This was the move about which we felt serious apprehension," Longstreet admitted.[11]

By dismissing McClellan at this juncture Lincoln committed one of the grave errors which mar his career as commander-in-chief. The reason for his change in general was twofold. Beside seeing in McClellan a dangerous opponent at the next Presidential election, he wished to appease the Radicals, who hated the general, because he promised to gain an early victory. His dismissal placated them, and his replacement by a military misfit added to their satisfaction. Thus Lincoln brought about a political victory at the price of stopping a campaign while it was getting into full swing and its prospects were favorable.

A Pennsylvania congressman named William Darrah Kelley suggested Hooker as McClellan's successor, but Lincoln preferred Burnside because, he said, Burnside was a better housekeeper, fed his men well, cared for them better and therefore would get more fight out of them than Hooker could.[12] Lincoln probably was guided by Napoleon's epigram that an army marches on its stomach. This doctrine notwithstanding, he complained bitterly that the Confederate soldiers marched and fought exceedingly well without much food or care. He was right in reproving his generals for this disparity in performances, but he missed one important point: the Southern soldiers were defending their homes against invaders, while the Federals had no such powerful incentive to inspire them.

It was the President's privilege to discharge generals at any time, but prudence demanded that McClellan's campaign, which had been approved, be carried on without losing the momentum already gained, unless the new commander had a better plan. If so, it should have been ready at the time of his appointment. Lincoln neglected this elementary precaution. It developed that Burnside had no plan at all, and when he did evolve one, he had to take it up with Washington before executing it.[13] Pride or vanity had kept him from pursuing the campaign of his predecessor, and so several weeks elapsed before he got into action. The year before McClellan had been abused for spending the Indian summer in idleness, but the army then had not been fully organized. In November 1862 it was in perfect condition, well-trained, war-wise. Even if Burnside had won at Fredericksburg, the season had so far advanced by that time that it would have been impossible to exploit his success.

Burnside was defeated; Hooker, who took his place, lost his nerve, and with it the battle of Chancellorsville. His loss of self-confidence might have been forgiven, for this was his first big command. Many a private had lost his nerve in his first battle and become a good soldier later on. But Hooker followed his first error with one which was much less pardonable: he withdrew his troops from almost impregnable entrenchments, just as Lee was ready to make one of his headlong assaults against them. Yet Hooker was allowed to remain in command. Then, at the moment when another collision of the two armies was imminent, he was summarily fired and Meade, one of his corps commanders, was made head of the army. Once more Lincoln had swapped horses in the middle of a stream without urgent cause. If Hooker could not be trusted, as might have been assumed after his behavior at Chancellorsville, he should have been discharged at once; to wait till the Confederate army was almost in sight was challenging Fortune. Meade did not even know the disposition of the various army corps, nor did he have time to install his own chief of staff. Luckily for Lincoln, Fortune declined the challenge, and Meade won over Lee. But had he not been bewildered by the suddenness of his appointment, he might have turned Gettysburg from an empty victory into a Confederate debacle.

Lincoln should by now have realized that he was a bad judge of commanders, as he was of men in general. "My husband placed great reliance in my knowledge of human nature," his wife recalled, . . . "he had no knowledge of men."[14] Lincoln could be excused for misjudging Hooker, who had misjudged himself, but

Burnside had stated frankly that he lacked the qualifications for a commander-in-chief, and had twice refused to take command of the army. Lincoln had misinterpreted Burnside's confession, believing it a sign of modesty, and the mistake had had tragic consequences.

Meade, the President's next choice, was a dependable, although not brilliant officer, but he started out under the handicap of having to improvise his movements, with no time to spare. The laurels he gathered at Gettysburg were well earned, but it is understandable that he hesitated to risk losing them in an uncertain pursuit. Lincoln should have sensed this, and by failing to do so he muffed the greatest opportunity that ever came his way as commander-in-chief. With the swollen Potomac behind them, the Confederates were in an unprecedentedly precarious position. Lincoln, appraising the situation correctly, not only visualized the capture of their best army, but the end of the war. On July 7 he wrote to Halleck, "Now if General Meade can complete his work, the rebellion will be over." Halleck immediately wired to the front, "Push forward and fight Lee before he can cross the Potomac."[15] Then, undercutting the President, he advised Meade not "to be influenced by any dispatch from here against your own judgment. . . . Regard them as suggestions only."[16] To top his deceit, he counseled the commanding general that he had best postpone a general battle until everything was ready—whatever that meant.[17] Meade was only too willing to be overcautious. When one of his generals had urged him to follow the repulse of George E. Pickett's charge with an immediate counterattack, he replied, "We have done well enough."[18] In these five words he described his mental attitude better than he could have done in a two-hour speech.

Welles was disheartened. ". . . Halleck stays here . . . within four hours of the army . . . why does he not remove to headquarters in the field?"[19] The Secretary of the Navy remonstrated with his chief, but Lincoln had relapsed into his former awe of West Pointers and could not be moved. "It is proper," he said, "that I should defer to Halleck, whom I have called here to counsel, advise and direct in these matters, where he is an expert." To which Welles remarked sourly, "I question whether he should be considered an expert."[20] The answer to this question was obvious to everyone, the President alone excepted.

Where was Stanton during these days of decision? Had he not proclaimed "that battles are to be won . . . by boldly pursuing and striking the foe?" Now was the time to put this principle to work. Why was it not done? Had Halleck, Stanton's tool, sent his treacherous messages without his superior's knowledge and approval?

Welles guessed what was in the wind, and the reason behind it. "I fear the Rebel army will escape," he wrote three days before the escape took place, "and I am compelled to believe that some of the generals are willing it should."[21] Strange that the levelheaded Lincoln did not see how he was being victimized by the marplots in his entourage.

Not all the Union commanders deserved Welles's low estimate. General Alfred Pleasanton, who headed the Union cavalry, begged Meade to let him fall on Lee's rear, but was met by a rebuff.[22] General William H. French, stationed at Frederick with a few thousand men,[23] and acting on an order from Meade, had destroyed a pontoon bridge over the Potomac, on which Lee had depended for his retreat. But French could have done much better. Had he crossed to the other side before destroying the bridge, and subsequently frustrated any effort to rebuild it, he might have achieved lasting fame. General Abner Doubleday was the only one who suggested a similar plan which, simple though it was, bore the earmarks of a master stroke: he wanted to block Lee's escape route south of the river. "I do not see," he argued, "why a force could not have been formed on the Virginia side of the Potomac . . . and have cut off [Lee's] ammunition. . . . The enemy had but a few rounds . . . and our artillery could have opened a destructive fire . . . from a distance.[24] Troops could have been dispatched to Lee's rear from several points and reached their destination ahead of him. Colonel Herman Haupt assured Meade that, if necessary, he could build a bridge across the Potomac at some convenient place in less than forty-eight hours, with material from near-by houses or trees.[25] His offer was ignored. But there really was no need for a bridge, because there was no want of troops on the Virginia side or in a position to get there speedily.

The colonel of a Vermont regiment, which was garrisoning Yorktown to no purpose, wrote hopefully on July 8: "It looks very probable that one grand effort will be made to support and strengthen Meade, while he has Lee so 'in chancery,' and . . . give him no excuse for failing to annihilate Lee utterly; we have 20,000 troops that . . . could easily be spared."[26] Welles remarked that men had been ordered up from Pamunkey to reinforce "the great army, which is already too large."[27] If these troops had been kept south of the Potomac, they would have been of much greater service.

A frontal attack, although less desirable than the blocking of Lee's retreat route, also held out hope for a decisive victory. Lincoln himself belatedly pointed out that Meade had had all the men he needed for a *coup de grâce*. "You had at least 20,000 veteran troops directly with you," he wrote in a letter which he did not send, "and as many more raw ones within supporting distance, all in addition to those who fought with you at Gettysburg; while it was not possible that [the enemy] had received a single recruit; and yet you stood and let . . . the enemy move away at his leisure. . . ."[28] Doubleday supported Lincoln's statement. "Meade had [Charles B.] Sedgwick's fresh corps, and was reinforced by a division of 11,000

men. . . . Troops of Baltimore and Washington were also available."
The fact has remained undisputed that, no matter what course
might have been chosen, Lee was in a most serious predicament.

"Why did Lee escape?" someone asked a high Federal officer.
"Because nobody stopped him" was the reply.[29]
The aftermath of Gettysburg has never been described more
concisely, nor more truthfully.

When the President received the news that Lee had safely
crossed into Virginia, he was heartbroken. "We had only to stretch
out our hands," he wailed, "and they were ours, [but] nothing
I could say or do could make the Army move."[30] Then he made a
graver accusation against himself than anyone else could have done.
"I regret that I did not myself go to the army and personally
issue the order for an attack." According to Hay, he had at one time
entertained that thought in earnest. But no regrets could turn back
the clock. Perhaps, in the privacy of his thoughts, Lincoln condemned himself still more severely. Just as no captain leaves the
bridge during a storm, so Lincoln's place as commander-in-chief
had been at Gettysburg, not at the Soldiers' Home. "I could have
whipped them myself," he told one of his secretaries after everything was over.[31] There is little doubt that he could have.

History has dealt gently with the men who did not reach for
the rich prize which was within their grasp. No one but himself
has ever blamed Lincoln for his failure to go to the front. Stanton's part in the affair was not questioned. Halleck's incompetency
has been condoned, his underhanded conduct overlooked. Meade
retained his military status. But it was not only the North which

would have been benefited by the elimination of Lee's army, because if the war had ended then, an untold number of lives would have been spared to both sides. Moreover, the bitter feelings between them had not yet arrived at the point of no return, nor were the Northern Radicals yet numerically strong enough to obstruct reconciliation.

In July 1863 the difference between ending the war or prolonging it for almost two years measured less than 100 miles; for if Lincoln had personally seen to it that his orders were being obeyed, the loss of the South's principal army, together with her defeat at Vicksburg, most likely would have broken both her power and her will to resist.

After the debris of Gettysburg had been cleared away, and Lincoln realized that the half-baked victory was not the end but only a bloody episode in a long war, his state of mind descended to a new low. He had perceived the chance of dealing the enemy a knockout blow, had impressed it on his generals, and had been thwarted. He looked with dismay at Halleck, who sat on his chair like a pagan idol, doing nothing. Later in the year he tried in vain to goad Meade into action against Lee by offering to take full responsibility for a possible defeat, then watched him squander the remaining months of 1863 in useless maneuvers, and fretted in silence.

Welles never faltered in the belief that Lincoln underestimated his capabilities and should have used them to better advantage. When the President reminded Halleck that the officers of the Army had not shown the right spirit, he received "a short and curt reply," which incensed the faithful Secretary of the Navy. "This is the President's error," he sighed. "His own convictions and conclusions are infinitely superior to Halleck's—even in military operations more sensible and more correct always. . . ."[32] Welles's diagnosis unquestionably was correct, but superiority to the dull-witted general-in-chief did not necessarily denote great military capability.

By this time Lincoln should have realized that he had been most unfortunate in his efforts to run the war. He had ruined McClellan's campaign by meddling, when he should have stood aside, but had not meddled with Burnside's suicidal battle plan, and therefore had to some degree made himself reponsible for the Fredericksburg slaughter. He had not intervened when, after the fall of Corinth in the spring of 1862, Halleck had scattered a mobile army of 80,000 men, with which, as Grant rightly pointed out, Vicksburg or Atlanta or any point south of Corinth could have been occupied without bloodshed.[33] But at Gettysburg, when his meddling might have ended the war, he had failed to interfere with three-starred incompetence.

The failure to occupy Vicksburg in 1862 was one of the most inexcusable bunglings of the war. Halleck was mainly responsible for it, but Lincoln was not without guilt. In July of that year the President himself had asked General Mitchel if he could take Vicksburg, and had received the reply that with the aid of General Samuel R. Curtis' army he could do it.[34] The subject had then been debated in a Cabinet meeting, of which Secretary Chase wrote an extended account on August 2, 1862: "The . . . capture of Vicksburg was discussed. I reminded the President that after the evacuation of Corinth [on May 29, 1862] it would have been an easy matter to send down a few thousand men and complete our possession of the river; and of his own plan of putting Gen. Mitchell [Mitchel] at the head of his own division and Curtis' army . . . to take Vicksburgh, almost adopted more than two weeks ago. . . . Gen. Halleck had decided against this plan, on the ground that Mitchell's division could not be spared . . . and Curtis' army was needed to prevent a foray from Arkansas into Missouri. . . ."[35]

How little these two generals were needed in the manner Halleck indicated was soon demonstrated. Mitchel was sent to Tennessee, tried unsuccessfully to take Chattanooga, and on his retreat burned an important bridge without necessity. He was "without any ulterior purpose," his commanding general commented caustically.[36] Later he descended on northern Alabama, where his troops extinguished the prevailing Union sentiment by unheard-of depredations.

Curtis meandered through Arkansas, then lay idle at Batesville most of the time,[37] and finally holed up in Helena. In January 1863 the bulk of his force was, after all, ordered to support Grant in the Vicksburg campaign.[38] What so easily could have been accomplished half a year sooner was now attempted in most unfavorable circumstances. Lincoln, after asking Mitchel to try occupying Vicksburg the previous summer, had refused to meddle with the contrary decision of his woodenheaded and procrastinating general-in-chief, and so another opportunity to shorten the war had gone down the drain.

Reports from the west did not tend to lift the President's spirit, and a few months later he took to meddling again, and with very serious results.

On October 25, 1862, Grant had been given the command of the Department of the Tennessee, and the next day he wrote to Halleck that, since no plan of operations had been suggested to him, he proposed to "move down the Mississippi Central road, and cause the evacuation of Vicksburg."[39] Receiving no reply, he

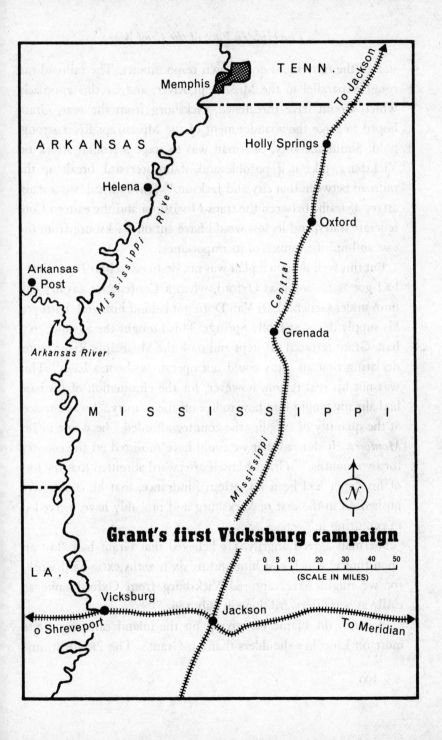

Grant's first Vicksburg campaign

TENN.

Memphis

To Jackson

ARKANSAS

Holly Springs

Helena

Oxford

Mississippi River

Arkansas Post

Central

Arkansas River

Grenada

MISSISSIPPI

Mississippi

N

0 5 10 20 30 40 50
(SCALE IN MILES)

LA.

Vicksburg

Jackson

o Shreveport

To Meridian

started the movement on his own responsibility. The railroad ran roughly parallel to the Mississippi River, and by this approach, which would have threatened Vicksburg from the rear, Grant hoped to force the abandonment of the Mississippi River stronghold. Simultaneously, Sherman was to stage a frontal attack on Vicksburg, take it if possible and, if unsuccessful, break up the railroad between that city and Jackson.[40] This railroad was a main artery of traffic between the trans-Mississippi and the eastern Confederate states, and its loss would have cut off Vicksburg from the east and nullified much of its importance.

But this well-designed plan was not destined to bear fruit. Grant had got as far south as Oxford, when a Confederate cavalry column under General Earl Van Dorn got behind him and destroyed his supply depot at Holly Springs. This brought the advance to a halt. Grant retraced his steps and took the Mississippi River route, declaring that an army could not operate without a base.[41] This was not his real reason, however, for the elimination of his base had already taught him how to live off the country. "I was amazed at the quantity of supplies the country afforded," he wrote in his *Memoirs*. "It showed that we could have subsisted off the country for two months."[42] Grant himself afterward admitted that the loss of his depot had been no serious hindrance, that he could have pushed on to the rear of Vicksburg and probably have succeeded in capturing it.[43]

Sherman agreed angrily. He believed that Grant had "lost an opportunity, which cost him and us six months extra-hard work, for we might have captured Vicksburg from Oxford quite as easily as was afterward done in July 1863."[44]

In truth, the blame for giving up the inland campaign rests more on Lincoln's shoulders than on Grant's. The President, impatient for the occupation of Vicksburg, which he should have ordered a year sooner, had lent an ear to the tales of an old friend, the Illinois politician-turned-soldier John A. McClernand. According to him, all the Union states which depended on the Mississippi for the transportation of their products were disgruntled, due to the interrupted navigation. To remedy this situation, he volunteered to raise 30,000 men and take Vicksburg, provided he were to be put in command of the expedition.[45] It was a bold request, but since McClernand was an influential politician, and voluntary enrollments had become scarce, Lincoln yielded to his blandishments. McClernand proved himself a good recruiter, and in a confidential order dated October 21, 1862, the President put him at the head of the troops he had assembled.[46] Of these backstage doings Grant had not been advised, but learned of them through newspaper gossip.[47]

Grant naturally was greatly concerned. Apparently the Vicksburg campaign was to be taken out of his hands. To forestall McClernand he gave up his promising flanking movement for the dubious and difficult venture down the Mississippi. Disregarding Lincoln's commitment, he kept the command of the campaign for himself, absorbed McClernand and his men, reduced him to the rank of a corps commander, and proceeded to take Vicksburg the hard way. Had he known of the intrigue in October, before he started on his inland campaign, he might have changed at once to the river route, with fair prospects for a successful outcome. Running the gauntlet of the Vicksburg batteries at that time would have presented much less of a hazard than it did next spring, and the roads on the Louisiana side, over which the troops had to march, were dry in the fall. As matters stood, Grant had to start the river campaign in January, when the waters were rising, making the roads alongside it impassable until April.[48] In the interval the Confederates had greatly strengthened their shore batteries and made the city itself well-nigh impregnable. And so six months were wasted, and thousands of men died of disease, while Grant waited for a return of the same favorable weather conditions he had passed up while trying to execute a far better strategy.

It was another example of Lincoln's meddling—muddling would be a more appropriate word in this case—and did as much damage to the Northern cause as his failure to meddle after Gettysburg. Yet in this instance it would be unfair to criticize him too harshly, because the temptation to add 30,000 men to the army was not easy to resist, and if Lincoln had foreseen the unfortunate consequences of his interference, he might have acted differently.

A few months later Lincoln tried his hand again in directing field operations by ordering Judson Kilpatrick's raid on Richmond, allegedly for the purpose of circulating the amnesty proclamation and liberating the Union prisoners on Belle Isle. The raid was ordered without Meade's approval, and all it accomplished was a loss in men and the temporary disability of from 3000 to 4000 horses, "the very flower of our cavalry," according to Brevet Major General Martin T. McMahon.[49]

At least one of Lincoln's Cabinet members regretted that the President took it upon himself to inaugurate campaigns or interfere with those already in progress. On February 27, 1864, Seward told Welles in a whisper that "we had met a serious reverse in Florida." Welles's comments, as usual, showed his keen insight: "The . . . expedition has been one of the secret movements that have been projected, I know not by whom, but suspect the President has been trying a game himself. He has done such things, I believe, always unfortunately."[50]

The last sentence, written by one of Lincoln's most loyal supporters, is an excellent summary of the President's achievements, whenever he overexercised his privilege as commander-in-chief.

The fall of Vicksburg was a great but not a decisive victory, and soon afterward the shadows descended again. Lincoln heard of Rosecrans going to pieces at Chickamauga and replaced him with Thomas, who took command of a starving army. But by the end of the year things looked up again. Grant relieved Chattanooga, then defeated Bragg at Missionary Ridge. Credit for these accomplishments did not properly belong to Grant, but that did not matter. In Lincoln's mind victory and Grant had become synonymous. Moreover, here was a general who, like the President, was not a slave to textbooks, but thought things out for himself. Grant had promised to stay out of politics, so he was to be the new general-in-chief, and Lincoln would stop trying to run the military side of the war. Experience had not only taught him that he could not control his generals, but also that military leadership must no longer be divided. One person, and one alone, would have to assume the burden. He shelved Halleck, whose uselessness had become a grim joke in the capital, and gave Grant almost unrestricted power. As to himself, he would confine his participation to the grand strategy of the war, where his clearheaded vision could be utilized to the best advantage.

One of the reasons for these drastic changes was that by this time the President had lost confidence in himself as commander-in-chief. "You know," he said to Stanton, "we have been trying to manage this army for nearly three years, and . . . we haven't done much with it."[51] It was an unusually candid confession.

When Grant decided on an overland attack against Richmond, Lincoln was delighted. He did not care to know the details,[52] but was happy that his favorite campaign plan was to be given the most thorough test yet undertaken. As heretofore, it met with calamitous results. Horror and shame must have overcome the President when Grant, after suffering unprecedented losses, decided to abandon his frontal attacks and try to cut Richmond's connections with its hinterland. As a result, the army had become stalled in front of Richmond, and month after month passed without further progress; yet Lincoln uttered no word of criticism, not even when Grant left Washington so denuded of troops that it might have fallen prey to a bolder raider than Early. On this occasion the President's failure to meddle almost led to disaster. He had insisted on keeping Washington fully garrisoned after Antietam, and again early in 1863, when an attack on Washington had been out of the question. But in 1864 he had idly stood by, while Grant siphoned off almost the entire garrison of the capital and left it unprotected, although the fighting had abated and he could easily have spared enough troops to guard it.

As the months rolled by without bringing victory appreciably closer, Lincoln felt that he had come to the end of his rope. Grant had been given the highest rank since George Washington, because he had established a reputation as a fighter; but lately he had made no worth-while progress. It was the old, old story again, delay following delay. Still, if Grant were dismissed, his successor might be worse, as had been the case in the past. Perhaps Welles was right when he claimed that all generals were procrastinators, because peace was bound to bring them either demotion or oblivion. Grant might have reasons to move slowly, and his obstacles might be insuperable, but Lincoln was sick of excuses and explanations. What he wanted, and what the country was crying for, was victories.

The victories came, but not from Grant; they came from Sherman. With the exception of Grant's Vicksburg campaign, Lincoln had paid little attention to the western scene of action, had never visited any of its battle fronts. On the whole, western campaigns had been mapped out without his interference. Aside from the Atlantic seaboard his main concern had been eastern Tennessee, and by insisting on its occupation he had upset much sound strategy. However, despite his resolution to stop giving strategical orders and his comparative indifference to the western theater, one more of his interventions was in the offing. He approved Banks's Red River campaign, although Grant opposed it strenuously.[53] Banks intended to penetrate into western Texas by means of a joint land and river operation. The campaign ended in a fiasco. The President at last saw the light. When he had left Grant to himself, Vicksburg had fallen, and the North had recorded its greatest triumph. He had left Sherman to his own devices, and everything was working out well in Georgia. Undisturbed by exhortations from Washington, uninfluenced by politics, Sherman was marching to Atlanta, to the sea, and to public acclaim.

Grant must have envied his subordinate, who could attend to the war without being shackled with political fetters; for though Lincoln no longer engaged in military back-seat driving, he still imposed his will on his general-in-chief whenever high politics demanded it. Grant's campaign plan for the spring of 1864 had been a copy of the President's original idea of attacking the South simultaneously on several fronts, and while Grant himself pounded the Confederates from the North, advances were to be made in other directions also. One of the armies was to move up from Bermuda Hundred, take Petersburg, and cut off the supplies of the Confederate capital. It was the stratagem Mahan had advocated from the start, and might have succeeded but for another of Lincoln's interpositions. Elections were coming up in the fall, and politics commanded top priority. The Army of the James, as the Bermuda Hundred force was called, was put under the incapable Butler, a Democrat who would attract many votes for the Administration. Grant could have dismissed him on his own initiative, and Sherman would have fired him in an instant; but Grant understood Lincoln's dilemma. Butler must be handled with silk gloves. The President had pledged himself to preserve the Union, and needed the support of both parties; also, he wanted to be re-elected.

As a consequence Butler remained, and promptly messed up the campaign. He did not take Petersburg, when it could have been done with ease, and then let himself be bottled up. After the election he was removed, but in the meantime thousands of needless casualties had been piled up on the altar of politics.

With the election out of the way, Lincoln definitely kept aloof from war operations. He still sent messages to Grant, but they were commonplace. "Wherever the enemy goes, let our troops go also,"[54] he wrote to Grant on August 3, 1864. Grant may have been astonished at such strange advice, since throughout the 1864 campaign he had forced the enemy to go wherever he himself was going, and was still holding the initiative at the time Lincoln penned this directive.

As the war approached its close, Lincoln withdrew more and more into the background. He kept in touch with the military situation, was informed of intended moves and let his generals know that he was eying them watchfully. To Grant he kept repeating the hard-earned lesson that the real goal of the war was not the occupation of Richmond, but the destruction of Lee's army; aside from that, he only sent out encouraging, but innocuous dispatches, and clothed his suggestions in inoffensive language. "If there is anything wanting which is within my power to give," he had written to Grant at the beginning of the Wilderness campaign, "do not fail to let me know it."[55] Later, when Grant, baffled and unhappy, crossed the James, Lincoln cheered him up: "I begin to see it; you will succeed."[56] And when Lee's army began to falter, and Sheridan thought that Lee would surrender, "if the thing is pressed," Grant received this admonition: "Let the *thing* be pressed."[57]

All this meant little, except in a psychological sense, but Lincoln could also let loose with a full blast when he thought the occasion demanded it. A year before Sheridan had beaten Early in the Valley, and the President, remembering Antietam and Gettysburg, had urged Grant to take no chances of losing the victory through a leisurely pursuit. "I repeat to you," he wired, "it will neither be done nor attempted, unless you watch it every day and hour, and force it."[58] Lincoln was speaking from bitter experience.

Aside from these occasional messages, Lincoln stuck to his resolution of noninterference. After Sherman had taken Savannah, he wrote to him very demurely: "But what next? I suppose it will be safer if I leave General Grant and yourself to decide."[59] No longer would he try to run the war from Washington, or issue specific orders and, best of all, he no longer changed generals on the eve of battle. Lincoln at last had found his niche as commander-in-chief. He applied his good sense to over-all strategy; Grant's business was to draw the noose around Lee; Sherman was marching victoriously through the Carolinas. And so, after four years of costly fumbling, for much of which Lincoln was responsible, the war came to the conclusion that, barring miracles, had been inevitable from the beginning.

⇒ 5 ⇐

NONMILITARY OVER-ALL STRATEGY

IN FAIRNESS to Lincoln it should be kept in mind that in his over-all planning he had to consider many factors besides those of a strictly military nature. Some of them ran counter to correct military thinking, yet each had to be weighed according to its relative importance in the general picture.

One of the conditions the President had to reckon with was the strong foreign element in the Northern states. In order to satisfy the Germans, the Irish, the Poles and other foreign-born recruits, especially the newly arrived immigrants, he thought it advisable to appoint generals from each national group, regardless of their ability. This led to the promotion of incompetents like Franz Sigel and Alexander Schimmelfennig, the latter, so it was said, having been chosen solely on account of his heavily accented name.[1] Furthermore, Lincoln felt he had to apportion high officers among the various states and, equally important, to gain the support of the Democrats by selecting some generals from their party. As a result, bungling field commanders like Butler were left in command long after they had demonstrated their worthlessness.[2]

In retrospect it appears that Lincoln would have been better off, had he concentrated on winning the war and paid less attention to these side issues. Victories would have made all critics and political opponents fold up. Trying to please everybody, Lincoln antagonized as many as he gratified, weakened the army, and so created to some extent many of his own vexations and troubles.

One important weapon which, surprisingly, Lincoln neglected, was psychological warfare. The term was yet unknown, but the underlying idea lay close to the surface. Conditions favored the use of it, especially in the beginning, when Union sentiment in the South still ran high. Unionists were scattered throughout the Confederacy, and in several localities lived in sizable groups. They formed the majority of the population in the western counties of Virginia, where they were powerful enough to secede and form a state of their own. Isolated eastern Tennessee, on the other hand, loyal to the Union, could offer no organized resistance, nor could the dissenters who lived in Northern Alabama, Northern Georgia and the hill districts of North Carolina. They, like some of the German and Scandinavian settlements in Texas, had to be held in check by force.

Gideon Welles saw through this situation with his usual perspicacity. He wrote in his diary that "a great majority [of Virginians] were opposed to . . . disunion sentiments, [but they] were passive, . . . while the Secession element was positive, violent and active. . . ."[3] Virginia and other Border States originally had voted against secession, and even the deep South had been far from unanimous in its desire to leave the Union. At the Georgia convention many delegates had been under the impression that secession was not to last long, but would serve only as a bargaining weapon. They acted as workmen do, who go on strike to better their conditions, but with no intention of destroying or harming the firm of which they are a part, and with which they expect to work in harmony again after an agreement has been reached. "The truth is," explained Alexander H. Stephens, Vice-President of the Confederacy, "in my judgment the wavering scale in Georgia was turned by . . . the words 'we can make better terms out of the Union than in·it.' . . . two thirds at least of those who voted for the Secession did so, I have but little doubt, with a view to a more certain reformation of the Union."[4]

In other Southern states similar conditions had prevailed, and Lincoln was convinced that, with the exception of South Carolina, no states had been anxious to secede.[5] One must wonder therefore why he, who was so clever in driving a wedge between England and France, did nothing to widen the rift between Secessionists and Southern Unionists. Welles constantly counseled endeavors along this line. "Instead of . . . treating as Rebels . . . all Union and disunion men in the insurrectory region," he advised, "we should . . . penetrate their territory, . . . protect the Union sentiment, and . . . strengthen a feeling counter to Secession."[6] He regretted that no friend of the Union in the South was offered protection.[7] He cited the specific instance of Norfolk, in the vicinity of which, he had been assured, a majority of the people were Unionists at heart, but "became cool, and were soon alienated by our abandonment."[8] The officers of the army, he complained, insisted on dividing the two belligerents by establishing artificial frontiers, as between the countries of continental Europe, "although large sections, and in some instances whole States, have a Union majority, occasionally . . . approaching unanimity."[9] He noted with dismay that apparently it was the military that was shaping the war policy of the Administration.

The Secretary of the Navy then tried to see matters from the viewpoint of a Southern Unionist. "No man in the South," he declared, "could avow himself as a friend of the Union without forfeiting his estate, his liberty, and perhaps his life. . . ." How, Welles asked pertinently, could he have remained loyal to the old Union in these circumstances without outside help? "The Federal government not only afforded him no protection, but under the military system of frontiers he was treated as a public enemy because he resided in his own home. . . ."[10] Senator John Brooks Henderson of Missouri shared Welles's opinion, and urged in 1862 that "the Union sentiment in the South should be cultivated."[11] Secretary of the Treasury Chase argued the case in a Cabinet meeting, as an entry in his diary shows. It is dated August 2, 1862, and reads: ". . . we had elected to act on the principles of a civil war, in which the whole population of every seceding State was engaged against the Federal Government . . . the bitterness of the conflict [has] now substantially united the white population of the rebel States against us. . . ."[12] This implied criticism found no response in Lincoln, not even during the final months of the war, when one touch of kindness, applied in the right place and in the right manner, might have been more effective in re-establishing the Union than all the victories of his generals.

Up to the last Welles was critical of Lincoln's uncompromising attitude. He regretted that in his December 1864 message to Congress the President had not appealed earnestly to the people within the Confederacy to come back into the Union, assured them that their states still were part of the nation, that after hostilities had ceased they were not to be treated as outlaws, and that their persons and property would be respected.[13] On the contrary, in his Second Inaugural the President uttered a veiled threat to the vanquished South, when he said, "Woe to the man by whom the offense cometh." In view of his well-known conciliatory intentions, what did he mean? Or was he carried away by his own poetical oratory?

That Welles had been appraising the situation correctly all along was shown by what was transpiring in some parts of the South. As early as June 1861 Union companies were formed in western North Carolina, and by November Unionists had become so strong that Confederate troops were asked for to protect the loyalists.[14] In the hill counties of Alabama the dissenting elements attempted to fly the Stars and the Stripes.[15] In the next year the Confederate General Gideon Johnson Pillow reported that the mountains harbored from 8,000 to 10,000 deserters and Southern Copperheads. In 1864 strong bands were assembling in Alabama to resist the government.[16] When a convalescent officer returned home, he found rebellious deserters terrorizing the southeast counties of the State.[17] In Texas some young Germans tried to reach the Mexican border to sit the war out, but were overtaken and slaughtered by local militia. When the war was two years old local judges in Georgia, North Carolina and Tennessee were trying to defeat conscription and encourage desertion.[18] At the same time secret societies to stop the war were being formed in Northern Alabama, and even within the army of the Tennessee.[19] In September 1863 Union meetings were openly held in North Carolina under the auspices of a society calling itself the Order of the Heroes of America. It soon found adherents as far north as southern Virginia.[20]

Jefferson Davis was incensed about several public meetings, in which treasonable designs were openly discussed and secret leagues were formed. He lashed out against "men of no mean position, [who] do not hesitate to avow their disloyalty and hostility to our cause, and their advocacy of peace on the terms of submission. . . ."[21]

Lincoln could not have been ignorant of these developments, and it is difficult to understand why he failed to take advantage of them. Had he adopted Welles's proposals, Southern peace advocates would have been encouraged, and might have prompted their government to make the best bargain possible.

The question why Lincoln, who tried honestly and desperately to speed the advent of peace, disregarded one of the best means to achieve this end, is one of the Civil War's most puzzling enigmas.

Psychological warfare, however, even though intelligently directed from Washington, would have been useless, unless the army had been imbued with the same humane spirit in which McClellan, Lee and other generals conducted the war. Unfortunately, this was not the case. The majority of Northern troops and officers had been indoctrinated with hatred by the press and radical politicians, as was illustrated by the experience of a cavalry officer from Chicago, who had served eight months in Arkansas. Returning in October 1862, he related that when he arrived in Arkansas, the majority of the people had been Unionists, but when he left, not one man in 10,000 still sympathized with the North, because Federal soldiers had been plundering local citizens, no matter what their political persuasions. This officer felt certain that, had affairs in Arkansas been managed differently, the state at the next election would have chosen a legislature and a governor wedded to Union principles.[22]

The Reverend Mr. Emery and his wife, who had just visited Memphis and Helena, Arkansas, in November 1862, attested to the truth of this report. They told of "the wanton mischief" and "mercenary plundering" of which the soldiers were guilty. "They rob and steal for private gain," they related, ". . . utterly regardless of the loyalty or disloyalty of the person depredated upon."[23]

Neither the Union officers in Arkansas, nor the shameless Colonel Turchin who had looked the other way while his men pillaged the town of Athens, were by any means the only ones who encouraged the brutality of their soldiers, instead of restraining it. On August 11, 1862, Sherman sent these lines to Secretary Chase: "I will write plainly and slowly—this is no trifle . . . when one nation is at war with another, all the people of the one are enemies of the other; then the rules are plain. . . ."[24] What rules Sherman had in mind he did not spell out, and did not have to, for he was shortly to make them known on his march through Georgia and the Carolinas.

Lincoln, as Welles had observed, submitted to the doctrine of military boundaries, which Sherman was so heartily recommending. Although the President never would have sanctioned such brutalities as men like Turchin and Sherman committed, he seemed to consider them incidents of war, and did not disapprove them.

A strange case in which he could have rectified an iniquity of this kind has been recorded by his old friend Orville H. Browning, who represented a widow named Fitz as her attorney. Mrs. Fitz was a staunch Unionist, had owned a cotton plantation in Mississippi, and Federal soldiers had taken from her 10,000 bushels of corn and all her forty-seven slaves, without offering her payment for either. The impoverished woman had refugeed to St. Louis, and now asked no compensation for her slaves, but begged that a sufficient number of Negroes be allotted to her for the coming season to work her farm. She promised to pay them full wages for the produce raised. This reasonable request was warmly supported by Browning, but for no apparent reason Lincoln flew into a towering rage and expressed his refusal in unusually rude language. Rather than agree to make good losses occasioned by rebels, he declared, he would take a rope and hang himself. When Browning pointed out that the wrong had been committed by Federal soldiers, that her property had been taken from her by the Washington government and was now being used by it, Lincoln replied that she had lost no property, because her slaves had been free when taken. Browning, though, stated as a fact that at least a portion of them had been taken before the Emancipation Proclamation, whereupon the President, in a very excited manner, said that he would rather throw up than do anything about the matter.[25]

This spirit of remorselessness, issuing directly from the White House, severely handicapped those who wanted to disseminate conciliatory propaganda in the south. The roots of friendly feelings could have been preserved, if the Washington Administration had differentiated between the leaders and the led, with further differentiation among the latter between Unionists and Secessionists. No such distinctions were ever made, no hope ever held out to courageous dissenters.

Undaunted, Welles kept hammering at the desirability of fostering better relations with the civilian population of the Confederacy. In September 1864 he again diagnosed the situation, and this time prescribed practical remedies. "A large portion of the people in the Rebel region," he wrote, "are not enemies of the Union; they sincerely desire its restoration. . . . Give them . . . the opportunity. Promote friendly intercourse. Let the people in such portions of the country . . . come forward with their cotton and begin to feel that they are of us and we of them. Tennessee and Kentucky, northern Georgia and Alabama . . . can thus, under skillful and right treatment be soon reclaimed."[26] But by then sectional hatred had replaced calm judgment even in high quarters. William Whiting, solicitor of the War Department, urged that no exceptions be made in dealing out punishments after the war, and went so far as to include such a Union-minded Southerner as the Vice-Presidential candidate, Andrew Johnson, who had never wavered in his allegiance, in the list of those who were "to be treated like Rebels."[27]

This unreasoning lust for vengeance blinded Northern chauvinists to the fact that after the Confederate defeats in the summer of 1863 the time for a psychological victory was ripe. The citizens of the seceded states were worn out, hungry, desperate. In September of that year Sherman reported from Mississippi that "the smaller farmers, mechanics, merchants and laborers, . . . [which] class will probably number three-quarters of the whole, . . . are essentially tired of the war, and would slink back home if they could."[28] North Carolina was teetering on the brink of seceding from secession, and Georgia was in a state of unrest. Lack of food, clothing and other necessities was exerting an almost unbearable pressure on the entire population, and a fair offer for an honorable return to the Union might have led to a quick disintegration of the Confederacy. Yet the contrary of what Welles was striving for came to pass, because the North had constantly been waging psychological warfare in reverse, by irritating, torturing and antagonizing the people in the South through measures that had no influence on the armed conflict but prevented *rapprochement*. Although Lincoln in his message to Congress on December 3, 1861, had declared that he was "anxious and careful that . . . the conflict . . . shall not degenerate into a violent and remorseless . . . struggle,"[29] he did nothing to enforce this lofty principle. He had not protested against nor meted out drastic punishment for the depredations of the army in Arkansas, northern Alabama and other territories strong in Union sentiment. Not even Sherman's devastation in Georgia aroused his resentment, although these outrages tended to kill in the bud the good will he intended to engender by a generous peace.

Far from taking steps to aid and encourage Unionism in the opposite camp, the Washington government had early issued a decree that was bound to have the contrary effect and tended to solidify all Southerners into a hostile and unforgiving phalanx. This decree forbade the sending of medicines and surgical supplies into the Confederate states. As a war measure it was futile, because forcing wounded Confederate soldiers to undergo operations without the benefit of anesthetics would not bring victory nearer; the chief sufferers, however, were not soldiers but civilians. Most military hospitals fared fairly well, for they had first call on all medical supplies obtained through captures and blockade-runners. Nevertheless, they too often felt the shortage. In July 1862 the chaplain of a Northern regiment visited a Richmond hospital and reported that "all the sick . . . are suffering from scarcity of medicines, and the Confederates complain bitterly of the action of our Government in declaring medicines contraband of war."[30] What caused the greatest and most needless misery among civilians was the lack of quinine, especially in fever-ridden swamp districts; yet great suffering also was due to the inability of surgeons to obtain sufficient amounts of morphine, chloroform and calomel. Lack of replacements for their worn-out instruments further aggravated the situation. Some surgeons had to use table forks and knives for operations, and one was known to have used a penknife and a knitting needle.[31] People who saw their closest relatives burn themselves out due to lack of quinine, or tossing through sleepless, pain-filled nights because no morphine was available, would fight to the last against an enemy from whom they expected no mercy when the war was over.

The classification of medical supplies as contraband of war had its roots in Lincoln's "Proclamation Forbidding Intercourse with Rebel States," which he had signed on August 16, 1861.[32] The proclamation did not specifically mention medicines or medical instruments, and provided exemptions at the discretion of the Secretary of the Treasury. But by the way in which Secretary Chase interpreted the proclamation it grew into one of the most strictly enforced embargoes ever imposed against an enemy country.

Many Northern people, strange to say, endorsed this cruel measure without any pangs of conscience; worse, they actively supported it. The Louisville *Journal,* for example, warned detectives to be on the lookout for women whose crinolines might contain "contraband."[33] That the medicines they carried were intended to alleviate the pains of the sick did not matter to the writer.

The army was no more lenient than the police, and at least one Northern commander went to such an extreme that it bordered on the farcical. In October 1862 the Confederate General Earl Van Dorn had his headquarters in Holly Springs and, being "short of the comforts and luxuries of life," as General Sherman phrased it, endeavored to provide himself by having them smuggled out of Memphis. "I connived at his supplies of liquor, boots, gloves, etc for his individual use," Sherman confessed, "but medicines . . . were confiscated."[34] No doubt Sherman was proud of this heroic act.

General George Stoneman followed in Sherman's footsteps. On his cavalry raid in May 1863 he encountered Lee's supply of medical stores and ruthlessly destroyed it.[35] Not to be outdone, General Sheridan did the same a year later.[36] The depth of infamy, however, was reached by General Butler, when he sentenced a druggist to months of hard labor with ball and chains for sending a few ounces of quinine to his friends outside the city.[37]

The extreme severity with which the embargo was enforced was matched by the indifference of the North to the sufferings of its own prisoners. Unable to get medicine inside the Confederacy, the Richmond government offered to buy them from the North for gold, cotton or tobacco, and guaranteed that they would be used solely for the inmates of prison camps and under the supervision of Federal surgeons. The proposal did not even elicit a reply.[38]

How sadly the prevailing war psychosis had warped public thinking even in cultured circles was demonstrated at the annual meeting of the American Medical Association, held at New York in June 1864. One Dr. Augustus K. Gardener of New York City introduced a resolution, in which he set forth that "it is the duty and great distinction of Christian nations, and in conformity with the highest instincts of humanity, to assuage the sufferings and mitigate the horrors of war, . . . in which attempt the medical profession has ever been eminently conspicuous." He then pointed out that the blockade had, to a great extent, deprived "the sick and wounded, the feeble babe, the helpless woman, the aged man, as well as the sufferers . . . in the ranks of our enemies, of needful appliances," but that 10,000 Union soldiers, made prisoners, also "have been compelled to have operations performed without relief . . . which chloroform would bring" and without "many needful medicines and instruments."

Dr. Gardener proposed that the meeting urge the government to remember the universal brotherhood of man, and to "request the President to take such action as shall cause all medicines and medical surgical instruments and appliances to be excluded from the list called 'contraband of war.'"

Between the dry lines of the transactions one senses the chilly reception which was accorded to Dr. Gardener's resolution. One Dr. Silas L. Loomis of Washington moved to lay the whole matter on the table, but such a gentle disposition did not seem to please a Dr. A. Mayburry of Philadelphia, who suggested adding the word "indefinitely," in which form the resolution was carried. The record does not show how many, if any, of the physicians present sided with the humane Dr. Gardener, nor does it mention that he was said to have been hissed from the hall.[39]

Lincoln indirectly gave his stamp of approval to Chase's interpretation of the Trading with the Enemy Act. In April 1864 a half sister of his wife, who made no secret of her allegiance to the Confederacy, asked the President to give her a pass to go south. Her wish was granted, but she returned the pass with the further request for permission to take along her trunks, which were not to be examined. No one, of course, entertained any doubt about the contents of her luggage. Lincoln refused the request,[40] for he could hardly violate his own proclamation in favor of his wife's relative so long as it was being enforced against all other Confederates.

A Southern lady commented caustically on the edict. "Abraham Lincoln," she wrote, "professes to conduct his war on the most humane and merciful principles, yet he has declared all medicines and surgical instruments contrabands of war, a thing never before heard of among civilized people. . . ."[41]

Although the Southern population endured great hardships

from the lack of medical supplies, stricter regulations by the authorities might have provided some relief. As it was, speculators were able to contract with the captains or owners of the blockade-runners for their entire medical cargoes.[42] In cases where an auction was held at the port of entry, they usually outbid every outsider for the coveted goods, which they resold to the public, often heavily adulterated and at outrageous prices.[43] In July 1862 when the Confederate money had as yet only slightly deteriorated, the *New York Herald* reported that an ounce of quinine, priced at five dollars in New York, cost sixty dollars in Richmond.[44] A single quinine pill sold for one dollar, and at times was unobtainable at any price. One wonders if Lincoln and the outwardly pious Chase would have relented, had they read a letter written to Jefferson Davis by a disconsolate mother. "Twenty grains of quinine," she wailed, "would have saved our two children . . . they are now at rest . . . I have their little graves near me. . . ."[45]

To what degree the South was deprived of medicines is difficult to estimate, for contemporary reports are contradictory. One of the reasons for this uncertainty is that the shortages fluctuated both geographically and chronologically. Druggists near the seacoast were better off than those in the interior, and the over-all supplies varied from time to time. Whenever large captures were made or blockade-runners were especially successful, soldiers as well as civilians benefited. During the last two years of the war, however, captures were few, and even Lee's army had to depend almost entirely on blockade-runners for chloroform, morphine, quinine and digitalis.

It is understandable, though hardly excusable, that the medical embargo has virtually been ignored by Northern writers. It is less understandable why their Southern counterparts have given it little attention. Jefferson Davis in *The Rise and Fall of the Con-*

federate Government condensed his complaint about the matter into a few lines: "A petty war was made on the sick, including women and children, by carefully devised measures to prevent them from obtaining the necessary medicines. Were these the appropriate means by which to . . . preserve a voluntary Union?"[46]

Mrs. Davis made hardly any critical mention of the subject in her *Jefferson Davis, a Memoir by His Wife,* nor did the journalist Edward Alfred Pollard in his *The Lost Cause.* Southern newspaper editors seem to have been too busy publishing recipes for substitutes to devote much space to protestations. A search through diaries has been barren of important results, as has been one for letters written at the time. Among modern writers Mary Elizabeth Massey in her excellent book *Ersatz in the Confederacy* has a chapter on "Drugs and Medicine," and Dr. Norman H. Franke has written a scholarly article on *Pharmaceutical Conditions and Drug Supply in the Confederacy.*[47] Recently H. H. Cunningham has written a fine compendium on the subject in his *Doctors in Gray.*[48] While all these writers and a few others have made valuable contributions to our knowledge of the subject, Miss Massey seems the only one who commented adversely on the embargo. "Few war measures," she declared, "caused feeling to run so high in both the North and the South, for many felt this to be an inhuman, barbarous act."[49]

Is it possible that the want of medicines was not so acutely felt as one would assume? Dr. Franke suggests that people in the South were not so badly hurt as would have been the case elsewhere, because they were strongly addicted to homemade medicines.[50] One may add that their markets were swamped with substitutes and recipes; cultivation of medical plants also was encouraged and yielded some homemade opium of satisfactory quality. As to chloroform, it had not yet been universally adopted by the medical profession, and inhabitants of rural districts probably were scarcely aware of its existence. Clandestine procurements of all the materials in scant supply undoubtedly also did much to alleviate prevailing shortages. For some of these transactions permits were issued by Union generals, usually in order to obtain in exchange cotton and sugar.

On the other hand, it may be argued that most contemporaries who wrote on the subject lived in the larger cities, where the want was not so severely felt; that in the hardest-hit malaria-invested districts, which lay off the beaten path, parts of the population were illiterate or averse to letter writing, and were further restricted by the lack of paper and ink; that as a whole the Southern people were a rugged race, inured to hardships and not easily given to complaints. It is possible also that in all the misery which the Confederacy had to bear, the deficiency of medicines was only one of many evils, and so received less attention than it would have been accorded under normal conditions.

Vying in cruelty with the embargo on medicines were the efforts of the Washington government to deprive the Confederacy of salt. There was one noteworthy difference, though. Lack of medicines affected only a limited number of people, while lack of salt affected the well-being of the entire population. The struggle for this precious mineral was so widespread and intense that it developed into a veritable salt war, a sort of war within the war, which was fought with ferocity on one side, with desperation on the other. Although rarely touched on by historians, it approached in drama, persistency and importance the clash of arms on the battle fronts.

A few years after the return of peace an ex-Confederate gave a lecture in New York State, and startled his audience with this opening sentence: "Do you know why you Northerners whipped us? Because you had salt."[51] This statement was not so gross an exaggeration as it appears at first glance. A Union officer, returning from a raid on some saltworks near Pensacola, boasted that their destruction had hurt the South more than would have the loss of Charleston. And the *New York Herald* hailed the demolition of saltworks on St. Joseph's Bay in Florida as a greater blow than capturing 20,000 troops.[52]

Aside from its use for human consumption, salt was indispensable for curing pork and beef, also for packing eggs, butter and other edibles. Immense quantities of badly needed food were lost to the South because of the inability of farmers to obtain enough of this preservative. Without salt, Sherman wrote to Chase in August 1862, the Confederates "could not have moved their armies in mass."[53]

The North did not immediately interfere with Southern salt supplies, because their impact on the conflict apparently was not realized until later; but this complacency did not last long. On July 30, 1862, General Sherman complained to Grant's aide John A. Rawlins that "salt is as much contraband as powder. All Boards of Trade are shipping salt South. . . ."[54]

By December of that year the Federal authorities had become thoroughly aroused, and General Daniel Ruggles wrote that stringent orders had been received by Major General Butler and Commodore Farragut from Washington, prohibiting the shipment of salt.[55]

Nine months afterward Sherman still was not satisfied with the way these orders were being enforced, and on October 25, 1863, he sent to Secretary Chase a copy of what he had written to Admiral Porter at Cairo: "There are some things such as salt for curing meats, medicines for curing wounds and sickness, that I am not clear about and care less. . . . If you will prepare a list of Contraband, and send it to Secretary Chase he will make it public and save us a lot of trouble."[56] What trouble this order would have saved the North is obscure, but there was no obscurity about the suffering it was bound to cause in the South, especially among noncombatants. It is also noteworthy that Sherman held salt as important as medicines.

At the beginning of the war the seceded states had been able to obtain sufficient quantities of salt from large brine lakes in western Virginia and Kentucky, and no shortage was felt until these passed into Union hands, never to be recovered. Smaller deposits of salt existed near Mobile, Alabama, and in other parts of the South, but these were barely sufficient to take care of the adjoining communities. The Confederacy therefore had to depend mainly on its two remaining large-sized sources: one at Saltville in southwestern Virginia, the other in Louisiana. Some salt also kept filtering through the lines, some was secured from blockade-runners, and more was extracted from sea water.

Saltville was situated in a territory difficult of access, and for three years no serious attempts were made by the Federal armies to rob the South of this source. Nevertheless, transportation problems proved almost as great an obstacle to the distribution of the salt as enemy action. Due to inadequate rolling stock the railways could not handle the traffic efficiently, and wagons were lined up for miles along the roads leading to the saltworks. At times only about one third of the mined product could be taken away, and some salt purchased in October 1863 still remained unshipped by the next March.[57]

The relative peace at Saltville was not destined to last. In May 1864, General William W. Averell, heading a body of cavalry, threatened the place, but was successfully opposed by a Confederate cavalry brigade under General Albert G. Jenkins, who was severely wounded in the ensuing fight.[58] In September of that year General Stephen G. Burbridge with 5,000 men again made an attack, when Virginia Reserves, composed almost entirely of boys and old men, managed to hold the Union forces at bay. But three months later General Stoneman with 4,000 men finally succeeded in destroying much of the works, having only a handful of militia and teamsters to contend with.[59]

The source next in size was located on a small island in Louisiana, at the head of Vermilion Bay, near the town of New Iberia. It had long been known that brine wells existed there, but the owner of the island, while deepening them, unexpectedly struck a bed of pure rock salt. A packing establishment was erected near by, and considerable quantities of the commodity were transported by steamers to Vicksburg and Port Hudson, whence they were transshipped to eastern points.

A few months after the opening of the mine it was shelled by a Union gunboat, but the vessel became entangled in the marshes and had to abandon its aggression.[60] In April 1863, however, General Banks succeeded in wrecking the works, which were protected by only a small force of infantry and a section of artillery.[61] Shortly afterward Vicksburg and Port Hudson surrendered, and from then on what was left of the deposit could benefit only the trans-Mississippi portion of the Confederacy.

Sea water, subjected to a boiling process, furnishes a salty residue; but while the utmost efforts were made to exploit this source, lack of utensils and bags hampered continuous production. Moreover, the ocean beds were favorite targets for the Federal Navy. On the Florida coast it demolished hundreds of saltworks in one raid alone, but they were back in operation within a short time, whereupon they were destroyed again. The Union officers seemed to consider these intermittent attacks an amusing sport. In January 1864 an otherwise humane and fair-minded officer reported, without regret, the destruction of four large saltworks, plus a quantity of imported salt, along the North Carolina coast.

No substitute for salt was ever found. Saltpeter, which might have been used, commanded top priority for the manufacture of gunpowder, and the dirt from the floors of smokehouses, which also proved fairly acceptable, was soon exhausted. Several other substitutes were tried, but none of them proved satisfactory.[62]

The scarcity of salt in the South was reflected in the prices it commanded during the course of the war. Before the conflict it sold in New Orleans for one-fourth cent per pound, by September of 1861 it cost three cents a pound in Richmond, and by the following January the price had risen to twelve cents in Savannah. In November of that year people paid $1.30 for a pound in the black market.[63] In 1865 salt had risen to $5.00 a pound, but by then the debasement of the Confederate currency had proceeded so far that it makes a proper evaluation of this price difficult.

A quaint sidelight is thrown on the situation by a report of the wedding of General Pickett, which took place on September 15, 1863: one of the most precious gifts was a small package of salt.[64]

Equally significant is a letter which General Forrest sent General Taylor in the fall of 1864. He had been ordered to gather supplies in West Tennessee, but found that the natives would hide them rather than give them up or accept Confederate money in payment; but, he added, if they could be paid in salt or anything else of use to the people in their homes, the supplies might be forthcoming.[65] From the fact that Forrest put salt first, it may be assumed that he considered it the most desirable item on his barter list.

This is only one instance which shows that from a military point of view the damage resulting from the salt shortage was far from negligible. Aside from the inability to cure and store meat needed by the Army, and its interference with the manufacture of various products, such as leather, it necessitated the detachment of troops that could ill be spared. Its chief effect, however, was the spoilage of valuable food products, which contributed materially to the undernourishment of both soldiers and civilians. As might be expected, the main blow fell on the poorest classes, who could not afford to pay the prices demanded by speculators for what little salt was for sale, and were rarely able to obtain it through the ordinary channels of trade.

A strange feature of the medical contraband measure was that no one in the Washington administration, not even Welles, recognized or exploited its potentialities as a propaganda weapon. After the battle of Gettysburg the government missed a rare chance to undermine the Southern war spirit. Morale in Richmond then was extremely low; adding to the gloom, the hospitals were overflowing with wounded soldiers, who could not be properly cared for. At this juncture Lincoln might have sent several trainloads of medical supplies and salt to the enemy capital, together with one of his poetical messages, saying that he was not fighting sick or wounded men; that, after all, both sections would again be brothers some day, and that love for their estranged fellow citizens had never died in Northern hearts. Such a gesture might well have started a grass-root peace movement of such magnitude that the Confederate authorities could not have stemmed it. But supposing that this was too much to hope for, what possible damage could have resulted? If nothing else, the shipment might have revived some of the mutual feeling of kinship that had previously existed on both sides. No doubt skeptics would have ascribed sinister motives to Lincoln and warned the people against Greeks offering presents. But for the first time Southern Unionists would have had an answer to scoffers, who sneered that Lincoln was preaching charity in the North while practicing malice in the South.

SCIENTIFIC AND TECHNOLOGICAL WARFARE

ONE of the most interesting aspects of the Civil War was the attitude of both combatants toward military improvements and inventions. The world stood at the threshold of a scientific and technological revolution, but few of those in authority seemed to realize it. One of the reasons for this apathy no doubt was that no member in the two rival cabinets had a scientific or technical background. Lincoln shared this handicap, but made up for it by eagerly following and encouraging developments in these fields. The President was an inventor in his own right, and his interest, despite his skimpy education, was not limited to powder, firearms, ships and other matters with which one would expect him to be familiar. In fact, in his search for new and better tools of war he may be said to have stood in a class by himself, with Welles running a close second.

The primary and most obvious aim of both sides was, or should have been, to procure the best possible firearms, and as soon as possible. The North, although boasting many long-established manufacturers of these weapons, and able to shop in the world's markets, failed to lengthen its favorable odds at the right time. If the Federal soldiers had been fully armed in 1861 with whatever breechloaders were available then, the war would have been over in less than a year. So thought General Edward P. Alexander, Longstreet's capable chief of artillery,[1] and his opinion is supported by evidence that the war itself furnished.

While the war might not have ended in one year, because enough breechloaders could hardly have been produced or procured within this short period, the psychological effect of such a superior weapon would have been of incalculable value, even before the supply could have caught up with the demand.

The Washington administration had no excuse for not ordering breechloaders right from the start, because this type of weapon was neither new nor untested. In 1860 John B. Floyd, Secretary of War under Buchanan, had tried out several types. Finding that they could be fired three times as fast as muzzle-loaders, and that a man could load them while lying down without exposing his body, he called them a great innovation, and predicted that they would replace muzzle-loaders when and if the ordnance officers would see the light.[2] One type, Sharp's, had been in production for twelve years and had proved its worth in "bloody Kansas."[3] Lincoln agreed that breechloaders should be bought, but complained bitterly that "the Bureau Officials" were against him. Complaining, of course, did not help matters. If he had acted as energetically as he had in pushing the completion of the *Monitor,* the result probably would have come closer to confirming Alexander's statement.

Lincoln's interest in improved firearms never flagged. The belated introduction of breechloaders and subsequently of the almost irresistible Spencer rifles was largely due to his promptings, but in spite of his efforts, these and other repeating rifles did not make their appearance in fair quantities until about a year before the end of the conflict.

Lincoln turned his attention to almost any innovation that came along. He personally tried to evaluate guns, rifles, incendiary bombs, flame throwers and innumerable gadgets, most of them worthless. Sometimes his activities aroused the ire of Welles, who feared that the President's frequent "irregular proceedings," for which he had no authority, would create difficulties for himself and others. One of these cases involved a new gunpowder, for which Lincoln had given a man whom Welles called Dillon [his right name was Isaac R. Diller][4] a written promise of $150,000, provided the product should perform satisfactorily. Welles was sharply critical of this rash act, especially as the Navy Department, on which had been placed the financial obligation, had no appropriation for it. "The President," Welles complained, ". . . has a propensity to engage in matters of this kind, and is liable to be constantly imposed upon by sharpers and adventurers."[5]

It never seemed to dawn on Lincoln or the Ordnance Department that scientific and technical investigations are not a one-man task, but should be undertaken by a group of experts. The creation of an agency for this purpose had been recommended by the *Scientific American* as early as May 1861, and subsequently had been urged by it several times, without eliciting any response, except from Secretary Welles who, with Congressional approval, appointed a board to give its opinion on armoring battleships. The board consisted of three naval officers, who admitted frankly that they did not feel competent, "having no experience, and but scanty knowledge in this branch of naval architecture." Nevertheless, in obedience to orders, they deliberated for six weeks, and then came forth with the enlightening statement that "opinions differ . . . on armature for ships. . . ."[6] After the *Monitor-Merrimac* fight had settled this issue, Welles decided on a broader approach and asked Congress for $100,000, to be used in screening novel ideas and testing out those that looked promising. Congress refused the money, and the proposal died a-borning.[7] Had Congress shown greater foresight, this small sum, intelligently applied, might have proved a splendid investment. Few legislators evidently realized the interrelation between technology and modern warfare.

The appropriation that Welles had asked for could have been instrumental in forming the nucleus of a research center, for which purpose the Smithsonian Institution in Washington seemed as if made to order. It was presided over by Dr. Joseph Henry, a scientist of renown, who headed a staff of able assistants. His own specialty was electrodynamics, and it was said that but for his modesty he would have been credited with the invention of telegraphy. In addition, the country could have counted on many other scientists of high repute. Welles reported meeting several, among them the famous Professor Louis Agassiz, at a social gathering,[8] and may have speculated whether their gifts could not have been put to better use than parlor conversations.

Although Dr. Henry was not directly or officially connected with the war effort, he headed an informal club of high-grade scientists and engineers, who met every Saturday evening to discuss scientific subjects, usually such in which the public was interested at the time.[9] There is no reason to doubt that many pertaining to the war came under the scrutiny of this gathering, for one of the members was Quartermaster General Montgomery C. Meigs, an engineer of high repute, who had been instrumental in building the Washington aqueduct and parts of the enlarged Capitol. General Thomas, though not a member, was often invited to the meetings and participated in the discussion. Secretary of the Treasury Hugh McCulloch also was a frequent guest. Under these conditions debates on technical and scientific war problems could hardly have been avoided. But since the club kept no minutes, details of its proceedings are not available. Luckily, McCulloch recorded the names of the most prominent members, and they give a fair picture of the variety of talents represented in this illustrious group.

Dr. Henry's club was not the only informal association of scientists in Washington. Another group, which met fortnightly, was started by Spencer F. Baird, assistant secretary of the Smithsonian Institution, in the fall of 1861. This society, if it may be so called, consisted mainly of members who were interested in animal life. There is no indication that they played any active part in the war.[10]

While Stanton, the head of the War Department, remained indifferent to innovations, Welles marched on. Neither the ineptitude of the first board, nor the complacency of Congress, could thwart the energetic Secretary of the Navy. Before long he appointed another three-man board to consider inventions, and followed it with still another later that year.[11]

In the meantime the seeds planted by the *Scientific American* for a central research agency had taken root. In the fall of 1862 the President convened a council of engineers and naval constructors to collate "their practical results of experience and observations." This was a rather narrow field but, if properly expanded, the council might have harnessed much scientific aid and technical knowledge to the war effort. Although the top-flight engineer Haupt took the project in hand, nothing came of it.[12]

Perhaps the sensational *Monitor-Merrimac* fight helped make the Navy Department more receptive to new departures. By and by other government agencies followed suit, and February 1863 witnessed the organization of a "Permanent Commission," headed by Rear Admiral Charles H. Davis.[13] Unfortunately, this commission, of which Dr. Henry was a member, was given no funds to institute research problems on its own initiative, and therefore had to confine its activities to screening new ideas and to keeping inventors from boring or irritating officials holding key positions.[14]

Later that year Congress at last woke up to its duties and set up a National Academy of Sciences, which was to sit in judgment over scientific and technical proposals. Probably on account of poor publicity, this organization aroused no popular appeal and was largely ignored. Even Welles would not lay his problems at its doorstep and refused to support it financially.[15]

This ended the attempts to utilize the creative minds of the North systematically and to their fullest extent. Yet, contrary to the indifference or stupidity of most generals and others in high positions, the inventive spirit of the men in the ranks asserted itself and pointed strongly to neglected possibilities. It was a Wisconsin lumberman, Lieutenant Colonel Joseph Bailey, who saved the Federal fleet from ignominious disaster in the ill-conceived Red River campaign by means of a dam, which enabled the stranded ships to float downstream. It was a Pennsylvania mining engineer, Lieutenant Colonel Henry Pleasants, who not only conceived the plan to blow up one of the Petersburg forts, but also carried it to completion. It was no fault of his that the project failed to achieve its military objective.

Yankee ingenuity found many other ways to express itself. During the fighting in the Wilderness, where visibility was low and troops at rest were liable to be shot by either friend or foe, they protected themselves by improvised barricades. These consisted of horizontal logs loosely piled on top of one another, resembling the wall of a log cabin, and supported by two logs leaning against a tree.[16] The attackers of Charleston in 1863 played calcium lights on the walls of Fort Sumter to dazzle the garrison;[17] and an officer of the 48th New York suggested capturing the Confederate ironclad *Atlanta* by firing shot connected by chains to tangle her up and haul her to the shore. But then the question arose how the captors, if successful, would get inside their ironclad prize. The officer in command, knowing that the regiment had been recruited in the slums of New York, had an inspiration. "Let any of you who is a safeblower step two paces forward," he ordered; whereupon the whole detachment stepped forward with military precision. As it happened, the *Atlanta* backed off and thereby avoided what might have become an embarrassing entanglement for both sides.[18]

In May 1864 a similar scheme was proposed. This time the Confederate ram *Albemarle* was to become the victim. The Federal vessel *Miami* carried a net with which to foul the ram's propeller. Again unfavorable conditions interfered, and the usefulness of the stratagem remained undetermined.[19]

If the military had encouraged the dormant talents of the country with a modicum of sympathetic understanding, and combined them with sound tactics, it might have made a radical change in Union prospects. Even Grant, who was not partial to novelties, remembered the Petersburg mine fiasco with a sigh of regret. "Such an opportunity," he mused, ". . . I have never seen, and do not expect again to have."[20]

Lincoln's Secretary of War, whose martial mind still dwelt in the stone age, hindered rather than fostered the technical aspects of the war. Aside from taking little interest in improvements, he had no conception of how essential trained men were in operating the war machine. Taking advantage of the faulty draft law, he allowed experts from the Ordnance Department to be forced into the army as common soldiers, although it should have been obvious that Welles was right, when he complained that they were indispensable and ten times more valuable behind the lines than bearing arms.[21]

Reflecting Stanton's spirit, most high officers in the Union army looked at technical projects with indifference, not to say contempt. General Meade went a step farther; he was actively hostile, just when circumstances called for his wholehearted cooperation. Lieutenant Colonel Pleasants, who had suggested the digging of the Petersburg mine, was denied the necessary implements, simple though they were. The miners, for instance, had to carry out the earth in cracker boxes because they were given no buckets; they were allotted no lumber and had to prop up the roof of the mine with whatever scrap materials they could pick up in the camps. They were not even allowed the use of a theodolite, although one was available at headquarters. In spite of the obstacles thrown in their way, and the ridicule heaped on the idea by the corps engineer, Major James C. Duane, the mine was finished in record time. Then it developed that the electric wires needed to insure the explosion had not been supplied. To increase the difficulties, the fuse arrived in pieces, with no tools for splicing the ends together. A contemporary observer probably was right when he remarked, "It seemed as though General Meade had determined that the enterprise should fail."[22]

Among all the commanding officers of the Union Army only one showed a strong interest in scientific matters and, strange to say, it was one who was universally detested and whose performances in the field earned him few encomiums. General Butler had a nimble and restless brain out, being devoid of technical knowledge, many of his notions were of the crackpot variety. He proposed to wash down the Confederate trenches with a fire engine, envisioned a gun that would shoot seven miles, and a guided missile that was to be directed by compass. He even wanted to dig a tunnel into the heart of Richmond. On the other hand, Butler also took kindly to more practical schemes. He had an aerial reconnaissance made from a balloon as early as August 1861, purchased the first machine guns,[23] and experimented with incendiary missiles or so-called Greek fire.[24] He used wire entanglements along his front at Bermuda Hundred. He ordered a submarine to be built, and sponsored a steam-driven helicopter, which had been nearly completed when he quitted the army. He tried out ironclad artillery propelled by an armed locomotive, and his Dutch Gap canal, which eliminated a dangerously exposed portion of the James River, had considerable merit.[25]

If Butler had been able to turn his ideas over to a competent organization, some of them might have been developed into usefulness. In the Second World War this writer served on the Executive Committee of the Associated Defense Committee of the Chicago Technical Societies, of which Robert C. Brown, Jr., a prominent Chicago patent attorney, was the originator and chairman. It was the duty of the board to evaluate all new ideas submitted to it and, if considered promising, to have them carried to fruition. The Executive Committee found the number of crackpot projects surprisingly small, and even some of these sparked connecting ideas, and were brought to a successful conclusion by co-operating scientists and engineers.

If other generals had taken the kind of interest in innovations that Butler did, who can tell by how many months the war might have been shortened, and how many lives would have been saved?

⇝ 7 ⇜

HOW THE NORTH FINANCED
THE WAR

IT WAS up to Secretary of the Treasury Chase to finance the war, a task to which he brought neither training nor a natural inclination. Nonetheless, he tackled the job energetically, and trained his high intellect to bear on it. The only means immediately available to him for raising money were bank notes and coins, which together constituted the entire circulating media then in existence.[1] The notes, issued by some 1,600 banks from all over the country, varied in size, color and intrinsic value, and were of no use to him, because in 1846 Congress had passed a law forbidding the Treasury to accept them. It was not until February 1863 that national banks came into existence, the notes of which were uniform, and which in the course of time provided a dependable market for government bonds.[2]

If Chase had studied the history of previous wars, he would have foreseen that, due to hoarding by cautious people and the poor credit of the United States abroad, the hard money of the country would soon either be expended for imported war material or go into hiding. Instead of prohibiting the domestic circulation of coins at once, he did nothing, until in December 1861 the banks were forced to stop payments in specie. The abrupt disappearance of small coins affected everyone. Merchants could not make proper change on purchases, and all other business transactions were similarly hampered. "Shinplasters," mere I O U's, printed hurriedly on ordinary paper, and issued by states, towns and even individuals, were brought into play to fill the gap, but proved a poor makeshift. The situation was somewhat relieved when the post office printed postage stamps to be used in place of small coins. The Treasury itself, although not embarrassed by the coin shortage, had its own troubles, because it encountered increasing difficulties in selling its notes to the few banks which still had enough reserves to absorb them. Speedy and drastic measures therefore had to be enacted to avoid a complete breakdown of the nation's finances.

Thus it came about that Congress in February 1862 passed what became known as the Legal Tender Act, which allowed the Treasury to print $150,000,000 of fiat money—an amount which subsequently was tripled. This was a deliberate dilution of the currency, and its constitutionality was questionable. Congressman Elbridge Gerry Spaulding of New York, who had introduced the bill, admitted frankly that it was "a measure of necessity, not of choice."[3] Secretary Chase echoed this statement by asserting that "there was no help for it."[4] These notes were printed in denominations as low as three cents and, lawful or not, were heartily welcomed by the people for putting an end to the cumbersome "postage currency."

Lincoln had not signed the Legal Tender Act without serious

misgivings. "I do not like to say to a creditor you shall accept in payment of your debt something that was not money when it was contracted. That does not seem honest, and I do not believe the Constitution sanctions dishonesty."[5]

L. E. Chittenden, a high Treasury official, tried to allay the President's qualms by reminding him that self-preservation rates higher than the Constitution, but Lincoln remained uneasy. A committee of great financiers, he said, had told him that "by approving this act, I have wrecked the country. . . . They . . . have argued me almost blind. I am worse off than Saint Paul. He was in a strait betwixt two. I am in a strait betwixt twenty, and they are bankers and financiers."[6]

Welles had little sympathy with the dilemma of the President who, he thought, should have given more attention to the financial problems of the country. His total ignorance of them really was hard to excuse, and at times took on a semicomical aspect. After Chase's resignation in 1864 he first offered the Treasury's position to Governor David Tod of Ohio, who was a pronounced hard-money man, and after his refusal to Senator William Pitt Fessenden of Maine, who was an outspoken advocate of the fiat-money system. Welles felt sure that the President could not have any idea what was at stake, nor how big the stake was, if he could swing like this from one extreme to the other within twenty-four hours.[7]

Lincoln still felt apprehensive about the constitutionality of the Legal Tender Act when he was considering the appointment of the former Secretary of the Treasury to the Supreme Court. Might Chase not condemn the fiat money in his judicial capacity? But McCulloch, who eventually was given the Treasury post, dispelled the President's fears. "Chase," he said, ". . . favored and advised, as he himself has informed me, the dispersion by force of the Maryland legislature, and if anything more illegal than that . . . has been done, I have not heard it."[8] Lincoln laughed heartily, and there the matter rested for the time being. McCulloch's optimistic forecast notwithstanding, Chase did decide that the Legal Tender Act was unconstitutional after the war was over.

But fiat money was not the only measure employed to bolster the resources of the Treasury. Import duties were raised, income and excise taxes were imposed, and bonds were sold; but all this did not raise enough money to meet the growing demand. The Administration then took the only way out: with the consent of Congress, it raised the limit of legal tender or greenbacks, as the printing-press money was called, to a sum sufficient for the need of the Treasury.[9]

On the whole, this financial program proved successful, and was followed in principle by the U. S. Treasury during both World Wars. In some respects the Civil War methods were more honest, for they did not hide the debasement of the currency behind technicalities which the majority of the public did not understand. Free trading in gold was permitted, which indicated from day to day the dollar devaluation by the unbiased yardstick of the open market. If gold went from 100 to 200—or to a premium of 100—the value of the greenbacks was reduced by fifty per cent. This simple method for judging the course of inflation certainly was superior to our present one which, based as it is on the cost-of-living index, has two disadvantages: it does not include all items which go into the living cost, and their weighting does not affect all people alike; furthermore, the figures are not immediately available, and by the time they are announced may no longer reflect current conditions.

There was still another advantage in the Civil War method—it mirrored with speed and accuracy the ups and downs of the fortunes of war. Gold rose when the North suffered defeats, and fell with her victories. The highest premium for gold—185—was reached on July 11, 1864, the day Early threatened Washington, when the paper dollar fell to about one third of its gold value. It recovered to about forty cents before Lee's surrender. After that it fluctuated between forty and fifty cents, which does not differ materially from its purchasing power after the two World Wars.

When peace had been restored, Secretary McCulloch considered it his duty to retire the legal-tender notes as rapidly as possible, by withdrawing them from circulation.[10] By the end of 1866 the outstanding greenbacks had been substantially reduced, and the process continued until Congress stopped it in 1868.[11] A Greenback Party had been formed, the aim of which was to prevent a return to the gold standard. A new financial and political era had begun, which was to dominate the American scene for decades, until the defeat of William Jennings Bryan in three Presidential contests definitely decided the issue.

CONFEDERATE
OVER-ALL STRATEGY

➤➤➤ 8 ◄◄◄

CONFEDERATE MILITARY
STRATEGY

OVER-ALL strategy on the Confederate side was a much simpler problem than that with which Northern leaders had to wrestle, because against an opponent vastly superior in manpower and industrial capacity the South could do nothing but remain on the defensive. The Confederacy resembled a huge fortress under siege by land and sea. Occasionally it did engage in offensives, but they were defensive in character, being merely strong sorties, undertaken to relieve pressure at given points, retaliate for Northern depredations, secure provisions, or influence European governments.

As commander-in-chief of the Confederacy it devolved on Jefferson Davis to formulate broad plans for its effective defense. Those who had elected him President had reason to believe that he was well qualified to do so. He possessed a good educational background, was a graduate of West Point and had fought in the Black

Hawk War. His record as a colonel of the First Mississippi Volunteers in the Mexican War was an honorable one, and as President Franklin Pierce's Secretary of War he had proved himself an able organizer and administrator. He also had done well as chairman of the Senate Committee on Military Affairs. Davis was fond of everything pertaining to military matters, and would have preferred a position in the field to that of President.[1] He had no small opinion of his military capacity, for he boasted to his wife that he and Lee, each leading one wing of the Army of Northern Virginia, could "wrest a victory from those people."[2] Since he had never led more than one regiment in battle, his ability as a field commander of larger forces cannot be judged fairly.

Unfortunately, there was another side to Davis's qualifications. His years as Secretary of War had been largely spent in peacetime routine work, and this had given him and his followers a false idea of his martial talents. Neither his West Point training nor his experience in the Mexican War had broadened his naturally narrow and rigid mind, which had not changed perceptibly since the day he had received his diploma as second lieutenant. Gideon Welles, eying from Washington what was going on in Richmond, looked on him as a would-be successor to Calhoun, but without the endowments of the departed Southern leader.[3] Davis was extremely jealous of his Presidential privileges and despotic in upholding them. Prewar Southern celebrities were soon pushed into the background, until he, so Welles scoffed, was "the great 'I am.'"[4]

This overbearing attitude was a grave detriment to the efficacy of the chief executive, and stood in striking contrast to that of the President in the White House. While Lincoln was making friends and blunted the animosity of his opponents by tactful maneuvering, Davis seemed to go out of his way to make enemies. Where Lincoln liked common people and they liked him, they irritated

Davis, and he in turn offended them by his frigidity. Dispepsia and insomnia plagued him and kept him in a state of extreme nervousness, which he made little effort to control. As a result, the enthusiasm with which he had been welcomed to the Presidency waned rapidly. He had been installed only a few weeks when Mrs. James Chesnut of Charleston, wife of a prominent South Carolina politician, confided to her diary that some men were willing to hurt the Southern cause, if by doing so they could hurt the President.[5]

A Northern observer, writing without prejudice shortly after the war, gave this pen picture of the Confederate President: "He always seemed to delight in thwarting the wishes of others; and with a most mischievous obstinacy he followed the dictates of his own will, passions and caprice, rather than the councils of judicious advisers. This disposition was conspicuous in his appointment to important offices of his incapable personal and political friends; and the best of the Confederate army officers declare that, by his interference in details, he was a marplot in the way of military affairs. . . . At the beginning he appointed an incompetent and vicious companion-in-arms at a former period, named [Lucius B.] Northrup, to the vitally important post of Chief of Subsistence. This was done in the face of earnest protests."[6] It was characteristic of many other appointments, and therefore deserves a closer examination.

Northrup had been a practicing physician before his appointment, and demonstrated his incompetence early in the war. "He refused to allow his subordinates to purchase supplies for the army at Manassas in the fertile country adjacent, but sent others to gather them in the rear of the army, and forward them in daily doles. . . . On the day of the battle, Beauregard had only a single day's rations for his troops. . . . Flour bought by speculators in the [Shenandoah]

Valley and Loudon [County] was carried to Richmond, sold to the Subsistence Bureau, and transported back to Manassas." So it was stated by Beauregard's chief of staff, General Thomas Jordan, after the war.[7]

One of Northrup's first acts was to erect a meat-packing plant at Thoroughfare Gap, a place so close to the northern border of the Confederacy that it was in danger of loss sooner or later, at least temporarily. It was lost sooner and permanently, together with large food supplies. The newly erected buildings of the plant were burned or torn down.[8]

Northrup's inefficiency, of which the foregoing citations are samples, continued to be an insuperable burden for the Confederate generals. Yet Davis kept him on to the last days, and when he finally let him go, it was too late to repair the damage done. Many Southerners were convinced that Northrup was one of the main factors in the downfall of their cause.

The task of evolving and co-ordinating the over-all planning of the war carried Davis far beyond his depth. The former Supreme Court Justice John A. Campbell, who had thrown in his lot with the Confederacy, after watching for two years the way Davis discharged his duties, rendered his verdict in harsh words: "The President . . . seem[s] to have no plan, . . . This is characteristic of the President. He is not a comprehensive man. He has no broad policy, either of finance, strategy or supply."[9]

Judge Campbell's summary was not quite correct. Davis did have plans, but they were mostly of the wrong kind. His fundamental policy was trying to defend every square inch of Confederate territory, and he deluded himself into believing that it could be done. This ill-conceived principle had disastrous consequences. In order to make it work, he divided the South into military districts, each with its own garrison, the commanding general of which had to report directly to the President. In addition, troops under independent commands were assigned to guard isolated spots. Robert G. H. Kean, head of the Confederate Bureau of War, called it a "fatal notion" to make "each military Department a separate nation for military purposes, without subordination, co-operation or concert."[10]

The result of this impracticable arrangement was that the district commanders, bent on protecting their own posts, were loath to collaborate, no matter how urgently the occasion demanded it. This was maladministration at its worst. It was as if a town divided its water supply among its householders, leaving each to fight his own fires. There would never be enough water in anyone's house to quench a serious blaze, yet people would be afraid to relinquish to their neighbors what little they had; the fire department, without a central reservoir from which to draw, would be hamstrung. So it went with the armies of the Confederacy. Troops were scattered throughout Arkansas, Louisiana and other relatively unimportant points while the main armies were crying for reinforcements. The local soldiery may have given the favored sections a temporary illusion of security, but in reality deprived them as well as the rest of the country of defensive strength where it would have done the most good.

Aside from the foolhardy dispersion of manpower, this checkerboard system of defense sorely hampered the Southern military leaders, because they exercised no authority over the scattered detachments. When Lee started on his Gettysburg campaign, he asked Davis to assemble a force of 40,000 under Beauregard at Culpeper, the men to be taken from places which were not in immediate danger. Davis refused the request; had he granted it, the

Northern general would have had to immobilize two or three army corps to hold Beauregard in check, and Lee's prospects for the impending battle would have been greatly improved.

A few months before the Gettysburg campaign the faultiness of the system already had done irreparable harm in the west, and had practically assured Grant's success in his Vicksburg campaign. The Confederate commander in Arkansas, General Theophilus H. Holmes, whose troops were not engaged in any useful enterprise, had been ordered by Secretary of War George Wythe Randolph to join General John C. Pemberton, the defender of Vicksburg, when Grant's army still was comparatively small, and might have been overpowered by their combined forces. Davis, however, who had not been consulted, countermanded the movement for no other apparent reason than that Randolph had infringed Presidential prerogatives. Randolph promptly resigned.[11] A major in the Commissary Department expressed impolitely what some officers in Richmond thought of the way their President was handling matters, by remarking that he used to consider Jefferson Davis a mule, but a good mule. Now he had come to think of him as a jackass.[12]

Following Davis's instructions, Holmes refused to aid Pemberton and, on the day Vicksburg was surrendered, made a useless and hopeless attack on the heavily fortified town of Helena, probably because he did not know what else to do with his soldiers. He lost twenty per cent of them[13] to no purpose, because the attack failed miserably and would not have produced worth-while results had it succeeded.

Vicksburg was doomed when Grant gained a firm foothold on the left bank of the Mississippi, but its garrison of over 30,000 veterans could have been saved, had it not been for Davis's insistence on hanging on to places. Johnston instructed Pemberton to aban-

don Vicksburg and join him, whereupon Davis once more countermanded a sensible order, and sent Pemberton back into the city and
to certain surrender. If Davis had kept his hands off, the united
armies of Johnston and Pemberton would have become a weighty
factor on the western front, and made the loss of Vicksburg easier
to bear.

The maxim of defending the entire Confederate territory and
the creation of military districts comprise all the positive measures
Davis contributed to the over-all Confederate strategy. The rest, as
they developed during the war, were mostly negative, but equally
calamitous.

Lee had not been invited to participate in the initial planning,
but if he had been, his ideas would have conformed to an important part of Scott's Anaconda Plan. In a letter written on April 25,
1861, he wrote that "our policy should be purely on the defensive
. . . allow time to allay the passions and permit Reason to resume
her sway." He hoped also, perhaps with dark forebodings, that the
policy of the Confederacy would "be shaped by united counsels."[14]

Edward A. Pollard, wartime editor of the Richmond *Examiner,*
viewing the situation at the beginning of the war, considered the
outlook for the South by no means hopeless, despite the "vast
superiority of the North in material resources and apparatus of
war." He pointed out that against these unfavorable factors the
Confederacy had on its side "one single advantage which should
have been decisive . . . an advantage which no numbers could really
surmount [nor] skill effectively circumvent. This advantage was
space." Space, Pollard said, had defeated Napoleon in Russia, Great
Britain in America; therefore "it might safely be predicted that the
South, . . . occupying more than 728,000 square miles," and protected as it was by mountains, rivers and swamps, which "were
equivalent to successive lines of fortifications, would be victor in

the contest." But Pollard too seemed to have had some disturbing premonitions, for he dampened his hopes with a provision. The South, he said, would win, *"unless the management of her affairs should became insane."*[15] Pollard was one of Davis' bitterest enemies, but in this case it does not appear that his feelings influenced his judgment.

The opinion of the Richmond editor was shared by General Armistead L. Long, Lee's military secretary, who enlarged on it. "The interior rivers, such as the Rappahannock and the Rapidan, furnished good defensive lines and convenient intermediate bases for aggressive operations, and the York and the James became important auxiliaries to the armies that operated on the peninsula lying between those rivers. The Dismal Swamp, the Blue Ridge, and the successive ridges of the Allegheny Mountains were adapted to serve, in the hands of an able general, as powerful batteries and impenetrable masks for secret or delicate maneuverings."[16]

One of the best suggestions to bolster Confederate over-all strategy was made by Colonel William C. Oates of Alabama, one of the most intelligent Confederate officers. Writing after the war, he asserted that the effect of Lincoln's emancipation proclamation could not only have been nullified, but actually turned against him, by having the South counter it with one of her own. What he had in mind was a gradual and limited liberation of the slaves.[17] In this manner, he figured, the enemy would have lost his strongest propaganda weapon, while the Confederate armies could have been augmented by 300,000 Negro soldiers.

"This policy," he expounded . . . "would have terrorized the North. [It] could no longer have enthused the abolitionists, and . . . would have wonderfully enhanced the prospects . . . of early recognition of the Confederacy by European Governments." Limited emancipation, Oates claimed, was favored also by some of the leading generals, such as Lee, Richard S. Ewell, Johnston, Hood, Patrick R. Cleburne, John B. Gordon and others.[18] Cleburne is reported to have actively agitated for the enlistment of Negro soldiers in the spring of 1863.[19] Lee and Davis are said to have leaned toward arming the Negroes in 1863, but wondered whether they would stay on the Southern side or desert,[20] which indicates that Davis at least had contemplated recruiting them, but without the incentive of subsequent liberation.

Could the Negroes have been induced to volunteer for military service? Oates was convinced of an affirmative answer, provided that, after receiving an honorable discharge from the army, they should be forever free and be given eighty acres of public lands. Gradual emancipation of their families would have to follow.[21]

How well Oates had appraised the situation was proved by General Forrest, who had put this very idea into practice. When he entered the army, he told his forty-five slaves that if they went with him, he would set them free after the end of hostilities. As a matter of fact, he did better than he had promised. He gave them their freedom eighteen months sooner, and they remained with him to the end.[22]

Pollard shared Oates's opinion and argued plausibly that if the armies of the South had been strengthened by Negro troops at an early stage of the war, the scales would have turned in her favor, considering how evenly the balance had hung in the early campaigns.[23]

Despite these alluring possibilities, the Confederate Congress never seriously considered enlisting Negroes until late in the fall of 1864, and then debated it until next March. By that time, Pollard wrote, the measure had become "puerile, absurd and contemptible."[24]

The great obstacle to Southern emancipation, of course, was the monetary value of the slaves which was to be sacrificed, and which Oates estimated at twenty-eight hundred million dollars. Yet he felt certain that this hurdle could have been overcome, had the seriousness of the exigency been impressed on the public mind: "There was unfortunately no Danton, no Patrick Henry in that Congress to awaken its members from the sleep of fancied security and to stir . . . people to a realization of their real danger. . . . Had the alternative . . . been presented [to them] to give up slavery or the Confederacy, . . . the people would have said, "Let slavery go."[25]

But during the war neither Oates nor Pollard publicly proposed emancipation of the Negroes. So far as is known, only General Johnston had the foresight and the courage to do so, although not until the beginning of January 1864, and then only obliquely. In a letter to Davis he urged the substitution of Negroes for all soldiers on detached duty. Then he hinted gently at their liberation by recommending "judicious legislation," and made his meaning clearer by citing his experience with impressed Negroes, who "run away whenever it is possible."[26] Yet it is unthinkable that Davis would have reacted favorably to this suggestion, or that the Southern Congress, which was too deeply committed, would have enacted emancipation into law, although militarily it would have been of immense import; politically it would have been a thunderbolt. While it would not have terrified the abolitionists, as Oates predicted, it would have checkmated them. They and the Northern propagandists in England would have been left without ammunition, while the abolition-minded soldiers would have lost much of their zeal, inasmuch as the purpose of the war, as they saw it, had been accomplished.

It was not a Danton or a Patrick Henry, though, whom the South needed for such a bold stroke, but a man of action, one whom the masses would have followed, if he had led them out of a war of which they had sickened, and accomplished it by freeing the slaves, whom most of them did not possess. The only man in the Confederacy who might have carried the people with him was Lee; but Davis would never have abdicated of his own volition, and it is very unlikely that Lee would have accepted the Presidency or a dictatorship, if either had been offered to him.

One serious mistake the Confederacy committed and for which not Davis but the members of the Provisional Congress were to blame, was the exchange of Montgomery, its first capital, for the highly vulnerable Richmond. The Federal government erred by staying in Washington, but could at least argue that its prestige would have suffered by abandoning it. The Confederates had no such justification. They deliberately gave up a capital which was so securely located that no Union forces came near it until the last days of the war. By moving to Richmond the government fastened the same fetters of restricted mobility on its generals that plagued their Federal adversaries. Various reasons were given for this decision, none valid. Some sycophants claimed that Davis' presence so close to the fighting front would insure victory. Davis himself, in a message to his Congress on July 20, 1861, declared that, since the impending attacks of the enemy would be directed against Virginia, defensive measures had best be worked out in her capital.[27] This contention, endorsed by the majority of his contemporaries, was the most insipid that could have been put forth. Quite on the contrary, the very prospect that much of the coming conflict would be fought on Virginia soil should have shown the fallacy of transfering the capital to Richmond, which was as easily accessible by land as by water and was bare of natural defenses. In fact, the peninsula on which it was situated, surrounded as it was by water on three sides, without a navy to defend it, fairly invited enemy attacks.

Those who had chosen the new capital on account of its proximity to the battle zone may have been haunted by memories of the distant past when, before the advent of telegraphy, messages to the front had to be dispatched by horsemen. Wagging tongues had it, however, that Richmond had been picked by the wives of congressmen, who would not willingly adjust themselves to the discomforts of a provincial and overcrowded community. "Mosquitoes, want of neatness and want of good things to eat, drove us away," is the way one prominent lady put it.[28] But these inconveniences were hardly a compelling reason to take a step of such far-reaching importance.

Most likely the exodus from Alabama was at least in part prompted by political considerations. Not only did Virginia enjoy high public esteem, but before the Fort Sumter affair the state had been strongly antisecessionist. The excitement of the moment had swept the Unionists off their feet or stilled their opposition, but had it been permanently suppressed? A relapse could best be prevented by selecting the Old Dominion as the seat of the government. This would flatter the Virginians and would also allow keeping dissenters under close observation.

But why choose Richmond, when Lynchburg, Staunton or Danville would have been plainly preferable? These towns boasted excellent communications, and their inland locations made them safe against naval attacks. Their selection would also have confronted the North with a problem of logistics that did not exist so long as its troops and supplies could be transported most of the way by water, without fear of attacks. Other and very important advantages were that the Confederate Army would have had more elbow room for operations, and that the mountainous country around and beyond these outlying places was ideally adapted for defensive warfare.

To aggravate the error of selecting Richmond, the Tredegar Ironworks, which in any case should have been dismantled and set up in the interior, were built up to big proportions, and other war installations were added. By these means Richmond grew more and more essential for the survival of the Confederacy, so that its abandonment at a later date would have crippled the Southern war potential.

Of all the Confederate statesmen and military leaders Lee seems to have been the only one to foresee the fatal weakness the new capital infused into the war prospect. At any rate, he was the only one who was not afraid to speak out. As early as June 5, 1862, he wrote to Davis that it would take 100,000 men to hold the city, and even they might not be able to save it, but only postpone its surrender.[29] The President disregarded this plain hint that the seat of the government should be moved inland before it was too late.

General Hood asserted that Joe Johnston also considered Richmond a drag on the military situation. While retreating from Yorktown in the spring of 1862, Johnston is alleged to have told one Mr. McFarland, a volunteer aide on his staff, that "he expected or intended to give up" the capital. Hood's evidence is based on hearsay, but in all likelihood Johnston did agree with Lee that, if the Southern troops had to retreat, they must at all costs avoid being immobilized in a besieged city.[30]

A situation which arose at this time offers a striking example of the burden imposed on Southern strategy by having to protect the capital. Lee had suggested a bold plan that "would change the character of the war": strengthen Jackson with large reinforcements from the deep South and have him undertake an all-out offensive through the Shenandoah Valley into Maryland and Pennsylvania, while Lee was holding McClellan in check.[31] The suggestion was turned down by Davis, who was unwilling to denude the deep South of troops. Jackson was allotted only some 16,000 men, with whom he performed brilliantly; but how much more effective his coup would have been, had the capital simultaneously been transferred into the interior, out of McClellan's immediate reach! In that case Lee with most of his troops could have joined Jackson at once; their combined forces would undoubtedly have overwhelmed the resistance of the scattered Union army corps, while McClellan with the bulk of the Union forces was left hundreds of miles behind, out of contact with other commands, and with nothing left to conquer but the swamps of the Chickahominy and an empty city.[32]

As the years went by, Lee's anxiety about Richmond grew. On September 11, 1863, he wrote to Davis that the Ordnance Department should enlarge its manufacturing facilities in the interior, so as not to be destitute "if Richmond should fall."[33] In March 1864 he wanted to send everything not immediately required out of the capital.[34] On May 22 of that year he nudged the President again, telling him that solicitude for Richmond had compelled him to disarrange his plan for resisting Grant's advance.[35]

Matters kept going from bad to worse, and in October Lee was more anxious than ever to see Richmond evacuated. He knew that his talents could be utilized to their fullest extent only in a war of movement, and he dreaded the prospect of being pinned down on the narrow peninsula housing the capital.

General Long was disgusted with this state of affairs. "To add to the embarrassment of the army," he complained, "it was confined to one line of operations—the defense of Richmond. Both the State and Confederate governments demanded with Quixotic persistency the defense of a place that had been rendered almost untenable since the Federals had gained possession of the James and York rivers. The general [Lee] had been heard to say that Richmond was the millstone that was dragging down the army."[36]

During the winter of '64-'65 Lee again wanted the seat of government moved. Long, who shared his chief's conviction that the siege of Richmond could have only one ending, reported him as desiring to take up a new line behind the Staunton River. There he could harass Grant, who would find it more difficult to perform offensive operations with a longer line of communications to protect. In this way Lee thought he might keep the war going indefinitely, because, if need be, he could retreat into Tennessee, or move south, with little or no danger of interception. Moreover, he could readily draw in enough detachments from West Virginia, the Carolinas and other states, to provide him with quite a powerful army.

As might have been expected, Lee's recommendation was overruled. Davis decided that the Confederacy should live or die in Richmond, and so it died there,[37] while he himself made an ill-advised and unsuccessful attempt to prolong its life by making the trans-Mississippi a last-ditch battleground.

As in the case of Washington, it was feared by many that giving up Richmond during the war would hurt Southern prestige; and just as with the Northern capital, the fear was shown to be imaginary. When Richmond was endangered in May 1862, with nothing but a small, unfinished battery and a few sunken ships in the James blocking the path of the Union fleet, the Confederate Congress adjourned hurriedly, and its members scrambled to safety. Davis sent his family to North Carolina and ordered the archives to be readied for removal to Lynchburg. But the river obstacles proved sufficient, and the danger was averted. This half-finished flight was accepted by the people with quiet resignation and did not injure the reputation of the government either at home or elsewhere.

It would be interesting to speculate how the war would have been fought in the east had both capitals been removed from the fighting zone, so that the two hostile armies in the eastern theater would have been footloose. There certainly would have been no campaign on the peninsula, because minus Richmond it was not worth campaigning for. For the same reason there would have been no battle at Fredericksburg or Chancellorsville. Union strategy would probably have been directed against southern Virginia, the Carolinas and Georgia. The Confederate offensives, on the other hand, would have more or less followed the lines they did in 1862 and 1863, except that their goal would not have been Washington, but Maryland and Pennsylvania, with Harrisburg and Baltimore as ultimate objectives. The outcome of the conflict would hardly have been affected, but the end probably would have been reached at a much earlier date.

CHAPTER

➤➤➤ 9 ≪≪≪

DIPLOMACY, FINANCES AND ANTIBLOCKADE MEASURES

DIPLOMACY and finances formed as vital a part of the Confederate over-all strategy as they did with that of the North, but in the Confederacy they were so closely entwined with the blockade that they can best be discussed in connection with one another. President Davis took it on himself to manage all three, and nobody, not even the least capable of his fellow-citizens, could have done worse.

The disposable wealth of the South, on which her financial staying power depended, was founded mainly on cotton, tobacco and naval stores, with cotton overshadowing the rest in quantity and value. To utilize this staple to the best advantage, three courses were under consideration. The first was to prevent its export, so as to coerce the Western European countries into recognizing the Confederacy as an independent nation. The second called for acquiring all available cotton by the government, storing it at home, and using it as collateral for a foreign loan. The third course contemplated transferring as much of it as possible to foreign warehouses, and keeping it there to provide funds for the purchase of goods as they were needed.

The first course, that of withholding cotton from the European markets, was in truth a gamble on a gamble. "The President and his advisers," his wife remembered, "looked to the stringency of the English cotton market . . . to send up a ground-swell from the English operatives, . . . and grudged every pound of cotton exported."[1] This was the first gamble, for the British might not allow themselves to be browbeaten; but if they did—and this was the second gamble—would the stringency develop soon enough to frighten them into an early recognition of the Confederacy, which was what Davis demanded?

The first of the two alternate plans, a foreign loan secured by cotton stored inside the seceded states, had few supporters, since the collateral was exposed to the vicissitudes of war. Moreover, this course required that the government-owned cotton be taken inland, where it was not accessible to raids by the Union fleet, and that the army detach troops, who should have done field duty, to protect the warehouses. The scheme subsequently was tried in a limited way, but failed dismally, because European investors exacted such usurious discounts that little of the borrowed money was left for the Confederate treasury.

The third plan, the export of enough cotton to establish a European credit of at least $500,000,000, unquestionably held the greatest attraction. It was heartily endorsed by Vice-President Stephens[2] and most other Southern men of experience and foresight. With large supplies of the commodity stored where they were readily available, the work of the Confederate purchasing and diplomatic agents abroad would have been greatly facilitated. The cotton would not only have been as good as but better than gold, because its price was bound to rise when the expected shortage developed. Despite the obvious advantages of the project, Davis rejected it summarily. The arguments advanced against it were twofold. One was the hazard of running the blockade, the other the alleged insufficiency of ship bottoms.[3] Neither argument was convincing. The blockade certainly could not function very effectively for some months, and a great deal might be accomplished in the meantime; nor was the alleged scarcity of ocean-going vessels an insurmountable obstacle, for sufficient ships could have been bought, and storage facilities were close at hand, in Cuba, in the West Indies, in Mexico, whence reshipments to Europe could be made leisurely and safely. They did serve this purpose after the blockade had tightened, but by then their usefulness had appreciably lessened.

General Johnston wrote in later years that "the blockade . . . was . . . not at all effective until the end of the following winter; so that there was a period of about twelve months for . . . converting four or five million bales of cotton into money. The sum raised . . . would have [procured] arms enough for half a million of men, . . . and the Confederate treasury [still] would have been much richer than that of the United States."[4] Whether or not Johnston indulged in second-guessing when he penned these lines, they did epitomize the cotton problem precisely.

It is difficult to understand why Davis was willing to forego these tangible benefits for the hollow prestige of recognition. The Confederacy already had been conceded the status of a belligerent, which gave it all the essential rights it needed, except that of appointing full-fledged diplomatic representatives, and their duties were taken over by Confederate emissaries, who performed them informally as well as they could have done formally.

In reality recognition was of little practical value, but Davis was a stranger to realities and practicalities. He wanted it for the sake of prestige, and wanted it at once. As the difficulties to attain it mounted, so did his eagerness and persistency. He never realized that any newborn nation, even if not at war, had to prove that it could sustain itself, before it might expect international recognition. Lord John Russell, the British foreign secretary, made this quite clear in a letter written on August 2, 1862, to Mason, the Confederate representative in London: "In order to be entitled to a place among . . . independent nations . . . a State ought to . . . afford promise of stability and permanence." He then added that "independence [must be] achieved by victory, and maintained by a successful resistance to all attempts to overthrow it. That time," he concluded, ". . . has not, in the judgment of Her Majesty's government, yet arrived."[5] But to Davis recognition had become an obsession, and to gain it he was willing to sacrifice the cotton trade which, by providing ample purchasing power abroad, could have built up enough armed strength to "achieve independence by victory," as Lord Russell had specified.

To the masses recognition never was more than a nebulous, undefined something. They confused it with foreign intervention which, in turn, was supposed to mean breaking the blockade, or even furnishing active military support. This interpretation was far from the way the British and French governments construed it. They had no intention of going farther than to propose a six-months armistice, during which time peace terms might be arranged between the two contending sections. Even had such a suggestion been made, however, it is highly improbable that either side would have accepted it.

In fairness to the Confederate President it must be recorded that his decision to put an unofficial embargo on cotton met with the enthusiastic approval of his people, including those who were making their living by planting, transporting or merchandising it.[6] But the public was unaware that he was staking not only recognition, but also the financial and military future of the seceded states on this measure, the effectiveness of which rested, aside from the question of its coercive power, on two other shaky premises—that the war would not last more than one year, and that during this period England and France would run out of cotton.

In the South it was considered certain that the war would be over within twelve months. Two years after peace had been restored, Christopher G. Memminger, Davis's slow-witted Secretary of the Treasury, still defended the Confederate cotton policy on this basis.[7] Blind faith in the early success of Southern valor, although imprudent, was understandable, but what challenges one's credulity is that the quick impact of the embargo on European industries was universally taken for granted, so much so that no one thought of inquiring into the supply-and-demand situation abroad. Yet even a cursory investigation would have disclosed that the supply aspect presented a discouraging picture. The 1859 and 1860 crops in the South had been unusually large,[8] and textile factories in Great Britain were bulging with cheaply bought cotton. The demand prospect was as bad or worse, because domestic consumers as well as those of foreign countries, such as China and India, had been overstocked with finished fabrics.[9] English operators, far from being anxious to obtain cotton, were anxious to get rid of it. Mills were shutting down, not for lack of material, but on account of top-heavy inventories and glutted markets. During 1861 sizable quantities of cotton actually were reshipped to the United States, partly to relieve the overabundance, partly in the belief that the war would soon be over, and that the next crop would cause a further break in prices.

A businessman who does not study foreign markets before committing himself there would be considered incompetent, if not downright stupid. Yet no member of the Confederate cabinet possessed sense enough to order an expert survey of the European cotton markets before resorting to the embargo. The means for such a survey were readily at hand. In March 1861, while America was still at peace, Davis had sent three commissioners to Europe, Pierre A. Rost, Ambrose Dudley Mann and William L. Yancey. Foolishly, they had been given orders only to seek foreign recognition and conclude treaties of commerce,[10] but they were also allowed to hint at a stoppage of cotton shipments in case of a war with the North.[11] In view of these instructions it is hard to see how they could have helped taking notice of the cotton situation; nevertheless, they did ignore it completely. Yancey was an orator of the fire-eating type who, with secession accomplished, had lost his zeal and purpose in life. He was versed solely in agitation and did not know how to handle down-to-earth problems. Mann was a socialite, who had served much of his life in European diplomatic posts of postage-stamp size. Rost had no qualifications at all. One experienced cotton merchant, added to the commission as a commercial attaché, might have changed the course of the war; but such unorthodoxy was beyond Davis' mental horizon.

Thanks to the shortsightedness of Davis and his cabinet, Yancey afterward could offer the excuse that the commission had received no instructions to look into export problems.[12] But he certainly must have sensed from the cool reception he had received that something was wrong because, after his resignation in September

1861, he remarked pensively that cotton was not king; it was an influential factor of commerce, but not its dictator.[13]

If the negative results of his commission gave Yancey something to think about, they certainly should have opened Davis' eyes, and made him draw the inevitable conclusion that his cotton policy was unworkable. There still was time to reverse it; but his mind was cast in an iron mold, and he continued the embargo until it hurt the Confederacy far more than it did European countries.

In the second year of the war the Richmond authorities finally became realistic by force of circumstances, and turned a complete somersault. With all other sources of financing foreign purchases exhausted, they abandoned the embargo on cotton, and instead encouraged its export. Unfortunately, the product now had to be shipped from inland depots to seaports, which put a severe strain on the overworked railroads. The tightening of the blockade, which by then had taken place, did not help matters. These, however, were minor evils compared to one of far greater magnitude. Inconceivably, no one had worked out a plan for the new order of things; none was proposed, and none went into effect. The blockade-runners, who controlled the largest part of the clandestine ocean traffic, did as they pleased and mainly brought in luxury articles which yielded them the biggest profit, such as wines, coffee and cosmetics. And as if this practice were not harmful enough, they converted their profits into gold, thus further depreciating the currency, which already was sliding downhill on a greased toboggan. Not until March 1864 did the government compel blockade-runners to reserve half of their cargo space for war implements and other necessities, and to invest their profits not in gold, but in cotton for the return trip.

Davis, after proving that he was a poor merchandiser, now

showed that he was an equally wretched financier—in other words, that he was not fit to run a war. If regulations of blockade-running had been formulated while ships still were sailing back and forth without much hindrance, erosion of the Confederacy's currency could have been held within bounds, its armies would have suffered less from lack of matériel, and the civilian population would have been spared many of the shortages that made its life nearly intolerable.

One of the defensive-offensive measures Davis undertook was the issuance of letters of marque. The Washington government waited only two days before it delivered a counterstroke. In a proclamation delivered on April 19, Lincoln threatened that "any person who, under the pretended authority of the said [Confederate] States, should molest a vessel of the United States would be treated as a pirate,"[14] meaning that he would be hanged. Lincoln clung to this view, even after it had been pointed out to him that it was he who had given the South the right of privateering by his declaration of a blockade, without having informed himself of its legal pitfalls. A few proceedings against privateers were instituted, and some convictions were obtained, but no prisoner was hanged or kept captive for any length of time. The Northern people did not approve Lincoln's severity, and one of the judges who tried a case mirrored the prevailing opinion, when he declared that he could not see any difference between those fighting on sea and those fighting on land, that it was unfair to condemn a few unfortunates, when half a million others went unpunished, although in arms against the Federal Government, and that it was the last case of this kind over which he would preside.[15] Surprisingly, the stern Chase took a similar view. Admitting that the blockade order had made the South a belligerent, he remarked at a cabinet meeting that the Union might as well face privateering as it did the war on land. Seward, who shared with the President the blame for the ill-considered blockade edict, objected, but did not press the point.[16]

Another reason why Lincoln finally had to unbend was the power of the South to retaliate. On June 3, 1861, the privateering *Savannah* had been captured, and its crew were treated as criminals. Davis immediately announced that his government would deal out the same fate to the same number of war prisoners.[17] This thrust was more persuasive than long-winded legal arguments. By and by all pending cases against privateers were quietly dismissed, and the prisoners given their freedom, either by exchange or otherwise. Lincoln's stand on this question had been logical, but untenable. He had steadfastly refused to recognize the Confederates as anything but rebels, and even refused to exchange prisoners with them; but after fourteen months, mounting public indignation forced him to sanction an exchange cartel in which privateers were put into the same category as soldiers in the army. It was one of Davis' few political victories.

The summer of 1862 marked the high point of Southern prospects militarily, and also in the use of cotton as a diplomatic weapon. From then on the stringency of the staple abroad was being gradually overcome. Due to its exorbitant price, linen and wool were coming into vogue; furthermore, Egypt, China and Brazil had stepped up their cotton production, which began to undermine the quasi-monopoly the American product had so long enjoyed.[19] Davis had to play a hand which, while still strong, was steadily growing weaker, and he played it badly. Early in the year he had demanded that his European representatives press for declaring the blockade ineffective and therefore not binding. Probably much against their own judgment they complied with this unreasonable directive, and thereby succeeded only in making themselves ridiculous. They were offering proof that the blockade was inoperative, but when foreign diplomats asked why no cotton was being shipped out, they had no answer.[20] Their embarrassment, of course, was a godsend to the Washington government, which stressed that the lack of cotton exports did prove the blockade successful, although in fact the blockade was yet as leaky as a fish net. The Queen's advisers must have learned this from their consular agents, yet the equivocation of the Southern emissaries gave England's authorities a way out, and on February 27, 1862, they officially recognized the blockade as in force.[21] Guided by their own interests, they gave the South tit for tat: no cotton, no easy imports of what she needed most.

England's decision in favor of the North notwithstanding, the general situation in the summer of 1862 offered the Confederates the best chance of securing European intervention. The long-delayed cotton shortage had at last set in, and competition from other sources had not yet gained much headway. The fortunes of war also smiled on the Confederacy. In the west Braxton Bragg was knocking on the doors of Louisville, and in the east Lee had defeated the Union army at Bull Run and driven it into the fortifications of Washington. It looked as if the seceded states were going to win recognition through their own efforts after all. The British government, strongly urged by France, was seriously considering interposition. It awaited only the outcome of Lee's Maryland campaign; if Lee should continue victorious, but only then, England was willing to act.[22]

At this crucial juncture Davis held the course of future events in the palm of his hand. Lee had climaxed his Bull Run victory with the capture of Harper's Ferry, which netted him 11,000 prisoners and much war material, and stood behind Antietam Creek, facing General McClellan, who commanded about twice as many troops. The President, whose duty it was to look at the war from all angles, now should have given Lee strict orders not to fight another battle. Bull Run and Harper's Ferry were enough glory for the time being; even another victory could add nothing to Southern renown or to the halo of Lee's near invincibility. This was no time to take needless risks. The conviction of the Queen's cabinet, which from the beginning had cherished the thought that the Confederates would eventually win their independence, had to be upheld above everything else.

But Davis, who ordinarily loved nothing better than to meddle in military affairs, did nothing at all. Neither did the British government, when the news reached London that Lee had failed to score against McClellan. Thus the only real opportunity of the South to gain recognition, perhaps even intervention, was passed up. From a diplomatic view the Confederates lost the war on the banks of Antietam Creek.

While Davis usually managed diplomatic affairs poorly, he occasionally showed good judgment in his selection of foreign representatives. Mason and Slidell, often forced to try the impossible by Davis' orders, did fairly well in their uncomfortable posts, but someone was needed who did not wear striped pants and could fight with no holds barred. Davis found such a man in the person of a twenty-seven-year-old journalist of Swiss birth named Henry Hotze. It was an excellent appointment, but it came too late, as did so many other things in the Confederacy. The critical time had been August and September 1862, when the British government was wavering, and might have been pushed into action by public opinion. In November 1862, when Hotze entered the scene, the golden hours were gone. Furthermore, his initial salary of only $1500, with a measly expense account of $750 per annum, drastically limited the scope of his activities. Nevertheless, Hotze surprised everybody with his accomplishments, so much so that at the end of the year his expense account was increased to $10,000, and before long rose to three times this figure.[23] Among other things he started a high-class newspaper, the *Index,* which catered to England's intelligentsia and was read even by members of Parliament and the cabinet. He sent agents through Germany and Italy to combat Northern recruiting, pointing out that their young men were wanted only as cannon fodder for the Union armies.

Hotze also kept hammering with gusto at the vulnerable facets of the Northern administration. He undid much of its propaganda talk that the war was a moral undertaking, by citing the President's repeated promises not to interfere with slavery where it existed. He harped on Lincoln's arbitrary arrests and his high-tariff policy, and counteracted Northern-inspired mass meetings against slavery by arranging mass meetings of his own which passed resolutions demanding the lifting of the blockade. He gained the support of the venal French press by judicial use of slush money. All in all, he was a one-man counter-propaganda army. Had his talents been put to use earlier in the war, he might have fought Lincoln's emissaries to a standstill.

Toward the end of December 1864 Davis, in a last desperate attempt, asked Mason and Slidell to find out if the Confederacy could gain recognition, provided it abolished slavery. Whether he believed that this offer would be accepted when his country already was tottering toward its collapse, or what good it would do if it were accepted at this late hour, is not known. England's reply was polite, but devastating. It hinted that, inasmuch as the seceded states had "given up" their seaports and had not been able to stop Sherman on his march through Georgia, they could scarcely hope to maintain their independence in the future.

The cotton fiasco and the gradual military breakdown of the Confederacy were accompanied by a steady deterioration of its finances. For some time Southern patriotism had kept the currency close to par, but the fact that many imports had to be paid for in specie, that exports were insufficient to earn enough foreign exchange, added to the inroads blockade-runners and speculators made on the gold reserve, led to a disastrous drop in the value of the Confederate dollar. By the time these errors were partly remedied, the credit of the country had sunk so low that no other expedient was left but to print paper money. The unbridled inflation which followed burdened the army with obstacles that neither generalship nor bravery could overcome. "The result of the war," wrote Pollard in 1866, "was powerfully influenced by the condition of Confederate finances." The Richmond editor was putting it mildly. Even had the Confederacy not been crushed militarily, it must sooner or later have died of the financial cancer which had been embedded into its body at birth.

In his memoirs Jefferson Davis said very little about his faulty over-all strategy, including the boomeranging cotton embargo, and skipped lightly over the way he handled, or rather mishandled, Confederate finances and foreign affairs. He probably realized what events had abundantly shown, that he had failed tragically in all three.

NONMILITARY AND TECHNOLOGICAL
PROBLEMS OF THE SOUTH

JEFFERSON DAVIS' nonmilitary problems were of a somewhat different character from those of Lincoln, but he too had to consider them carefully before arriving at his military decisions. Foreign-born citizens in the South were smaller in numbers, and political parties less sharply defined, which practically eliminated two potential sources of trouble. On the other hand, Davis was cramped by the doctrine of State rights, one of the pillars of the Confederate constitution. The seceded states formed a rather loose organization, and state-rights-conscious governors, particularly Joseph E. Brown of Georgia and Zebulon B. Vance of North Carolina, were perpetual thorns in the side of the Richmond administration. At one time Vance's opposition to the central government became so pronounced that he was on the brink of negotiating a separate peace.[1]

Contrary to conditions in the North, this emphasis on State-rights generated much friction and was detrimental to the successful conduct of the war. Where Lincoln could order troops from one state to another without encountering opposition, Davis always had to be careful not to step on oversensitive toes. Some of the Confederate states considered it a favor if they let their soldiers cross home boundaries, or allowed a regiment from another state to use weapons from their arsenals. When in February 1865 General Johnston was reinstated as army commander, he was joined by 1,100 South Carolina militia and reserves, but was afraid he would not be permitted to take them with him into North Carolina.[2] On the other hand, while the two Presidents shared the political necessity of having to select generals with regard to an equitable geographical distribution, Davis had no need to satisfy racial minorities.

One matter in regard to which Davis had to make decisions which might be wrong militarily but right politically, was the protection of border states which were loyal to his side, or whose allegiance was divided. Davis was particularly worried about Missouri and Arkansas, where Confederate troops might never accomplish anything worth while, yet where their withdrawal might discourage friends or turn them into active enemies. Davis' reluctance to evacuate Harper's Ferry was another case in point. Strategically the town was a trap, but he wished to hold onto it as a link with the secessionists in western Maryland. In all such cases the military and political importance had to be carefully weighed against each other. It was unfortunate for the Confederacy that its President was an incompetent weighmaster, who was unwilling to deviate from adopted policies when changed circumstances demanded it.

Later in the war a factor which caused Davis deep concern, and which reacted unfavorably on Southern strategy, was the growing shortage of provisions. Every time a piece of territory had to be given up, it reduced the productive acreage from which people and animals could be fed. When Davis made Lee fight Burnside on the

Rappahannock rather than on the North Anna, he was militarily wrong, but economically right, for the retreat would have cut off a substantial source of supplies.

Unfortunately, the scarcity of food was not the only one that had to be reckoned with. The shortage of iron required allotments among railroads, foundries, munition factories and numerous other war plants, all of which were starved for the precious metal. As to copper, lead, leather and other scarce materials, priorities had to be set up, which called for keen judgment, with many contestants vying with one another to keep their end of the war effort from getting stranded.

In one respect Davis did decidedly better than his White House enemy. While the latter neglected to foster or sustain Union sentiment in the South, Davis ardently wooed Lincoln's political opponents and made good use of them. Foremost among them were the Northern Peace Democrats. They openly opposed the war, yet were a faction of a legitimate political party, and aimed at peace by negotiation through Congressional action. They had no counterpart in the South, where any overt opposition to the war would have been considered akin to treason, if not treason itself.

The radical wing of the Peace Democrats, however, the so-called Copperheads, went far beyond lawful opposition in their attempts to bring the war to a close. Like similar organizations within the Confederacy, they formed secret societies of considerable numerical strength, but their activities were more destructive and they were much more than mere gadflies. They incited riots and murdered members of the draft boards; they destroyed warehouses, interrupted communications, burned river transports, induced men to shirk military duty, and terrorized loyal citizens. They also acted as spies or couriers, and even did recruiting for the Confederate army.[3] After the battle of Fredericksburg, so a contemporary observer wrote, they "filled the express trains with packages containing citizens' clothing, in which [soldiers] might escape from the service."[4] Due to this scheme the number of deserters rose to an average of 200 a day. The situation became so serious that General Hooker had all incoming trains searched by provost marshals, and ordered the burning of all civilian clothing found.[5]

Northern opposition to the war gained in strength as the conflict dragged on. After the Wilderness campaign with its heartbreaking casualties, a fervent desire to end the bloodletting swept over the country, regardless of party lines. By the summer of 1864 one commentator friendly to the government recorded that "the most hopeful had become weary, the most determined were depressed and disappointed. . . ."[6] The elements hostile to the Administration, aided by Confederate agents, did all they could to intensify the general dissatisfaction. They blackened the reputation of Union generals, misrepresented their movements, belittled their successes and magnified their losses. "The enemies of the nation at home did it nearly as much harm as Lee," wrote the same commentator. "They stimulated the South . . . , they invited foreign sympathizers to active interference, and did their best to hinder recruiting, to withhold supplies, to damage the financial credit of the country, and to discourage the armies in the field."[7] Even the stolid Halleck noted the growing disaffection. "The people in many parts of the North and West," he confided to Grant in August 1864, "now talk openly and boldly of resisting the draft. . . . It is probably thought that such a thing will have its effect . . . by showing the inability of the present administration to carry on the war, with an armed opposition in the loyal states."[8] In some localities the work of the obstructionists was so effective that, according to the *Chicago Tribune,* Grant disbanded the 109th Illinois Volunteers, because he considered them a branch of the Copperhead organization.[9]

Contrary to the indifference of the Washington administration toward counterbalancing developments in the South, Davis' governnment skillfully fanned these antiwar sentiments in the North. It maintained there a large network of secret agents, and sustained them by liberal gifts of money and arms. In November 1864 Southern saboteurs tried to burn New York City. The plot, although cleverly conceived, was only partly successful, on account of inept handling; nevertheless, much damage was done. Another plot that might have had serious consequences was an attempt to liberate thousands of Confederate prisoners from Camp Douglas in Chicago. Had it succeeded—and it came close—the great fire, which wiped out large sections of the city, might well have occurred in 1864 instead of 1871. Moreover, the released veterans might have broken into local arsenals and wreaked havoc in the rear of the Union armies, who at that time had their hands full, with Thomas fighting in Tennessee, Sherman in Georgia and Grant in Virginia. As it was, the threat of such exploits kept sizable garrisons away from the battlegrounds.

The Confederates, however, committed a grave error in failing to co-ordinate their military efforts with their subversive activities. In 1863 they allowed John Hunt Morgan to undertake a raid through the very parts of Indiana and Ohio which were friendliest to the South, and where the secret societies had the largest following. No record exists of how many of those whose horses and provisions Morgan's men requisitioned changed their point of view, but the sobering effect of his pillages could not have been inconsequential.

Although Davis deserves full credit for a goodly part of the internal troubles that were heaped on the North, in the end it was he who helped bring about the downfall of the Copperhead movement and the defeat of the Peace Democrats at the polls. In July 1864, when the November elections were not far off, Lincoln's opponents smelled victory in the air. Grant was stalled in front of Richmond, and Sherman faced a similar situation as he approached Atlanta, which was protected by an undefeated army. Peace by conquest seemed as far away as ever. At this critical moment Davis dismissed the skillful and popular Johnston. Within a few days the fruits of his masterly strategy were dissipated by his successor, and a few weeks later Atlanta fell. If the city had held out until the November elections, which very likely would have been the case if Johnston had been retained, the conciliatory Democratic party, which could count on the votes of the war-weary, might have won; but with the fall of Atlanta all opposition to Lincoln collapsed; he was re-elected, and the South lost its best chance for a negotiated peace.

The advantages to be gained by the proper application of science and technology to warfare were well understood in the Confederacy, despite the fact that neither its President nor its leading statesmen and politicians had much knowledge of or took great interest in the subject. The Southern setup differed from the Northern, because the underlying conditions were dissimilar. First of all, the seceded states began without even the shadow of a military organization. The Ordnance Department existed only on paper, and the country had few industrial establishments able or ready to supply the instruments of war. Furthermore, while all the efforts of creative technical talent in the North could be directed toward inventions and improvements, those of the Confederacy had to be partially diverted to a continuous search for substitutes, or switched into unpredictable emergencies, caused by the shortages of vital materials. That the south succeeded in overcoming these handicaps was largely due to the chief of the newly created Ordnance Department, Josiah Gorgas. A Pennsylvanian by birth, and formerly a captain in the Ordnance Department of the United States Army, he undertook the almost superhuman task of creating a war industry out of nothing, and of keeping it going. His name never became widely known, and today no statue perpetuates his memory; yet without his ingenuity, persistence and inspiring leadership it is doubtful that the war could have lasted long enough for Lee, Jackson and Forrest to have statues erected in their honor. In this respect Gorgas suffered the same fate as most others who did their war work back of the front. McCulloch, one of Lincoln's financial secretaries, expressed it pointedly: "It was the successful general who was the recipient of public honors, not the man by whose agency the sinews of war were supplied."[10]

But not even Gorgas could have provided the Southern armies with the sinews of war, had he not surrounded himself with a galaxy of scientists, technologists and administrators. Outstanding among them was John W. Mallet, a chemist of Irish origin and German training, who had charge of all government laboratories and manufacturing centers. He was responsible for the preparation of ammunition, explosive shells, fuses and a long list of other war matériel. Traveling much of the time, and attending besides his other duties to such wearisome collateral problems as allaying labor troubles, obtaining subsistence for workers, devising safe methods of packing and transporting ammunition, he invented, among other things, the "polygonal shell," which made it possible to predetermine the number and size of the pieces into which it would burst.[11] Shortly after the war, while Northern politicians still were waving the "bloody shirt," he was elected president of the American Chemical Society. It was the highest honor the chemical profession could bestow on one of its members at that time.[12]

The third prominent man in this group was George W. Rains, who could be called the chief chemist of the Confederacy. Among other things he built a powder plant at Augusta, and its excellent products became the main reliance of Confederate firearms throughout the war. Other bright stars in the Southern constellation were I. M. St. John, Chief of the Nitre and Mining Bureau, and James H. Burton, who headed the Department of Armories. Highest merit was earned also by Commander John M. Brooke, chief of Navy Ordnance, who designed the famous *Merrimac* and invented the banded rifle gun named after him. The great Matthew Fontaine Maury likewise added luster to the roster of Confederate scientists. There were many others too numerous to mention, whose brains and skills were of immeasurable value to the war effort.

Both Gorgas and Mallet recognized the necessity of screening new ideas, and in September 1862 a committee was appointed for this purpose. Its first object was the examination of an invention using steam for the moving of field artillery.[13] What became of this project and others that followed, is not known. At any rate, with or without this committee, the work of the Southern miracle workers went on. As the outlook assumed a darker hue, it seemed at times as though they had come to the end of the road, but they always managed somehow to stave off the threatening debacle.

One might assume that as a talented engineer Lee would have

been on the lookout for new weapons or other technical innovations, but the records do not bear out this expectation, although he himself designed an armored car that went into action during the Seven Days battles.

Probably the most effective defensive weapon the South employed was the underwater torpedo. Rudimentary torpedoes, constructed from tar-covered beer barrels or glass demijohns, were used by the Confederates as early as 1861,[14] to obstruct shipping in the Potomac below Washington. A torpedo found in the Tennessee River in February 1862 indicated that considerable improvements had been made in the short interval;[15] nevertheless, the weapon was still far from perfect. After the surrender of Fort Donelson in February 1862, Junius Henri Browne, a war correspondent for the *New York Tribune,* was asked by a Confederate captain how the Federal boats had contrived to escape the many torpedoes which had been placed in the Cumberland and Tennessee rivers; he had thought that they would blow the entire enemy fleet to atoms.[16] The most likely cause of their failure was that they had not been properly anchored, and had been carried away by the current.

Further refinements soon made the torpedoes a dreaded destructive instrument. Among the men chiefly responsible for their development were Professor Maury and General Gabriel J. Rains, but many others, like one Captain F. D. Lee, and a humble lieutenant named Hunter Davidson,[17] also contributed profitable ideas. The efficacy of underwater torpedoes was demonstrated time and again, as when a number of them, planted in the Roanoke River and detonated from shore, destroyed six out of twelve Federal vessels, which had started out to capture Fort Branch.[18] Aside from the material damage inflicted by this type of weapon, it exerted a strong psychological influence, and often made Union naval commanders exercise greater caution than conditions warranted. General Gillmore reported in April 1862 that at Fort Pulaski "the probability of encountering torpedoes . . . determined a change of plan."[19] And on March 12, 1863, Welles wrote in his diary that "the attack on Charleston will be delayed. . . . Of obstructions and torpedoes little is known, but great apprehensions are entertained."[20] Lincoln's Secretary of the Navy greatly overestimated the number of torpedoes in the harbor, perhaps because the Confederates practiced the simple trick of dumping empty barrels into the harbor, thus creating the appearance of floating mines.[21]

Forced to minimize the threat of torpedoes, the North met the challenge by constructing mine sweepers,[22] and by installing protective instruments on ships themselves. At Mobile Bay in August 1864 the *Brooklyn* was given the lead because she was equipped with an apparatus for picking up torpedoes.[23] These devices, however, were only partially successful, and on the whole the advantage lay with the torpedoes, especially when they were used in the form of floating mines, or were electrically exploded from land. Before the attack on Fort Blakely, near Mobile, during the last days of the war, the mine sweepers of the Union fleet functioned well, for they picked up 150 large torpedoes in the Blakely River and adjacent waters. This achievement notwithstanding, the *Milwaukee* struck a torpedo on March 28, 1865, and sank in three minutes. Next day the *Osage* met a like fate, and so did the tinclad *Rodolph*. Shortly afterward the gunboat *Sciola,* the tugs *Ida* and *Althea* and a launch belonging to the *Cincinnati* fell victims of these obstructions.[24] Small wonder that Professor James Russell Soley, a Northern observer, wrote after the war that "the torpedo service . . . probably contributed more to the defense of the Confederacy than all the vessels of the navy."[25]

Land torpedoes also were in vogue, and it was a Union officer who was the first to use them. Captain John G. Foster of the Engineers Corps planted some shells at the landing wharf of Fort Sumter, even before the first shot had been fired.[26] The Confederates were aware of this mode of warfare, and when they took over Fort Moultrie brought ladders along, for fear that explosives had been buried in front of the main gate.[27]

Later in the war Gabriel Rains was appointed head of the Confederate Torpedo Bureau because of his accomplishments along this line. Like his brother George W., he preferred scientific work to soldiering. He had been accused of having used "sub-terra shells" as booby traps at Yorktown in May 1862, killing several Union soldiers when they entered the abandoned fortifications. McClellan was so incensed about this act that he threatened to employ prisoners of war to remove them. Attorney General Bates also waxed indignant about the "devilish devices." Two and a half years later Sherman still considered land mines illegitimate, and served notice that he would have prisoners march ahead of his troops unless their use was stopped.[28]

Gabriel Rains strenuously denied that he had planted booby traps in Yorktown. He did claim, though, that he had been the first to make effective use of land torpedoes. It had happened during the Confederate retreat from Williamsburg, when he had hit on the idea accidentally by finding some shells on a broken-down abandoned ammunition wagon. Harassed by pursuing Union cavalry and unable to bring his guns to bear on them, he buried four shells on the road, creating havoc and confusion among the pursuers.[29] If booby traps had been found in the works of Yorktown, he declared, they had been planted by his soldiers without his knowledge.[30]

The sentiments of McClellan and Bates toward torpedoes were shared by the Confederate high command, and Rains was forbidden to use them as booby traps.[31] They were considered permissible otherwise, and during the Vicksburg campaign Rains was ordered to give torpedoes a fair trial by planting them in Grant's path to keep him from reaching Jackson,[32] where Johnston was assembling an army. Whatever the result of this expedient was, it did not greatly hinder Grant, if it hindered him at all.

After his experience during the retreat from Williamsburg, Rains became quite enthusiastic about land torpedoes. "No soldier will march over mined land," he predicted, "and a corps of sappers, each man having two ten-inch shells, two primers, and a mule to carry them, could stop an army."[33] This was far too optimistic a forecast, for the weapon did not come up to his expectations. On open roads the troops, after some insignificant losses, simply detoured around the mined areas. More promising was the use of this weapon in guarding fortified places, but even there they sometimes had drawbacks. During the siege of Charleston, for instance, the Confederates laid out a large minefield on James Island to protect Fort Wagner. The mines had been planted thickly and close to the surface, so that the tread of a man would explode them. These "subsurface torpedo mines," did furnish protection to the fort, but the protection worked both ways. "The mines," wrote the Federal general, "were a defense to us as well as to the besieged garrison, as they brought a sense of security from sorties. . . ."[34]

At Fort Fisher, too, a vast system of torpedoes had been laid out, extending across the peninsula on which the work was situated.

They were to be exploded by electricity, and were so arranged that the explosion of one would not affect the others.[35] But when Union troops finally stormed the fort, the mines failed of their purpose for an unexpected reason. Before the attack a heavy bombardment by the fleet had cut the connecting wires, making the torpedoes impotent. On the other hand, land torpedoes worked well at Fort McAllister, for Sherman reported that they "killed more men than the heavy guns of the fort."[36]

With Lee apparently too busy to take much interest in innovations, Jefferson Davis might have lent a helping hand to Southern inventors; but he held technical and scientific personnel in small esteem. It is significant that Gorgas, the kingpin of the all-important Ordnance Department, started out as a major and was not promoted to the rank of a brigadier general until the end of 1864.[37] The brilliant Mallett joined the department as a captain and never rose beyond the rank of lieutenant colonel.

Despite such want of recognition, Southerners who possessed inventive minds and scientific know-how performed exceptionally well. Unfortunately, their number was small, and their facilities were limited. Davis, who once had been a regent of the Smithsonian Institution, and a friend of its administrator, Dr. Henry, should have realized that the Confederacy, weaker in manpower and resources, might have offset these drawbacks by scientific superiority. Qualified men might have been brought from Europe and given the opportunity to work in well-equipped laboratories, located in Mexico or other neutral territory, where their work could have proceeded without impediment. A relatively minor improvement in torpedoes alone might have had a strong impact on the outcome of the war. Underwater torpedoes, good as they were, suffered from one weakness—they were not corrosion-proof, and lost their effectiveness after prolonged immersion. This imperfection may have saved Farragut's fleet when it forced its entry into Mobile Bay. The officers of the *Hartford* and the *Richmond* heard the snapping of torpedo primers under the bottom of their ships, but the torpedoes failed to explode, "having probably been corroded by lying a long time in the water."[38] The entire bay had been heavily mined, and if the torpedoes had been in working order, Farragut's famous "Damn the torpedoes!" might have made him a prototype of criminal recklessness rather than one of daredevil heroism.

While the scientists and technologists of the South furnished the means for prolonging and strengthening her resistance, the medical profession, under the able leadership of Surgeon General Samuel Preston Moore, fought the shortage of medical supplies valiantly and intelligently. Aside from suggesting substitutes and the cultivation of indigenous plants, Dr. Moore instituted an underground exchange of cotton for medicines and appliances. This issue became so important that General Beauregard urged the government to sanction an "interior black trade" for the good of the army. The Richmond bureaucrats disagreed, and the Attorney General even sued several drug firms for trading with the enemy, although they produced permits from General Pemberton. One general actually captured and imprisoned one of Dr. Moore's agents. Other commanders took a more reasonable view, winked at the trade, and were glad to get badly needed medicines.[39]

Where Dr. Moore got his medical goods can only be surmised, although it is well known that Memphis was one of the important trading centers for clandestine transactions. The city was, so an indignant Northern general declared, "of more value to the . . .

Confederacy since it fell into Federal hands than Nassau."[40] That the system worked well by the end of the war may be gleaned from a report filed in February 1865, when Dr. Moore stated that "the Department had on hand of some articles a twelve-months supply, of others a limited supply; but if allowed to retain its skilled workers at the various laboratories, and to import medicines freely through our lines in Mississippi and Alabama, no fear need be entertained that the sick and wounded of the army will suffer for want of the essential articles. . . ."[41] This would indicate that some supplies had been procured from Mexico. The boats which the smugglers used probably discharged their cargoes at some desolate spots along the Gulf coast, whence further transportation into the interior could easily be arranged.

Strangely enough, the contraband measure in some respects benefited the South. When sponges became unobtainable, the surgeons used cotton wads to clean open wounds. These wads were then thrown away, thus preventing pus to be carried from one patient to another. When bandages also were getting scarce, raw cotton was introduced in their stead. Inasmuch as the cotton had first to be baked, it was thereby rendered aseptic. Another step which, unbeknown to the surgeons, led them in the right direction, was the use of boiled horsehair in place of silk sutures. The Southern medicos may have been puzzled by the diminishing cases of blood poisoning, but the apparent mystery remained unexplained until Pasteur's discoveries were given to the world a short time later.[42]

The Confederate government, like the Northern, might have used the medical embargo as an effective psychological weapon, but with the added advantage that the attacker of an inhumane measure has over its defender. The theme song of Lincoln's foreign propagandists was the brutality of the slave system, but the emotions on which they played might have been reversed by showing the cruel picture of the medical edict, which was directed against white people, mostly of British stock who, far more than their opponents, had nurtured the time-honored culture of their motherland. Yet all the government did was to have Judah P. Benjamin, Davis' Secretary of State, send a dispatch to the Confederate emissaries abroad, in which a casual reference was made to Lincoln's "fell purpose by declaring medicines contraband of war." Moreover, this dispatch was sent on December 27, 1864, when nothing any longer mattered.[43]

It appears probable, although it seems incredible, that Hotze, Davis' adroit agent in Europe, did not know of the medical embargo, because he could have done wonders with such fruitful material. With a free hand he might have turned the opinion of the entire world in favor of the South, if in addition the Richmond authorities had given him the necessary support for a bold stroke. He could have chartered a boat, put it into a European harbor, then broadcast an appeal for contributions of medical supplies. All that was needed to arouse universal indignation was to draw an eloquent portrayal of the sufferings inside the Confederacy, due to a ruthless enemy who deprived the country of the means to aid the sick and the wounded.

The loading of the mercy boat should have been unhurried, so that its mission might sink in. When at last she would be ready to leave, the second lap of the venture might have begun. If the Washington government had let the cargo go through, it would have broken its own medical embargo and admitted the guilt of having imposed it; if it had stopped the vessel, it would have been held guilty of making war on men, women and children. No matter which course Lincoln's administration chose, its action would have undone much of what its propagandists had accomplished.

Only three men in the Confederacy had the necessary imaginative powers to put such a scheme into effect—Alexander Stephens, Benjamin and Henry Hotze. There is no record that either one of them gave it a thought at any time.

THE GENERALSHIP OF
JEFFERSON DAVIS

DAVIS' field strategy was as faulty as his over-all planning. The war was less than a year old when the Confederacy had to pay its first installment on his incompetence.

In order to protect the ingress into the South by two tempting waterways, Fort Henry had been erected on the Tennessee and Fort Donelson on the Cumberland River. Fort Henry, which was an isolated work, fell on February 5, 1862, after a few hours of bombardment by gunboats; the garrison fled before Union land forces could go into action. If Davis had subjected this setback even to a cursory analysis, he should have apprehended that neighboring Fort Donelson, which was equally isolated, also might fall, unless help from the outside—which was not available—could scatter the besieging army. But what neither Davis nor the commanding General Albert Sidney Johnston realized, its defenders did, after Federal troops and gunboats had closed in on them. Although they had repulsed the first day's attacks, they lost no time in trying to emulate the example of their comrades in Fort Henry. Their attempt to break out of their trap miscarried, and the Confederacy lost some 14,000 men and much war material.

In later years Davis admitted that this disaster should have been foreseen. "Many, wise after the event," he wrote plaintively, "have shown their skill in telling what all knew afterward, but nobody told before."[1] Davis was wrong. The disaster had been told before, not by men, but by events. As early as August 1861 a Union fleet, supported by the army, had taken the North Carolina Forts Clark and Hatteras after a short fight, capturing 670 men and thirty-five cannon. They then occupied near-by Beacon Island and Portsmouth, the garrisons of which decamped, thereby showing better sense than their government; but they left twenty-two guns of heavy caliber in the hands of their victors. On February 8, 1862, five forts on Roanoke Island with 2675 men and 32 guns were taken by a combined army and navy attack.

The outcome of these one-sided engagements showed clearly that forts on a sea front could not be held, provided the enemy commanded the waterside and had sufficient force on land to back up the fleet. They would be subdued either by guns or by hunger. There was no reason to believe that river forts would fare differently. Fort Henry proved the correctness of this assumption, but had already been lost by the time news of the Roanoke surrender reached Richmond. Fort Donelson, though, could yet have been evacuated and the garrison saved. Nevertheless, Davis, instead of ordering Johnston to abandon it, allowed him to strengthen the garrison, thereby accomplishing nothing but to accentuate the severity of the loss.

Still Davis could not read the handwriting on the wall, for he believed that Johnston's left flank had been made secure by the fortified Mississippi River Island No. 10. He soon was disillusioned, for once more a combined Union army and fleet forced its surrender, further weakening the Confederates by 6,000 men and twenty cannon. Forts St. Philip and Jackson on the lower Mississippi had to strike their flags the same month, leaving New Orleans defenseless. But Davis, who never learned from past mistakes, kept his blinders on, and a year later lost Arkansas Post in the same fashion. This fort had been built on the left bank of the Arkansas River to protect the strategically unimportant city of Little Rock, and was one of the many military luxuries in which the Confederacy so often indulged. Early in January 1863 the Union General McClernand, "having nothing better to do," as one of his officers wrote,[2] determined to capture it and, after a short engagement, scooped up what was left of its 5,000 men.

In spite of the ruinous defeats Davis' policy had brought about, he never seemed to grasp that isolated river forts could not be successfully defended. In December 1862 he ordered Bragg to send 10,000 troops to help defend Vicksburg. This weakening of his army may well have been the decisive factor in the drawn battle at Stone River a few days afterward, for with this additional force the Confederates might have won. The fall of Vicksburg and Port Hudson, with a loss of over 35,000 men and a whole arsenal of guns and other equipment, followed within half a year. Among those captured were the 10,000 men taken from Bragg.

The only river forts that withstood enemy attacks were those securely protected on the land side and not within reach of Federal warships. Two works that met these requirements had been erected on Drewry's Bluff and Chaffin's Bluff on the James. Both remained in Confederate hands during the four years of fighting.

The validity of this military principle was demonstrated by the fact that the vulnerability of isolated water-front forts worked both ways. On April 12, 1864, General Forrest turned the tables on the North by taking Fort Pillow on the Mississippi after a short struggle, in which a single Federal gunboat was of no help to the defenders.[3] A few days later the Confederates recaptured Plymouth, North Carolina, on the Roanoke River, where a Union fleet of eight warships was neutralized by the Confederate ram *Albemarle*.[4] Thus the Union high command showed that it could be no less obtuse than the one in Richmond. It was a race between the military incompetence of Halleck and Davis, with honors about even but with one difference: the North could afford to make mistakes; the South could not.

In 1863 Davis upheld the cantankerous and unfit Bragg against the angry protests of his subordinates, and left him in his position long enough to be crushed at Missionary Ridge. Then, instead of dismissing the discredited general, he called him to Richmond as general-in-chief. It looked as if Davis could not resist the temptation to copy Lincoln's error. Lincoln had chosen a bungling chief of staff, so why not he?

On the day after Bragg's promotion the Richmond *Enquirer* commented on it with biting sarcasm: "The judicious and opportune appointment of General Bragg to the post of Commander-in-Chief . . . will be appreciated as an illustration of that strong common-sense which forms the basis of the President's character, that regard for the opinions and feelings of the country. . . . The Confederate armies cannot fail to be well pleased. Every soldier's heart feels that merit is the true title to promotion, and that glorious service should insure a splendid reward. From Lookout Mountain, a step to the highest military honor and power is natural and inevitable. . . . This happy announcement should enliven the fires of confidence and enthusiasm . . . like a bucket of water on a newly-kindled grate."[5] And just as Lincoln had interfered with Grant's Vicksburg campaign in the fall of 1862 by giving McClernand an independent mission, Davis interfered with Lee's Gettysburg campaign in 1863 by refusing his request to put Beauregard at Culpeper. "Davis has undoubtedly committed a mistake,"[6] reads Welles's dry comment in his diary.

The Confederate President seemed to think of the war as his private affair and let personal feelings influence his military decisions, including the appointment and removal of officers. He disliked Joseph Johnston, a top-notch general, but out of necessity placed him at the head of the Army of Tennessee after Bragg's ignominious departure. During the winter of 1863-64 Davis urged Johnston repeatedly to attack Sherman's army of some 80,000 men, bountifully provided and heavily fortified,[7] although Johnston commanded only 36,000 effectives, who lacked arms, equipment and transportation.[8] He naturally demurred, but a few days later Davis again "hoped" that operations would soon be commenced, "to regain possession of the territory from which we have been driven."[9] After more irksome needling of this kind, Johnston lost patience and returned a reply bristling with verbal barbs: "Your Excellency well impresses upon me the importance of recovering the territory we have lost, . . . but difficulties appear to me in the way."[10]

Flying in the face of the common good, but always with an eye on the interest of his friends, Davis' orders became more and more obnoxious. In the spring of 1864, instead of allowing Forrest to cut Sherman's life line, as he was about to do, he was directed to stop Sturgis' unimportant raid into Mississippi, the President's home state. The order led to the battle of Brice's Cross Roads, bringing Forrest undying fame, and unrestrained joy to Sherman, who was happy to see his redoubtable opponent sidetracked on an assignment which could have no influence on the course of the war. Then Davis reached the apex of his maladministration: with a stroke of the pen he practically blotted out what remained of the western half of the Confederacy by removing Johnston, and replaced him with the impetuous Hood. "This was just what we wanted," Sherman wrote jubilantly in his *Memoirs*.[11]

As if he had not done enough damage, Davis now added one more blunder to his growing collection. In the hope of instilling new confidence into troops dispirited by his irrational leadership, he treated them to a speech, in which he hinted at Hood's next move. This enabled Sherman to block it by sending reinforcements to where Hood intended to go. The upshot was that the remnants of a brave army were pushed into useless slaughter.

The true measure of Jefferson Davis' mind could not have been better illustrated than by his first and last official acts. Shortly after his inauguration, while pressing state affairs awaited his decision, he spent much time writing out detailed specifications for caps, friction primers and rifling machines;[12] and on the eve of evacuating Richmond, when the end of the war was in plain sight, he went on signing promotions of junior officers, and sent a letter to Lee in which he expressed anxiety whether sufficient material for the Tredegar Ironworks was on hand to keep them going.[13]

It seems that during the four years of his incumbency President Davis was living in a dream world of his own making, from which he did not emerge until it toppled over. After that he became the gentle, kind and considerate man he was at heart; adversity had not humbled his pride, but it had cracked his crust of aloofness. The more of his associates left him, the higher his spirits rose. Many years later a friend of his drew a touching picture of the defeated President. "Still the head [of what had been a powerful government]," he wrote, "he moved, calm, self-poised, giving way to no petulance of temper . . . advising and consoling, laying aside all thought of self, planning and doing what was best, . . . he filled my own distressed heart so full of emotion and love and admiration, that it could hardly contain them. . . . He then appeared incomparably grander . . . than when he reviewed victorious armies from well-won fields."[14]

As a President, Jefferson Davis had been a tragic failure, who left behind him an unbroken record of errors and lost opportunities; but in the loneliness of his flight he redeemed himself. A man who could bear up so gallantly under misfortune must have had some greatness in him, his many adverse traits notwithstanding.

BOOK

III

CIVIL WAR GENERALS

*

THE generals of the Civil War ranged from near geniuses to men of shocking incompetence. A partial list of the more prominent ones is herewith presented, together with an attempted rating, based on their abilities and performances.

For the sake of simplicity, a star system has been adopted:

> Four Stars—Military ability near genius
> Three Stars—Extraordinary ability
> Two Stars—Competent, dependable
> One Star—Erratic, but with a high average
> One Star with a question mark—Undetermined
> One minus star—Bad

Union Generals	*Confederate Generals*
**** None	**** Nathan B. Forrest
*** None	*** Stonewall Jackson
** George H. Thomas	** Joseph E. Johnston
** Fitz John Porter	** James Longstreet
* George B. McClellan	* Pierre G. T. Beauregard
*(?) U. S. Grant	* Robert E. Lee
—* Henry W. Halleck	—* Braxton Bragg
—* Ambrose E. Burnside	

HOW GREAT A GENERAL
WAS GRANT?

MOST writers rank Grant with the great military leaders of all times. This is to be expected. To the victor belong the spoils and the glory. However, the winner of a war is not necessarily a great general. Whether or not Grant had outstanding military qualities cannot be judged equitably without taking into account that superiority in manpower and matériel tipped the scales heavily in his favor.

Grant fought only two battles, Belmont and the first day of Shiloh, where the number of men engaged and the quality of their weapons were approximately equal on both sides. At Belmont he acquitted himself well, but was compelled to retreat. He had gone into the battle against orders and despite the pleadings of his friend John A. Rawlins, whose protest that the soldiers had not had sufficient training, he met with the rejoinder that nothing could fill that want better than actual combat. On the first day at

Shiloh Grant behaved abominably and came within a hairbreadth of being annihilated, due to excessive carelessness on his part. Shiloh also demonstrated another of his defects—lack of imagination, for he had failed to anticipate what his opponent was almost certain to do: attack him before Buell's arrival would almost double the strength of his forces.

On the second day of the battle Grant beat Beauregard by sheer weight of numbers, but inexcusably did not follow up his advantage. If he had, he might have eliminated the only sizable Confederate army on the western front. The reasons Grant gave for his neglect were trivial—bad roads, softened by recent rains; his unwillingness to order his tired troops to pursue; his reluctance to give orders to Buell, whose superior he had become only a short time ago. These arguments are unimpressive. Most likely he was so shaken by his narrow escape from utter defeat that he shared the feelings of Sherman, who admitted frankly that "we had [had] quite enough of [the Confederates'] society for two whole days, and were only too glad to be rid of them on any terms."[1]

Grant's earliest exploits deserve acclaim. His unauthorized occupation of Paducah and his threat against Columbus were bold strokes, well carried out. This kind of initiative and an urge to keep busy characterized his leadership throughout, while his ability to think clearly, act calmly, and persevere in what he had set out to do, were and remained his prime assets. Inherently he was a simple, modest man of moderate intelligence, whose army life had fostered his native tendency toward devotion to duty and unquestioning obedience. He had scraped pelts in his brother's store, because that was what he was being paid for, and when asked to do a clerk's job in his Springfield days, he did it without flinching. In war he fought because it was his business to fight, not because he was fond of it; and in the words of an erstwhile enemy he did it "in the true spirit of a soldier, never by deed or word inflicting wrong on non-combatants."[2] Robert E. Lee's nephew W. H. Fitzhugh Lee, also had words of praise for his former opponent: "[Grant] had . . . many excellent qualities for a soldier. He was taciturn, sturdy, plucky, not afraid of public responsibility or affected by public opinion. There was no ostentation in his position, and to an outsider he was not as showy as a corporal of the guard."[3]

Besides Belmont and the first day of Shiloh, Grant started the Vicksburg campaign also on even terms and did well, but toward the end he greatly outnumbered his enemy. In all other battles Grant had the odds in his favor, overwhelmingly. Even so, the credit for his first great victory, the surrender of Fort Donelson, was not rightfully his, for when the Confederates tried to break through his army, which was twice as strong, their repulse was not due to anything he did, because he was not present at that time. The Vicksburg campaign gave Grant a great opportunity, and his original intention to operate against the city from the east showed excellent generalship. Due to Lincoln's interference, however, he had to engage in the long and arduous task of taking Vicksburg by an approach down the river. It was more dramatic, but strategically far inferior to his first plan.

The running of the Vicksburg batteries on April 16, 1863, which has been widely extolled as one of his finest achievements, was in fact neither novel nor unduly hazardous. Some two months before, the Federal gunboat *Queen of the West* had successfully defied the Confederate shore guns, and soon afterward the ironclad *Indianola* had passed Vicksburg "without a scratch."[4] In contrast to the army, navy men always looked at land batteries with disdain, and even before the outbreak of the war, when the fleet had boasted no armed vessels, they had been willing to run the gauntlet of the Charleston harbor batteries to relieve Fort Sumter. They had silenced the guns of several North Carolina forts without taking serious punishment and—what was still more noteworthy—had passed the two strong masonry forts guarding New Orleans. Moreover, in the latter case they had had to sail upstream and overcome enemy gunboats, fire barges and heavy chains across the river. None of such obstacles had to be overcome by the Union fleet at Vicksburg.

The remainder of the Vicksburg campaign was a masterly performance on Grant's part. Clinging to his idea that the occupation of Jackson was the cornerstone of victory, he took that town by a series of brilliant movements. After this the fall of the river fortress was only a matter of time. But luck also played its part. What, for instance, would have happened if Pemberton had followed Johnston's instructions to meet the Union troops in full force, before they could get set on the eastern bank of the Mississippi? Or if Johnston's order to give up Vicksburg and save the army had not been thwarted by Jefferson Davis? Yet Grant must be given full credit for profiting by his opponents' errors and for exploiting them with deftness and energy.

After the twin victories of Gettysburg and Vicksburg the North could dispense with luck. Barring inconceivable blunders, it could no longer lose. The blockade alone, which was becoming more effective by the day, relegated Confederate victory into the realm of daydreaming. But despite Grant's growing fame, his rise to the highest rank was not entirely the result of his military accomplishments. He had learned from mistakes of others that it was good policy to humor Lincoln. Whether through meekness, training or native shrewdness, Grant always played up to the President. On April 30, 1864, on the eve of the spring campaign, he wrote to Lincoln that "should my success be less than I desire and

expect, the least I can say is, the fault is not with you."[5] And at
the Presidential election in the fall he did not object, when enough
soldiers of the right kind were furloughed to insure a Republican
victory in doubtful states.[6]

Unlike other generals, Grant never asked for more men than
he had been allotted, nor did he openly resent rebuffs. "Grant
quarrels with no one," John Hay wrote in his diary.[7] It was his
spirit of docility, mixed with intuitive political sense, that helped
him to gain and hold the good will of the Washington authorities,
although keen-eyed Welles suspected that he was not without
cunning and selfishness.[8]

Grant's servility paid off handsomely. In a conversation with
Sherman, Lincoln once revealed what had caused him to entertain
friendlier feelings toward Grant and his chief lieutenant than
toward other generals. "It was because you never found fault
with me . . . ," the President explained.[9]

Lincoln wanted a man who would fight; therefore Grant
fought, even when maneuvering would have served his purpose
as well. Lincoln was set on campaigning against Richmond via
the overland route; so Grant took it. His losses in the spring of
1864 were frightful, his results disappointing, but he knew that
he would be sustained because he was following the President's
wishes. Grant knew that the administration was behind him, and
that its powerful propaganda machine was working in his behalf.
In return he had given definite assurance that he was not after
the Presidency. "I aspire only to one political office," he was reported to have said. ". . . I mean to run for Mayor of Galena."[10]

So long as Lincoln submitted to Stanton's highhanded methods, Grant did the same, to the point of permitting the censoring
of his dispatches.[11] He accepted Robert Todd Lincoln as staff
captain, overlooking the boy's lack of qualifications. Had not

Lincoln overlooked Grant's failure to provide protection for Washington when Early threatened it? Lincoln and Grant understood each other and worked in perfect harmony.

The relief of beleaguered Chattanooga, for which Grant received the plaudits of the North, was not his doing, but must be credited to the foresight of General William F. Smith who, prior to Grant's arrival, had made preparatons for crossing the Tennessee at Brown's Ferry. The storming of Missionary Ridge, one of the most sensational victories of the war, was not undertaken on Grant's orders, and came as a complete surprise to him.

Severe blame attaches to Grant for not finishing the war in the west then and there, which he could have done by ordering a determined pursuit of Bragg's army before Halleck could have intervened. Sheridan wrote disappointedly that he "felt great results were in store for us, should the enemy be vigorously followed."[12] Grant himself subsequently admitted that he had missed this chance; he had dillydallied too long. "I was not right sure," he explained, "but that Bragg's troops might be over their stampede by the time they reached Dalton. . . . When I arrived at Ringgold, however, on the 27th [two days later], I saw that the retreat was most earnest. The enemy had been throwing away guns, caissons, . . . and, altogether seemed to be moving like a disorganized mob. . . ."[13] But by that time many of his troops were on the march to the relief of Burnside, who was being besieged by Longstreet in Knoxville.

Grant should have realized immediately after his unexpected victory at Missionary Ridge that nothing could be lost and much might be gained by following through; that in view of the great issue at stake Burnside's corps was expendable, and that a temporary abandonment of East Tennessee would be more than offset by the destruction of Bragg. But Lincoln was wiring "daily, almost hourly," that Burnside be not forgotten.[14] It was another case of the President's meddling, but Grant thought it best to give the hint priority over sound military thinking.

In the last year of the war the relative strength of Grant's adversaries diminished progressively and rapidly. Their man power was dwindling, his artillery outshot theirs, and his repeating rifles gave him an inestimable advantage. His soldiers were well-fed, well-shod, well-clad, and received adequate medical care. The Southerners always were ill-shod or barefoot and insufficiently clothed, but by the last year of the war the resources of the Confederacy had been depleted to such an extent that, in addition to these deficiencies, its armies were starving and could not replace their losses. Their cavalry lacked horses, their surgeons were short of instruments and medicines. Under these conditions there never was any doubt about Grant's eventual victory; the question was not *if,* but *how soon* he would achieve it. It took him nearly a year, which cannot be called *soon* by any stretch of the word's meaning.

On the credit side of Grant's military ledger the Vicksburg campaign, magnificently fought in its intermediate stages, takes first place. Another feat deserving encomium was the neatly executed transfer of his army across the James, after he had become convinced that his plan to reach Richmond from the north was not feasible. It also took considerable moral courage to recant his rash promise that he would fight it out along the inland route "if it took all summer." Had Butler at this juncture done his part at Petersburg, Lee would have been in trouble. For once, however, Dame Luck deserted her favorite, and Grant had to resort to trench warfare, which was slow and enervating.

Grant's bulldog tenacity and his imperturbability under trying conditions filled his troops with confidence. He never gained the popularity of McClellan, he lacked the glamour of Hooker, but there never was disaffection in his ranks. Under him the soldiers did their duty as he did his, without much enthusiasm, but without complaints. McClellan had built the Northern war machine, and Grant steered it toward its goal; but in justice to his predecessors it must be remembered that in the last year of the war he was allowed to operate with a minimum of interference from high quarters, a privilege that had not been granted to them.

From all this it appears that the question whether Grant was a great general cannot be answered by a simple yes or no. Lee expressed his opinion somewhat contemptuously: "Grant's talent and strategy consisted in accumulating numbers."[15] Other contemporaries were not so sure. Welles considered him dull and heavy, but at the end of the war conceded to him military talent and "some capacity," though considering him "slow and utterly destitute of genius." On the other hand, Sherman was his ardent admirer from start to finish. Obviously it was as difficult then as it is now to judge a general who was so stupid at Shiloh and so clever on the James; a butcher at Cold Harbor and careful of his men's lives at Petersburg; who was right in leaving the execution of the Georgia campaign to a subordinate, and wrong in doing the same at the Crater; who favored and employed unorthodox methods of fighting, but ignored the potentialities of scientific improvements.

The foregoing presents the composite picture of Grant as commanding general. It contains some bright spots, others less so. His own accounts are not dependable, for they are not free from bias. He gives generous praise to some, withholds it from others. One would never know from his reports that disaster at Fort Donelson was averted by the steadfastness of Wallace, or that he was saved at Shiloh by Benjamin M. Prentiss' stubborn gallantry and

Buell's decision to ignore Grant's advice for delay. Instead of paying respect to these men, Grant had only mild praise for Wallace,[16] blamed Prentiss for not retreating at the right time,[17] and belittled Buell's part in the battle.[18] Two of his most loyal and valuable generals, John A. Rawlins and James H. Wilson, got little mention in his *Memoirs*.

Grant's preponderance in men and equipment undoubtedly was the most important factor in his victories, but does not necessarily disparage his generalship. He might have been equally successful against a strong and well-provided opponent. Nevertheless, the fact remains that, figuratively speaking, he was a two-hundred-pound, fully equipped boxer, who fought a half-starved, barehanded man half his weight. Unless this parallel can be shown to lack pertinency, Grant's military capacity cannot be appraised judiciously.

⫸ 13 ⫷

HOW GREAT A GENERAL
WAS LEE?

LEE, the beau ideal of American manhood, the knight *sans peur et sans reproche,* is one of the noblemen of history. This view is universally held today, both North and South. One almost hesitates to examine his military qualities, for fear that evidence may be forthcoming which runs contrary to one's wishes. Nevertheless, the task must be undertaken.

Disregarding tradition, and guided solely by the verdict of the test tube, Lee's record as a general does not emerge on a par with his character. Rather does he resemble the little girl of whom it is said that when she was good, she was very, very good, but when she was bad, she was horrid. Most of the time his generalship was competent or brilliant, but he did have shortcomings, and their effect was costly.

Lee had three outstanding faults which dim the luster of his martial fame. The most excusable of them was his submissiveness to Jefferson Davis. Thirty years in the Army had left their impress on Lee, and all he saw in the President was his military superior, who had to be obeyed implicitly. Yet he should have realized that in a life-and-death struggle justifiable opposition should have out-weighed military etiquette. Reading Lee's letters and dispatches to Davis, one cannot help feeling that much harm to the Confederate cause would have been averted, had Lee asserted himself more aggressively. Yet even when drastic action was imperative, he could not overcome his inherent deference to authority.

Two instances will illustrate his inordinate humility. "For some few days past," he wrote to Davis on June 16, 1864, "we have been only able to get sufficient corn for our animals from day to day . . . unless some improvement is made, I do not know what will be-come of us—I am therefore obliged to appeal to your Excellency as reluctant as I am to trespass upon your time and attention . . ."[1]

The first part of Lee's message was couched in a tone commen-surate with the seriousness of the problem; then he vitiated his manly appeal by a needless apology. For what was he apologiz-ing? For "trespassing" on the President's time? What better use could Davis have made of his time than trying to alleviate the desperate feed shortage his general was pointing out to him?

Another case of this kind had tragic consequences. In July of the same year Lee was advised of Davis' intention to replace Johnston with Hood. Following his first outraged impulse, Lee expressed himself in punchy staccato sentences:

"Telegram of to-day received. I regret the fact stated. It is a bad time to release the commander of an army situated as is that of Tenne[ssee]. We may lose Atlanta and the army too. Hood is a bold fighter. I am doubtful as to other qualities necessary."[2]

Lee evidently foresaw the loss of "Atlanta and the army too," if

Hood were to replace Johnston. His vigorous protest, though delicately phrased, left no doubt as to its meaning; but in another wire, sent a few hours later, he reverted to his customary meekness.

"Still if necessary it ought to be done; I know nothing of the necessity. I had hoped that Johnston was strong enough to deliver battle.... General [William Joseph] Hardee has more experience in managing an army."[3]

Why did not Lee say outright what he evidently had in mind—that Davis was about to commit an irreparable blunder? Instead he sidestepped the issue by ending his message tamely:

"May God give you wisdom to decide in this momentous matter."

This pious wish, well-meant though it was, is not what Davis had asked for.

All through the war years Lee exerted far too little influence on the general situation. Had he used the power of public opinion, he could have forced Davis to consult him on all matters of general strategy. He could have objected to the President's folly of dispersing the army into small, separated units. He could have persuaded him to bring trans-Mississippi troops across the river to oppose Grant. At the beginning of the Gettysburg campaign he should have pressed his recommendation to post Beauregard at Culpeper. He should have followed his own and Jackson's inclination to fight Burnside on the North Anna instead of at Fredericksburg. In short, he should have tried to have Davis confine his activities to administrative duties, and leave the conduct of the war to those who had shown that they were capable of doing it competently. If Lee had applied his gifts on a larger scale, it would not only have helped the South militarily, but would also have greatly strengthened her morale. It was he, not Davis who had the people's confidence, and for this reason alone his opinions should have prevailed over those of the President. But the only one who could have brought this about was Lee himself.

Gideon Welles, looking critically from afar at the Richmond administration, was disgusted. "It is sad and humiliating," he wrote in his diary on July 18, 1863, "to see men of talents, capacity and independence, cower and shrink and humble themselves before the impervious master who dominates over the Confederacy."

There must have been many within the seceded states who agreed with Lincoln's Secretary of the Navy.

The second and more serious of Lee's weaknesses was his strange aversion to maps. He lost opportunity after opportunity through lack of correct road information, yet he never seemed able to overcome this failing.

Lee's disregard of maps is as hard to excuse as it is to understand. He was a trained engineer and had distinguished himself in the Mexican War by gathering important topographical information. The only mitigating circumstance, if it can be so considered, is that in the neglect of maps he did not stand alone. From the beginning of the war it had appeared highly probable that the Peninsula and the environs of Richmond would become battlegrounds; yet no one noted the lack of maps or took measures to correct the deficiency. While Johnston was commanding the Army of Northern Virginia, Davis asked him on what line he would retreat from Manassas, should retreat become necessary. Johnston replied that he was "ignorant of the topography of the country in his rear."[4] Davis acknowledged that he was equally ignorant, and unable to give advice[5] as to the selection of a new position for the army. Both men appeared satisfied to let it go at that.

A short time later, when the Union army was already within sight of Richmond, Davis wrote to his wife that "though . . . our army had retreated from Yorktown up to the Chickahominy . . . *we had no maps of the country in which we were operating; our generals were ignorant of the roads, and their guides knew little more than the way from their homes to Richmond.*"[6] Davis called this "an extraordinary fact," but did not say who was to blame. Evidently he, although commander-in-chief, held himself free from guilt.

What about Lee? When the Seven Days battle began, he had been in charge of the Virginia troops for over a year, and during much of this time had resided in Richmond; nevertheless, he had not even ordered a topographical survey of its suburban territory. During all the weeks while McClellan was creeping up the Peninsula, he did nothing to procure reliable maps and guides, or even collate whatever little information was on hand. Before the battle of Fair Oaks, General G. W. Smith told President Davis of having received a report from a private citizen that Beaver Dam Creek presented an impassable barrier.[7] What, if anything, Mr. Davis did to confirm this hearsay information he did not reveal, nor was he prompted to ascertain why important military information about a locality a few miles from the capital was unknown there and had to be obtained accidentally through civilian channels. At any rate, two months later the existence of this barrier must still have been unknown to Ambrose Powell Hill, for he ran head-on into it, with the result that 1400 brave soldiers were mutilated or killed.

More and greater misfortunes were to follow. The same Lee who rarely went into battle without the most careful preparations, sent more than two thirds of his forces into the battle of Gaines's Mill under generals who, in lieu of maps, had been furnished with a few lines drawn childishly and haphazardly on a piece of paper.[8] General Taylor still was enraged when he commented on this state of affairs fifteen years later: ". . . from Cold Harbor to Malvern Hill inclusive, . . . the Confederate commanders knew no more about the topography of the country than they did about Central Africa. . . . a day's march [from] . . . Richmond, . . . yet we were without maps. . . . nearly as helpless as if we had been suddenly transferred to the banks of the Lualaba. . . . Let it be remembered, too, that McClellan . . . weeks before [had indicated] this very region to be the necessary theatre of conflict; that . . . General Johnston had been a topographical engineer in the United States army; while . . . General Lee,—another engineer—had been on duty . . . in Richmond. . . . Everyone must agree that it was amazing."[9] General Daniel Harvey Hill seconded Taylor in few but stinging words: "The maps furnished the division commanders were worthless."[10] Jackson found them equally so and depended on a guide, who happened to misinterpret the orders given him. As a consequence Jackson took the wrong road and consumed valuable time in countermarching, which made it impossible for him to co-ordinate his attack in the way expected of him.

If the Confederate maps north of the Chickahominy were useless, those south of it were practically nonexistent. Lee himself possessed only one sketch, and no copies of it were issued to the commanders engaged in McClellan's pursuit. The guides were as much a hindrance as a help and added to the confusion.[11] And while the Union army was marching to Harrison's Landing on a road of which Lee had no knowledge, he must have been wondering how McClellan had managed to elude him.

The sole excuse Lee's biographer Douglas Southall Freeman offers for "a man so mindful of the value of military details," is that he chose to use "the means at hand, without waiting to perfect them," although "perhaps more might have been done."[12] Neither this explanation nor the slight reproach is persuasive. Far from being a military detail, maps are fundamentally important, especially in terrains where swamps, thickets and poor roads confuse even the natives. This confusion was doubly confounded by the fact that the names of roads around Richmond often bore the same names, the spelling of which, moreover, was perplexing. There were two Quaker Roads, and, so General Taylor recorded, "we came upon two ... [roads] leading in ... different directions, but bearing the same name, Grapevine. . . . The name Darby [Road] was ... written Enroughty."[13] All these conditions notwithstanding, Lee's mind remained afflicted with a blind spot in regard to maps. The "means" to prepare them could have been supplied by a few topographical engineers, who were on hand and need only have been detached for this duty.

Those of Lee's generals who participated in the pursuit of McClellan were hamstrung by the lack of guidance. "I had no one to show me what road to take," complained General Huger.[14] A major who served under General Magruder declared that he had never seen a map of the country in which his troops had to operate, except the one used by Lee, and that contained a gross error.

General Long, while admitting that the map situation was deplorable, took issue with those who held Lee responsible for it, and declared that "the blame ... [for] want of maps should be placed where it properly belongs—with the war-directing authority at

Richmond. It is from the topographical bureaus of government that the . . . knowledge . . . should be obtained, and . . . neither Johnston nor Lee had opportunities to cause reconnaissances and surveys to be made . . . for the construction of maps."[15]

It would seem that even though the responsibility for maps may have devolved on the War Department, Lee as commanding general should have insisted on their procurement as earnestly as he would have demanded cartridges, guns, horses or other indispensable instruments of war, had they not been supplied promptly.

In his zeal to defend his beloved chief, Long overshot his mark. He asserted that "the statement in regard to Lee's want of knowledge of the topography of his field of operations and the inferiority of his guides is incorrect. The blunders complained of were more the result of inattention to orders and want of proper energy on the part of a few subordinate commanders than lack of knowledge of the country."

Nevertheless, Long must have felt that his biased opinion, unsupported by tangible evidence, would not stand up under close scrutiny, and in trying to strengthen his argument he went still farther out on a limb, by trying to explain that "for years Lee had been accustomed to traverse the country between the White House and Richmond to the different estates . . . on the lower James. He was therefore well acquainted with the country on both sides of the Chickahominy, and it was natural that he should apply his previous information to his present purposes. The inhabitants of that region supplied efficient guides, and his staff officers had been employed in making themselves acquainted with the roads and natural features of the country over which the army was likely to operate."[16]

The weakness of this plea is so transparent that it hardly calls for comment. No one denied that Lee might have had personal knowledge of the country; but if so, he evidently did not impart it to his staff officers; or if they had made themselves acquainted with the region, as Long indicates, they must have kept the information to themselves. "If Lee . . . as General Long states, . . . was familiar with the country," the colonel of an Alabama regiment asked pertinently, "how was it that [he] was not aware of the existence of the road which McClellan took in effecting his retreat from Malvern Hill . . .?[17]

Long went still farther in bolstering his claims by asserting that a detailed map existed at that time and did service in the Seven Days battles. As proof he included in his book "a copy of the official map used by General Lee during his campaign. It was filed with his report of these operations in War Department, C.S.A., by the special direction of General Lee."

This is where Long went too far. The map was not made until after the Seven Days battles, as becomes plain from a study of the map itself and from the markings on it. It shows, for instance, the Federal fortifications at Harrison's Landing, which of course had not been built before the battle, and it designates the various battle-fields with their dates; most convincing of all, it is marked "made 1862 & '63," and "approved April 2, 1863 by *R. E. Lee*."[18]

With this map the superloyal Long effectively killed his own case.

When Jackson commanded in the Shenandoah Valley, he, too, found himself handicapped by the lack of maps. He did not know the passes over the Blue Ridge Mountains and was not acquainted with the roads but, in contrast to Lee, he lost no time in applying the proper remedy. He had his able topographical engineer Major Jed Hotchkiss make detailed maps of the Valley,[19] and ordered him "not to be afraid of making too many."[20] Before the invasion of Maryland, Hotchkiss prepared maps of that state also,[21] and at the start of the Chancellorsville campaign he provided Jackson with valuable topographical information.[22] But Jackson's foresight did not impel Lee to follow the example of his distinguished lieutenant, whose map-making proclivities could hardly have remained unknown to him.

In the summer of 1862 the war moved out of the Peninsula into the regions of Manassas, and the specter of missing maps once more lifted its ugly head. On August 28 Jackson was separated from Lee by Thoroughfare Gap and in danger of being overpowered. The main Confederate army was approaching and found the gap occupied by enemy troops. In desperation Lee sent reconnaissances to right and left in search of another pass.[23] Luckily two were found and, still more luckily, there was no need for them, because the Federals had obligingly vacated the passage. This contingency thus was successfully met, but was there any excuse for not having anticipated it?

At Antietam and Fredericksburg the absence of maps presented no serious problem; but it arose again when Hooker marched into the thickets around Chancellorsville. Had his sudden appearance come as a surprise, Lee's want of information about the Wilderness back roads could be condoned, but this was not the case, for Burnside already had foreshadowed Hooker's route by his ill-fated mud march. At any rate, it was plain that sooner or later the Wilderness might become a fighting arena, and that a minute mapping of its roads was vitally important. Yet when Jackson decided on his flanking march, no detailed maps were available, and he had to get last-minute road information from inhabitants of the region.[24] He lost so much time thereby that he did not strike the 11th Corps until too late to achieve a total victory. Sorrowfully he exclaimed that with one more hour of daylight he could have completed the destruction of the Federal army.[25]

After three years of fighting it should have been a well established principle that maps were as essential to an army as soldiers and guns, yet Lee did not profit by his past errors. In the fall of 1863 he had predicted that in the coming spring the Union army would be led through the Wilderness to Spotsylvania,[26] which would bring it near the terrain in which the Chancellorsville fighting had taken place. Therefore several months could have been used for a thorough topographical exploration. But when the moment of decision arrived, Lee came dangerously close to losing the campaign before it was more than a day old. The reason? No adequate maps.

Grant had crossed the Rapidan on May 4 and the next day fought his way into the Wilderness against Hill's and Ewell's corps. Longstreet had started from Gordonsville on the afternoon of the 4th, marched sixteen miles that day and, with a total of only twenty miles to cover, should have joined the rest of the army early on the fifth. He took the wrong road, however, consumed a day and a half for his march to the battleground, and arrived just when the Union forces were on the edge of victory. Lee stated afterward that he had provided Longstreet with a guide, but that his services were spurned.[27] Nevertheless, Lee was equally at fault with his general. Why was it necessary to wait till the last hour to show Longstreet the right road? With the outcome of the initial clash, perhaps the fate of the campaign at stake, some of Longstreet's men should have examined their route before the crisis of the conflict was reached. In this way they could have made themselves acquainted with the roads and determined the time it would take them to join their comrades.

Worse was to come. After Longstreet's last-minute arrival had warded off threatening disaster, Lee decided to throw him against Grant's exposed left corps, expecting to roll up his flank. If the plan succeeded, the story of Chancellorsville might be retold. Unfortunately, the two main roads through the Wilderness were crowded with A. P. Hill's and Ewell's troops, and Lee needed a third parallel route for Longstreet. The embankment of an abandoned railroad was close by and would serve this purpose well, but it did not show on Lee's map. Frantically he sent his chief engineer, General Martin Luther Smith, on a searching expedition. Smith had no trouble locating the embankment, which was only a mile away, but valuable time had been wasted[28] and Longstreet's attack failed. That Lee did not know of this route is the more incredible as General George T. Anderson, who replaced the wounded Longstreet that day, was fully aware of its existence, having marched his brigade on it the year before.[29]

Now at last it would seem that Lee should have learned his lesson; but a month later, when the opposing lines were fighting near the old battlefield of Gaines's Mill, his old weakness returned to plague him. The Confederate front was vulnerable on its right end, and had to be strengthened at all hazards. John C. Breckinridge's division, which held the left of the line, was ordered to march during the night to reinforce the right wing. To make certain that it would get there before dawn, Lee sent Major Henry B. McClellan of his own staff to direct it. Dawn came, but no Breckinridge, and Lee rode out to look for him. He found him and his troops at breakfast in Mechanicsville, miles from their destination. The delay was soon explained: Major McClellan had not been supplied with a map, although Lee possessed one. Fortunately for Lee, Grant failed to attack.[30]

When the war of movements flattened out into siege operations, Lee's need for maps subsided. However, it became an important factor again in the final days. The country between Richmond and the Appomattox had never been occupied by enemy troops. The possibility of a retreat through it had grown evident, and it might have been surveyed at leisure. Yet when Lee had to traverse it, neither he nor his officers had accurate maps. Local farmers, many of whom were awakened in the middle of the night, were of no more help than the guides had been on the Peninsula.[31]

Thus the story of Lee's maps ended on the same tragic note on which it had begun.

The third of Lee's faults, and the one that did the greatest harm to the South, was that he could not always control his fighting spirit. Though he was ordinarily a man of unshakable poise and calm judgment, the thundering of guns aroused him to such a degree that it undermined his reasoning power. He himself came close to acknowledging this during the battle of Fredericksburg when he said, "It is well that war is so terrible, or we should grow too fond of it."

For this failing Longstreet criticized his former commander mercilessly. At Gettysburg, he asserted, Lee had been "off his balance . . . and labored under that oppression until enough blood was shed to appease him."[32] Longstreet was not alone in believing that Lee was apt to lose his mental balance in the middle of a battle, but the claim that it was prompted by bloodthirstiness is entirely unwarranted and was shared by no other contemporary. It was not blood that Lee was after, but victory, and for no other purpose would he have allowed blood to flow freely.

The first demonstration Lee had given of this defect was at Malvern Hill. His decision to engage McClellan's army was justifiable on the assumption that it was demoralized and could be driven into the James; but after the unconquerable strength of Porter's position had manifested itself, the repeated Confederate charges were sheer slaughter.

The next case of needless bloodletting occurred at Antietam. Lee's apologists have offered the excuse for this battle that the invasion of Maryland should not have ended without at least one large-scale fight on Northern soil. But the arguments to the contrary are far more powerful, because in no conceivable circumstances could Lee hope to gain a worth-while victory.

Another example of Lee's fighting fury, in which he, as at Antietam, risked the loss of his whole army against the possibility of a hollow victory, occurred after the battle of Chancellorsville. Although Hooker had broken off the contest, he was far from beaten. The bulk of his force had scarcely been involved at all, and he had at least 70,000 men left to defend his five-mile bridgehead,[33] the front of which was to a large extent protected by streams, while both flanks rested securely on the Rappahannock. Besides, the entire position was so strongly fortified that after Hooker's departure Confederate engineers marveled at what they saw. The entire line was protected by impenetrable abatis, wrote Colonel [later General] Alexander. Head logs with loopholes offered further protection and fortified shelters were provided for officers.[34]

Against these formidable works Lee intended to hurl his little army, which Alexander estimated at no more than 35,000 battle-weary effectives.[35] It was a murderous plan, and only Hooker's timely retreat prevented it from being carried out.

The worst error due to Lee's impetuosity, however, was the battle of Gettysburg. It was not Pickett's charge on which should be heaped the greatest blame, nor the fact that Lee was beaten. His unpardonable blunder was that he fought the battle at all. By doing so he violated a policy to which he had agreed, and which was the only one holding out a promise for achieving the honorable peace for which the Confederacy was contending.

After Chancellorsville the economic situation within the Confederacy had been deteriorating rapidly. The food supplies of Virginia were nearly exhausted, and the army could not hope to sustain itself, unless it replenished its provisions in Northern territory. In the west, Grant was drawing an iron band around Vicksburg, and no relief for its defenders was in sight. But the Confederates held one last card—the Army of Northern Virginia. It had been well fitted out, was in the best of spirits and had been strengthened until it size approximated its opponent's. It was a trump card which had to be played with the utmost care, for it had to win more than a battle for the South. It had to win her independence.

Intelligent Southerners had warned against risking this army in battle unless it was attacked. Jefferson Davis conformed to this sensible idea, although he missed some of its implications. "The main purpose of the movement . . . ," he wrote later, "was to free Virginia from the enemy. If this could be done by maneuvering only, a most important result would be cheaply obtained." Lee concurred and added that "we should not conceal from ourselves that our resources in men are constantly shrinking, and the disproportion between us and our enemy is steadily augmenting." This touched the core of the problem which had to be faced. The South would have to stop frittering away her armies in worthless victories.

Longstreet, Lee's second-in-command, also thought that "the time had come when . . . strategy and tactics . . . should take the place of muscle against muscle."[36] Thus the Confederate leaders were in perfect accord. They knew that they had to conserve their strength, that a drawn battle would in reality be a defeat, and that even a victory was of no value unless it was so crushing that it ended the war. Despite the consensus of the leaders, Longstreet felt ill at ease and tried to have the understanding reduced to writing. He did not trust Lee, because he knew that Lee could not trust himself. All the details and purposes of the campaign, Longstreet insisted, should be impressed on the generals' minds, so that, when a critical situation arose, they could refer to their calmer moments and know that they were carrying out their original design.[37] Davis held the same view, though he expressed it somewhat ambiguously: "General Lee was not a man of hesitation, and they have been mistaken who suppose that caution was his vice."[38]

Whether or not Lee had definitely promised not to fight offensively is a moot question. Longstreet stated vigorously that Lee had accepted a "campaign offensive in strategy but defensive in tactics,"[39] but Lee is reported to have denied this. However, he did declare in his official report that he had not intended to "deliver a general battle so far from our base unless attacked," which statement harmonizes with Longstreet's recollection.[40]

The Confederate campaign plan was as nearly perfect as human brains could devise it, and at the start worked well. Minor successes were achieved in the Shenandoah Valley, Hooker was forced to retreat, and any hopes he may have entertained for a break-through were squelched. The Cumberland Valley of Pennsylvania, which Lee reached in June, furnished ample supplies, and the mountains that skirted it formed a natural fortress. Lodged firmly in the midst of enemy country, with his supply line well secured, Lee should have stopped there, because from this vantage point he posed a serious threat to several important coast cities, and a still greater one to Northern morale. Lee had only to remain where he was to dictate Hooker's next move, as Longstreet foresaw. "I suggested," he wrote, "that after . . . menacing Washington, we should choose a strong position, and force the Federals to attack us . . . the popular clamor throughout the North would speedily force the Federal general to attempt to drive us out."[41]

General Henry Jackson Hunt, Meade's chief of artillery, analyzed the situation concisely: ". . . the defiles of the South Mountain range close in [Lee's] rear . . . could be easily held by a small force," but "any position east of Gettysburg would deprive him of these advantages."[42]

Then Lee heard a few shots in the direction of Gettysburg, and his promise not to be lured into battle unless attacked, melted away. No one was attacking him. It was he who was doing the attacking and, once engaged, he was seized by that dangerous battlefield delirium which did not allow him to quit, even after the odds had turned decisively against him.

By attacking Meade, Lee tore up the concept for the campaign; compared to this fundamental error, the tactical errors of the battle itself were of minor importance. That J. E. B. Stuart deprived the army of its eyes by a useless raid, that the successes of the first day were not followed up, that Longstreet's assault on the second day came too late, all contributed to the outcome. Lee's order to send Pickett against Cemetery Ridge was so ill-advised that it would have brought any other general before a court-martial. Yet these incidents pale into insignificance against the fact that the battle should not have been fought at all because, in a larger sense, the South could not have won it. General Evander McIvor Law, one of the participants, declared: "Even if Lee had succeeded in driving the Federal army from its position, he would have found his army in the same condition in which Pyrrhus found his at Asculum." Longstreet saw things in the same light. "Even if we had won at Gettysburg, we should have won a fruitless victory. I do not think there was any necessity for giving battle at Gettysburg," he wrote.

General Fitzhugh Lee, who led one of the cavalry charges, clothed his criticism of Pickett's charge in angry words. "If every man in that assault had been bullet-proof," he asserted, "and if the whole of these fourteen thousand troops had arrived unharmed on Cemetery Ridge, what could have been accomplished? . . . There would have been time for the Federals to have seized, tied and taken them off in wagons, before their supports could have reached them. . . ."[43]

If the verdict of these generals erred, it erred on the conservative side. They might have gone further and argued that even if the entire Union line had crumbled, it would have availed Lee nothing. At Pipe Creek, a few miles beyond Gettysburg, an excellent defense line had been staked out, which could have been quickly manned by the remains of the retreating army and near-by reserves. Moreover, the Confederate army was depleted, disorganized, out of ammunition, and too far from its base for a fresh venture. Jefferson Davis conceded that if Meade had fallen back to Pipe Creek, it would have been impossible for Lee "to supply his army for any length of time."[44]

A Southern triumph at Gettysburg would not have won the war in any conceivable circumstances. Even though victorious, the army would have found it difficult to extricate itself from its precarious position. Besides, the Union forces were more than holding their own in Tennessee, Grant was closing in on Vicksburg, and the blockade was steadily tightening.

Lee's mistake in initiating the battle could still have been retrieved, had he broken it off after the first day and retreated to his mountain stronghold. He had beaten two Union corps and taken

5,000 prisoners. He had preserved his own strength, and his nimbus had remained untarnished. But Lee had his fighting blood up. He "seemed under a subdued excitement," as Longstreet put it, "which occasionally took possession of him . . . and threatened his superb equipoise. The sharp battle [of the first day] had given him a taste of victory."[45]

Freeman bent far over in an attempt to explain Lee's stubbornness in continuing the battle after the momentum of the first day had been lost. He claims that to retreat with the trains over the mountains in the face of a strong pursuit was risky, and that Lee could not stagnate long, because the enemy could limit his area of forage.[46] These points are not well taken. Since the successful Meade did not energetically pursue the beaten Lee, who was burdened with thousands of prisoners and his own wounded, the partially beaten Meade would hardly have been inclined to pursue the undefeated Lee before taking a breathing spell. As to forage, the rich Cumberland Valley was heavily stocked, the passes would be well protected, and Stuart, who by this time had joined the army, would have stood off enemy interference. Anyway, compared with the devastated regions from which Lee had drawn supplies before his Northern invasion, even a restricted area of the lush Pennsylvania meadows would have seemed a land of plenty.

The ever-faithful Long also tried to justify Lee's action, but again was refuted by his own arguments. "General Lee entertained the reasonable expectation," he asserted, "that with his powerful cavalry he would be able to obtain all necessary supplies in Pennsylvania . . . and he knew that the fertile Cumberland Valley could supply an army of any size."[47] Then, realizing that this premise did not suit his ends, he quickly backed away from it. In the absence of the cavalry, he said, Lee had not been able to accumulate provisions, and had had to use mounted infantry for this purpose. Illogically he concluded that "if Lee had . . . occupied one of the passes of South Mountain, he would have placed his army in a trap that would have, in the absence of a miracle, resulted in his destruction; for Meade with his superior forces could have enclosed him without supplies or the means of obtaining them."[48]

Long lost sight of two factors that made his conclusion illusory: after the second day of the battle Lee had the full use of Stuart's cavalry; furthermore, Meade's superiority in numbers was not large enough to encircle the Confederate army. His thinly spread ranks would have been at the mercy of Lee, who would not have hesitated to pounce on any weak spot that presented itself. The fact is, as Longstreet pointed out, that with Lee's army wedged like a thorn in Northern territory, public opinion eventually would have forced Meade to make a frontal attack to expel the invaders, at a cost that might have made Burnside's losses at Fredericksburg look puny.

Once more that year Lee's impetuosity threatened to get the best of him, and this was at Mine Run. Both armies were facing each other in strong positions. Meade tried a flanking movement, and when he discovered that it held out little hope for success, he folded his tents at night and silently stole away. Lee had intended to attack the next day and was bitterly disappointed when he found the enemy gone. It is impossible, of course, to say what the outcome of the fight would have been, had it taken place, but by withdrawing from the front of a strongly entrenched enemy the mediocre Meade showed more moral courage and better judgment than his famous opponent had shown at Gettysburg.

In the last few months of the war Lee's generalship rose to superlative heights, because all his three weaknesses were suppressed. His submissiveness to Davis diminished, and without the President's meddling Lee could follow his own inclinations. Maps played a minor part in the limited territory of his operations. Opportunities for battle in the open no longer existed, and so Lee's excessive fighting spirit was held in check. Freed from his shackles, he fought a defensive campaign that has become a classic in military history.

The conclusion is justified that Lee's weaknesses in reality were outgrowths of his virtues. His submissiveness was an exaggerated sense of duty and military obedience. His neglect of maps was at least in part due to the fact that he kept an inadequate staff, so as not to take officers away from combat duty. His excessive combativeness he had inherited from his fighting ancestors. It was imbedded in his blood and he could not resist it. Had he, not Grant, commanded the stronger forces, it would have paid rich dividends.

While these considerations do not excuse Lee's faults, they go far toward explaining them, and leave even the coolest analyst with a wistful admiration for the man who possessed them.

PROMINENT UNION GENERALS

A. George H. Thomas

After the first day of the battle of Stone River, during which the Union army had been hard pressed, General Rosecrans called his corps commanders into council. "General Thomas," he asked, "what have you to say?"

Thomas slowly rose to his feet, buttoned up his greatcoat and stood there, a statue of courage. "Gentlemen," he said, "I know of no better place to die than right here." With that he turned around and walked out into the night.[1]

This word portrait, painted by a young officer who was present, characterized Thomas as well as would a voluminous recital of his deeds, all of which were commendable. He defeated a Confederate force at Mill Springs, and distinguished himself at Perryville. Following that battle he was offered the command of the army, but declined, fearing that he might be suspected of having intrigued against his chief. At Stone River he held the center against fiery Confederate attacks. At Chickamauga he became the famous Rock, which barred the way to a complete rout and possible destruction of the Union army. Once more he was offered the top command, and again he refused, for the same reason that had prompted his refusal before.

Thomas next led one of Sherman's corps in the Atlanta campaign. Then he was entrusted with the defense of Nashville, where he was confronted by General Hood, whom he was ordered to attack without delay. Inclement weather made it necessary to postpone the attack, and Grant was on the point of replacing him.

Pestered by continuous prodding from his higher-ups, he responded with grim humor. "To one of General Grant's dispatches . . . ," he later told one of his friends, "I was strongly tempted . . . to ask why he was not fighting himself."[2]

When his proposed dismissal came to Lincoln's ears, he defended Thomas vigorously and pointed out to Grant that the judgment of a general on the battleground was probably better than that of others 500 miles away. And when Grant replied that Thomas was notoriously slow, the President had a ready reply: "But has he not always 'got there' in time?"[3]

Sherman, in a letter to Halleck, was equally laudatory: "Thomas is . . . a noble war horse. It is true . . . that he is slow, but he is always sure."[4] Grant assented: "When Thomas attacks, victory is sure."[5]

After the weather had cleared, Thomas attacked and practically annihilated Hood's army.

In the entire war Thomas never once gave way, never lost a fight and was always an inspiration to those around him. During every crisis, so one officer remembered, he looked calm, stern, determined, silent and perfectly self-possessed. It was a tonic to look at the man.[6] Charles A. Dana, the official observer for the War Department, paid him a rare compliment. "He had more the character of George Washington," he wrote, "than any man I ever knew."[7]

One cannot help thinking how well it would have been for the North, if Thomas had accepted the independent commands that he had so modestly and generously declined.

B. FITZ JOHN PORTER

Grant is reported to have told President Chester A. Arthur that if Fitz John Porter had commanded at Second Bull Run, there would have been no Chancellorsville, no Antietam, no Gettysburg and no Appomattox.[8] He might have added that there also might not have been a President Grant.

Catch phrases do not prove cases, however, and the *if's* of history are treacherous; but in this instance they are abundantly supported by Porter's record. As early as April 20, 1861, the day after the Baltimore riots, he showed his mettle by assmbling 3,000 men within fifteen miles of that city and was ready to move them into Washington. When he was restrained by higher authorities, his eyes flashed with indignation. "I would march the troops through Baltimore or its ashes," he exclaimed angrily.[9] At Gaines's Mill, with only 35,000 men, Porter stood off 55,000 Confederates, led by Lee, Jackson, Longstreet and the two Hills, and retired from the field with honor, after inflicting greater losses than he himself had sustained. At Malvern Hill he handed the formidable Lee-Jackson combination their only defeat. And at Second Bull Run, without waiting for orders, he covered the retreat of the Union army and stemmed its demoralization.

Porter was possessed of the same fiery spirit as Lee, but used greater caution; on the other hand, he frequently opposed McClellan's overcautiousness. After the battle of Malvern Hill he wanted to follow up the victory and protested strongly against a retreat to the James. He wished McClellan to act on Napoleon's principle that, no matter how confused and exhausted a victorious army might be, conditions in the defeated one must be a hundredfold worse. There was, he argued, every inducement to take the offensive, especially as in case of a reverse the Federal army could withdraw to the protection of the fleet. The two officers, close personal friends, sat up all night debating the problem, but McClellan could not be moved.[10]

Lincoln was looking desperately for a general who would fight, but overlooked Porter, who had all the fighting qualities of Grant and none of his drawbacks.

After less than two years of distinguished service Porter fell victim to a political conspiracy. He was falsely accused of having caused Pope's defeat at Second Bull Run by disobeying an order to attack Lee's right wing late in the afternoon of the first day. The order didn't reach him until dusk, and he knew, what Pope did not suspect, that Longstreet, with a far superior force, had arrived on the field and was confronting him. Concluding that the attack would be suicidal, he recalled it before it had made any headway. Although these explanatory circumstances were brought out at his trial, and confirmed by Lee and Longstreet, a packed court-martial sentenced him to a dishonorable discharge, which brought his military career to an early end. Neverthelss, during the comparatively short period of active service his conduct had been blameless, his successes outstanding.[11]

Eventually Porter was vindicated and reinstated in the Army, but by then he was advanced in age, and resigned at once.

Porter was not a brilliant general, but he made no mistakes and always managed to do the right thing at the right time. He was too strict a disciplinarian to be popular with his men, but they respected and trusted him. The greatest compliment to his ability, however, came from his political enemies, who insisted on his downfall, because they feared, rightly, that under his leadership the war would come to a speedier end.

C. GEORGE B. MCCLELLAN

> "Distorted by men's fitful passions,
> His character sways to and fro in history."[12]

THIS is what Friedrich von Schiller wrote about General Albrecht von Wallenstein, hero of the Thirty Years' War. Had he been able to envision the future, he might have penned the same words about General McClellan.

McClellan is adulated by some, and abused by others. The very mention of his name incites Civil War students to a heated discussion. One is either for him or against him; there are no neutrals. He arouses partisanship to such a degree that some authors have twisted evidence, juggled figures and suppressed vital facts to prove their partisan case. Where, then, does the truth lie?

McClellan can perhaps be best understood through a study of his background. By training and inclination he was an engineer, and as such ranked high. A man whom a leading railroad engaged as its chief engineer at the age of thirty-one, and made its president four years later, must have possessed outstanding professional and other talents.

To McClellan war represented in essence the engineering task of overcoming a given obstacle. The needed power for it could be calculated, after which means would have to be found to provide and use it. The North possessed both the power and the means; therefore the problem resolved itself into building a machine of such irresistible strength that it would overcome the calculated resistance. If this condition were met, generalship could be relegated to a subordinate role.

McClellan's theory was sound, as Grant was to prove later, but it would take considerable time to build this machine—more time than the public and the politicians were willing to grant him. Whether it would have worked under his guidance will never be known, for it was radically modified by Lincoln and the War Department. Good engineer that McClellan was, he lost faith in a mechanism from which numberless bolts and nuts had been removed. He fought on, but without confidence. When he finally was allowed to reassemble his machine and lead it into battle, he was summarily dismissed before he could get it into action.

This, in short, is the story of McClellan's part in the Civil War.

The arguments *pro* and *con* about McClellan can best be judged by putting them into juxtaposition.

1. *Con:* McClellan was vain, tactless, too fond of display and gay parties.

The *cons* win this point. It was especially his tactlessness that, by estranging Lincoln, contributed to his downfall.

2. *Pro:* McClellan conducted the war along the same humanitarian lines that he had recommended in his Harrison's Landing letter to Lincoln on July 7, 1862:

"[This war] should be conducted on the highest principles known to Christian civilization. . . . It should not be . . . a war upon the population, but against armed forces. . . . All private property should be strictly protected. . . ."[13]

The troops idolized McClellan more than any other Union general.

These two points are undisputed.

3. *Pro:* McClellan refused to use his machine, even for minor operations, before it was perfected, and so did not attack the Confederate batteries on the lower Potomac, declaring that the obstructions were a moral, not a physical factor.

Con: The batteries should have been removed, for in war moral factors are as important as physical ones.

The *cons* are entitled to the decision.

4. *Con:* McClellan's Peninsular campaign was stalled at the Warwick River because of the inaccuracy of available maps. There had been plenty of time to verify them by having the stream surveyed, for Fort Monroe was in Federal hands and only some fifteen miles distant. McClellan's ignorance of the topography is the more reprehensible as he had suffered from the same negligence a few months before, when he had authorized the ill-fated reconnaissance at Ball's Bluff without having checked the correctness of existing maps.[14]

Pro: Procurement of correct maps was the duty of the War Department.

Con: This is questionable. At any rate, considering their importance, as an engineer McClellan should have made it his duty to assure himself of their accuracy.

Pro: He never made this mistake again. By the time he came close to Richmond he had excellent maps of the entire Peninsula.

The arguments *pro* and *con* fairly balance one another.

5. *Con:* McClellan reneged on his promise to leave at least 35,000 men behind to guard Washington before he engaged in the Peninsular campaign.

Pro: Literally speaking this was true, but in a military sense it was not, for the well-manned outposts of the capital were in effect part of the garrison. Nevertheless, he should have explained to Lincoln his way of figuring.

The *pros* have slightly the better argument.

6. *Con:* He constantly overestimated the number of his enemies.

Pro: The art of sifting information on enemy strength had not yet been developed, and the Confederates used clever and heretofore unknown schemes to mislead him. Furthermore, McClellan was not the only one guilty in this respect. "We overrated each other's strength greatly, as was generally done by the opposing generals during the war," wrote the Confederate General Joe Johnston.[15] Instances to prove this pronouncement are plentiful. On the first day of Shiloh Grant sent a note to Buell, asserting that he was fighting more than 100,000 men, although they numbered no more than 45,000. These lines may have been written hastily amidst the excitement of the moment, but Grant affirmed his belief in Johnston's superiority after the fight with equal conviction: "Those people who expect a field of battle to be maintained for a whole day with about 30,000 troops . . . against 70,000, as was the case at Pittsburg Landing, . . . know little of war."[16] On the eve of the battle of Antietam, Halleck thought Lee had 150,000 men,[17] while in fact he had about 40,000. In 1862 Lincoln advised McClellan that Jackson had 30,000 men in the Valley; James Shields's estimate was from 20,000 to 40,000, Frémont's 30,000 to 60,000.[18] The truth was that Jackson had 16,000. Two years later, when the Intelligence service had made considerable progress, Secretary of War Stanton estimated that Early had 35,000 men,[19] while the actual figure was close to 12,000. On the eve of the battle of Chancellorsville Hooker advised Lincoln that the Confederates had received reinforcements and now outnumbered him. The fact was that Lee had received no reinforcements and commanded less than half as many men as Hooker. The doubtful honor of beating all others in overestimating enemy forces belongs to Governor Andrew G. Curtin of Pennsylvania, who wired the War Department on September 13, 1862, that Lee had 190,000 men in Maryland, and 250,000 on the other side of the Potomac, a total of 440,000 men, or about ten times the real number.[20]

The *cons* win, but by singling out McClellan as the chief sinner they distort the picture.

7. *Pro:* If McClellan had not been compelled to reveal his plan of the Peninsular campaign, he might have surprised the Confederates and wedged his army between that of Johnston and Richmond.[21]

Con: 100,000 men could not have been transported to the Peninsula unknown to the enemy.

The *cons* win.

8. *Con:* After the battle of Gaines's Mill McClellan sent a dispatch to Stanton, which contained these words: "If I save this army now, . . . I owe no thanks to you" (thereby admitting a defeat which he had not suffered); he then referred to the "sad remnants of my men" (although he had lost only 7,000 men out of 100,000), and finally spoke of his hopes "to retrieve our fortunes" (which had not been lost).[22]

For these defeatist statements there is no excuse, even though there is one for his intemperate language.

The *cons* have it.

9. *Pro:* Stanton deliberately sabotaged McClellan's Peninsular campaign by closing all recruiting offices, thereby stopping reinforcements; by forcing McClellan to split his army, making it vulnerable to attack; by taking from him McDowell's corps, Louis Blenker's division and the Fort Monroe garrison, reducing McClellan's forces far below the strength on which his campaign plan had been based.

The *cons* either ignore these claims or minimize their importance. They offer no explanation for the closing of the recruiting offices; some suppress Stanton's May 18 order,[23] which forced McClellan to split his army; they justify McDowell's detachment on the ground that McClellan had not furnished sufficient troops to protect the capital; they blame political expediency for the separation of Blenker, and that of Wool on mistrust of McClellan's generalship.

The *pros* here have an overwhelming advantage.

10. *Con:* With the exception of the battle of Antietam, McClellan never went near the fighting front.

Pro: The front is not the proper place for a commanding general.

The *Pros* should be awarded this point.

11. *Con:* McClellan should have attacked Richmond, and probably could have taken it, while most of Lee's army was fighting the battle of Gaines's Mill north of the Chickahominy.

Pro: Since McClellan already had decided on his new base, he had to get there before Lee could organize a successful pursuit. The occupation of Richmond would have been an empty victory, and would have caused a dangerous, perhaps a fatal loss of time, before connections with his new supply base were functioning.

The *pros* have decidedly the better of the argument.

12. *Con:* McClellan was defeated in the Seven Days battles; one writer headlines his defeat a flight;[24] another, going him one better, even calls the flight a cowardly one.[25]

Pro: McClellan was not defeated. During his "flight," he fought two battles, one of them a standoff, the other a smashing victory. In the Seven Days battles his losses totaled 15,000, those of the Confederates 20,000 men. At the end he occupied an ideal position for either offense or defense.

The decision goes to the *pros*.

13. *Con:* During the battle of Second Bull Run McClellan sent

a dispatch to Halleck, saying in effect that Pope should be left to get out of his scrape as best he could. The message proves his callousness and an implied wish that Pope would be defeated.

Pro: This quotation is taken out of context. What McClellan suggested was one of two possible courses: "First, to concentrate all our available sources to open communications with Pope; second, to leave Pope to get out of his scrape, and use all our means to make Washington perfectly safe. No middle ground will now answer." McClellan's language was rough, but the inference that he gloated over Pope's discomfort or wished for his defeat is unwarranted.

The *pros* have it.

14. *Con:* After discovering Lee's "lost order" No. 191, which showed that the Confederate army was widely dispersed, McClellan should have attacked with greater speed and vigor.

Pro: The order was dated September 9, 1862, and did not fall into McClellan's hands until the thirteenth. He could not tell whether it was a ruse, nor what if any changes in Lee's dispositions had taken place since. Nevertheless, he gave urgent orders to General William B. Franklin to cross Crampton's Gap and cut off Lafayette McLaws' troops on Maryland Heights. "I ask of you at this important moment," he wrote, "[for] all your intellect and the utmost activity. . . ."[26] It is difficult to see what more McClellan could have done to speed the movement.

The *pros* win this round.

15. *Con:* McClellan should have continued the battle of Antietam the next day.

Pro: McClellan gave as one of his reasons that the risk was too great, that if he had lost the battle, "Lee's army might . . . have marched as it pleased on Washington, Baltimore, Philadelphia, or New York."[27]

Con: This is sheer nonsense. Even though McClellan's entire army had been wiped out—which no one in his right mind will assume—Washington was defended by strong forts and 70,000 troops. As to the other cities, the results of an attack by Lee's decimated army far from home and out of ammunition and supplies might have been catastrophic for him.

The *cons* are right: this argument of McClellan's *is* sheer nonsense.

16. *Con:* McClellan could have won the battle of Antietam if he had put Porter's corps in.

Pro: The basis of this contention is factually wrong. He did put Porter's corps in, all but some 3,000 to 4,000 men, who were needed to guard the trains.[28]

The *pros* win.

17. *Con:* McClellan should have pursued Lee after the battle of Antietam.

Pro: McClellan had been given command of the troops for the defense of Washington only, and had already exceeded his authority under the conditions imposed on him.

The fault for this state of affairs lies equally with Lincoln and McClellan. Lincoln should either have given his commanding general free rein, or stopped him when he ventured outside the fortifications of the capital. On the other hand, McClellan, who had been president of a large railroad, should have acquired enough business experience to insist on a clear-cut, written designation of his powers. As it was, both parties had an ace in the hole for a future contingency. Had McClellan been beaten, Lincoln would have been able to accuse him of having exceeded his authority, while McClellan had an equally valid alibi for not exploiting his victory.

No decision.

18. *Con:* McClellan should have abided by Lincoln's urgings to cross into Virginia soon after the battle of Antietam, instead of

waiting until the last picayunish item of his requisition had been furnished him.

Pro: The "picayunish items" were of a very serious character, and the delay of the War Department in furnishing them never has been satisfactorily explained.

Lacking conclusive evidence on this point, no fair decision can be reached.

19. *Pro:* If McClellan, marching with a vigor that even Lee noted,[29] had not been removed, he would have forced Lee to fight at a great, perhaps ruinous disadvantage.

Con: This assertion cannot be proved. Before the battle of Chancellorsville, Hooker, too, thought he had forced Lee into a dilemma, but matters did not turn out the way he had figured.

This was the crucial moment when McClellan could have demonstrated whether or not he was a great general, because for the first and only time his machine was in perfect condition, he had taken the offensive, and he was in a favorable position.

His untimely dismissal makes it impossible to arrive at a decision.

20. *Pro:* McClellan was the first general to point out, as he did in a letter to Lincoln, the importance that the railroads were to play in the war by making it possible to concentrate large masses of troops speedily at given places and for other purposes.[30]

No counterarguments.

21. McClellan was the first to install competent medical service in the army.

No counterarguments.

McClellan deserves a place on the honor list of Civil War Generals, if for no other reason than that out of the rawest materials he organized an army that kept its spirit, coherence and fighting power throughout the war, despite bad commanders and repeated defeats.

The open market, which embodied the combined judgment of people who backed their opinion with money, must have considered McClellan an able general because, when a rumor was current in 1863 that he was about to be reappointed, gold suffered a break in price,[31] meaning that the market place expected a speedier end of the war under his leadership.

To summarize: McClellan's great ability is unquestioned, but his performance cannot be assessed precisely, because he was not given an opportunity to test his generalship under conditions that had been specified by himself, had been promised to him, but had never been complied with.

D.   HENRY W. HALLECK

ALTHOUGH Halleck held the rank of general-in-chief of all Northern armies from July 1862 until the advent of Grant, his capacity was not equal to his exalted post. McClellan regarded him as the most hopelessly stupid of all men in a high position whom he had ever encountered.[32] Admiral Andrew H. Foote called him a military imbecile.[33] It would be interesting to know why Lincoln selected such a man for his military adviser, and, still more, why he clung to him long after his inadequacy had become a matter of public scorn and ridicule.

The story of Halleck's appointment is shrouded in uncertainty. According to Dr. Asa Mahan, who had heard the story from Senator Sumner, who in turn had received it directly from Lincoln himself, the appointment originated during the President's visit to Harrison's Landing in July 1862. Back in Washington the President told Sumner that his "mind had become perfectly perplexed," that he needed a commander-in-chief, and that Halleck should be the man.[34]

Mahan's account lacks confirmation from other sources, but probably is true. At any rate, immediately after his return the President gave Halleck the appointment, and three days later wired an almost frantic appeal to him: "I am anxious—almost impatient—to have you. . . . when can you reach here?"[35]

Mahan's version is complemented by a belated entry in the diary of Gideon Welles, who claimed that Halleck's promotion was the result of "an intrigue of Stanton's and Chase's to get rid of McClellan." Chase had pointed out to the President that so long as McClellan was fighting on the Peninsula, Washington was exposed to an enemy attack. He therefore urged the recall of the army. General Pope, who was present, then made a fateful recommendation. "If Halleck were here, you would have . . . a competent adviser. . . ." Lincoln hastily called on General Scott, and a few days later Halleck became general-in-chief.[36]

One of Halleck's first decisions gave a clue to his mentality. After the army had left the Peninsula, Welles called on him one morning and found that the new chieftain "had forgotten, or was not aware, there was a naval force in the James River. . . ." Welles assured him that such was indeed a fact. The general, in doubt whether the vessels should be retained or withdrawn, "went to work up on his elbows, and rubbed out the conclusion that they should be withdrawn." Then Welles suggested that they might as well stay, and the general immediately thought so too.[37]

It took Halleck less than four months to rub off his initial glamour. At a Cabinet meeting in November it was suggested that he take command of the army in person. "The President said," Welles recorded, "and all of the Cabinet concurred in the opinion that [Halleck] . . . shirked responsibility . . . , is a moral coward, worth but little except as a critic and director of operations. . . ."[38] What operations Lincoln had in mind is not clear, nor why a man of Halleck's military caliber should be chosen to direct them.

Hay, Lincoln's junior secretary, not only looked on Halleck with contempt, but even suspected him of disloyalty to the President. When General Gillmore reported on an enterprise in which he was engaged during January 1864, and expressed the hope that it would advance a cause on which the President had set his heart, Hay scoffed at anyone who could be so naïve as to believe that any cause close to the President's fervent wish would find favor with his general-in-chief.[39] Lincoln's Attorney General went Hay one better. He accused Halleck of having given false testimony in the Almaden imbroglio,[40] and on another occasion of having tried to influence a St. Louis judge in a jury case.[41]

An instance of Halleck's total unfitness as a director of operations was related by General Jacob D. Cox. In August 1862 Halleck had ordered him from West Virginia to Charlottesville, where he was to join Pope. Halleck had directed him to march by way of Staunton, which would have meant fifteen days of uninterrupted mountain travel, most of it through a wilderness destitute of supplies, and with the enemy on his flank. Cox appealed to Pope and received permission to change the route. As a consequence he made the trip in ten days, and arrived in time to take part in Second Bull Run. If he had followed Halleck's orders, he and his exhausted troops would have found themselves in Charlottesville, over a hundred miles from Pope, who had since moved away from there, and with Lee's entire army separating the two Union commanders.[42]

All that can be said in Halleck's favor is that he was well versed in the history of past warfare. He was like a chess player who could correctly replay the games that had been played by others, but who himself could not win a game against a child. Perhaps nothing illustrates better his inability to think for himself than a letter he wrote to Lincoln in January 1862. Buell had suggested a movement against Bowling Green, Kentucky, and Halleck vetoed it, because "it is condemned in every military authority I have ever read."[43] To Halleck anything that was not in his textbooks was taboo.

Why Lincoln hung onto this caricature of a general has never been satisfactorily explained. Halleck practically confessed his incompetence when, after the battle of Fredericksburg, Lincoln asked him to go over the ground and come back with an opinion on Burnside's further plans. "Your military skill," Lincoln wrote, "is useless to me if you do not do this."[44] Halleck was not slow in replying—he offered his resignation. But Lincoln took Halleck's impertinence lying down and did not fire a military adviser who had so brazenly proclaimed his uselessness.

The Pennsylvania journalist Noah Brooks, who stood close to high personages in the capital, was sorely puzzled. He wrote that "Washington, . . . especially . . . Congress, resounded with complaints of [Halleck's] sluggishness, his unwillingness to take responsibilities, and his supposed incapacity to grasp the whole military situation."[45] One day he ventured to bring Halleck's unpopularity to the President's attention, and received an unexpected reply. Lincoln told with "a grave, almost severe expression, that he was Halleck's friend because nobody else was."[46] This somewhat puerile explanation explains little, if anything. To his friend Isaac N. Arnold the President gave another explanation, and it explained still less. "People believed Halleck had driven Frémont, Sigel and Butler from the service. If he were dismissed, other false accusations would be leveled against him."[47]

The real *why* of Halleck as a general-in-chief may never be known, though the suspicion lingers that he was the puppet of influential politicians who did not want to win the war until it suited their political aims, and kept him in his position because he was best fitted to serve their purpose.

E. Ambrose E. Burnside

When the final examination of the West Point class of 1847 had been finished, the examiners pronounced Burnside the finest-looking cadet of the corps.[48] He still was handsome as a general, which is about the best that can be said about him.

At the beginning of the war Burnside did fairly well. He commanded a brigade at the first battle of Bull Run, and managed to retire in comparative good order, partly due to the presence of Regular Army dragoons, who brought up his rear.[49]

In February 1862 Burnside headed a combined Army and Navy expedition down the North Carolina coast, and occupied Roanoke Island, New Bern, Elizabeth City, Edenton, Plymouth and Fort Macon in quick succession.[50] He fulfilled his duty satisfactorily, but the decided preponderance of Federal striking power precludes a conclusion regarding his own merit. He claimed to have originated the enterprise[51] which, if true, is a point in his favor.

After the Seven Days battles Burnside was offered the command of the Army of the Potomac. He promptly and peremptorily declined.[52] Instead he took command of the Ninth Corps under Pope,[53] and after Second Bull Run once more was invited to head the army; but he knew his limitations, and it is to his credit that he not only refused the offer but tried to have the President restore McClellan to the command.[54]

Then came the battle of Antietam, and with it the beginning of Burnside's downfall. His disobedience of repeated and urgent orders to cross the bridge which bears his name probably lost the battle for McClellan. Burnside offered various explanations for his delay, but there is more to the story than that. The bridge was not essential for the proposed attack, for Antietam Creek was fordable in several places above and below the bridge; yet Burnside, who had arrived at his station a full day before the battle, failed to reconnoiter for possible crossings. Lee quickly took advantage of Burnside's negligence and moved two thirds of the defending forces to his battered left wing. An attack across the lower Antietam early in the day would have met with little resistance, caught Lee in the rear right flank and cut him off from his line of retreat.[55]

Even though Burnside missed this opportunity, he still might have won the battle if he had crossed the Antietam even two hours sooner than he did.[56] The difficulties were not unsurmountable, because the span was eventually carried by only two regiments. Burnside himself never set foot on the bridge;[57] without him his men fought halfheartedly, and returned to the river bank at the end of the day.

Burnside's biographer and apologist, Ben: Perley Poore, tried to extract some salvage from his hero's muddling. After the Ninth Corps had retreated to the bridge, Burnside became nervous and asked for reinforcements—why is not clear, for the Confederates were completely fought out and had escaped annihilation by the narrowest of margins. Nevertheless, Poore found something to crow about. "The bridge was not lost," he boasted. "Every foot . . . was stubbornly contested." That the bridge was not even attacked failed to dampen his enthusiasm. "When the sun went down," he continued, "it was a source of gratification . . . to know that the Ninth Corps, after a hard day's fighting, held the bridge, and thus secured victory by remaining on the ground which the Confederates had occupied."[58]

One will not easily find another boast containing so much foam and so little substance.

For reasons difficult to fathom, Burnside now was again offered the command of the Army. Once more he pleaded his want of confidence in himself, but finally accepted, reluctantly.[59] As new commander, so his biographer notes, he "did everything in his power to show his respect and esteem for his predecessor";[60] unfortunately, the respect did not go so far as to carry out McClellan's excellent campaign plan. The consequence was the slaughter at Fredericksburg, the ill-fated mud march, and the removal of the hapless commander.

Despite these dismal failures Burnside was not dismissed. Instead he was transferred to the Department of the Ohio, where he showed that his prowess, while not sufficient to win in the field, still could give him distinction by downing opponents of the administration. He ordered the arrest of Clement L. Vallandigham, an extreme Peace Democrat, and the suppression of the *Chicago Times*. His superpatriotism embarrassed the Washington government, which now sent him to eastern Tennessee. He reached Knoxville in August 1863, and his march over the Cumberland Mountains, which met with no resistance, was called a brilliant achievement by his panegyrist.[61]

In September of that year Burnside had an opportunity to retrieve his fortunes. Bragg was being maneuvered out of Tennessee, and Burnside was ordered either to intercept Bragg's retreat or to beat him into Chattanooga. Burnside ignored these instructions, though they were repeated some fifteen times. He offered the foolish excuse that, inasmuch as Bragg was retreating, Rosecrans needed no reinforcements.[62] Had he carried out his orders, he might have brought about the end of Bragg's army; but Burnside had his own ideas about winning the war. He marched his men in the opposite direction on what John Hay called "a foolish affair . . . to capture a party of guerrillas."[63] Bragg crossed the Tennessee undisturbed and proceeded to defeat Rosecrans at Chickamauga.

Burnside now offered to resign, but his resignation was rejected. A few weeks later he defended Knoxville successfully against an attack by Longstreet. Ordered to join Grant in the spring of 1864, one of his officers, Lieutenant Colonel Henry Pleasants, initiated and conducted the famous mine explosion, which boomeranged. This time, however, Burnside was not the only one at fault, although a court of inquiry found him guilty.[64] The Joint Committee on the Conduct of the War then ordered a new inquiry, in which Grant testified that, if Burnside's recommendation to put his Negro division in the front, had been followed, the plan would have succeeded.[65] The reason Burnside was not without blame for the blunder was that, before selecting and training Negro troops for the assault, he should have realized that in case of failure the Administration would be bitterly attacked for exposing Negro soldiers, while keeping white troops out of the danger zone.

By the time the committee came to its decision, however, Burnside was no longer with the army. He had resigned on August 13, 1864, only two weeks after the Crater affair.

Despite his shortcomings as a military man, Burnside did not lack intelligence. In 1852, as a young officer, he had invented a breech-loading rifle, which was declared the best out of eighteen submitted to a board of officers. Strangely, the judges accompanied their award with an opinion that no breech-loading rifle was fit to replace muzzle loaders for foot troops, and this adverse development dashed Burnside's hopes. He had resigned from the army to establish a factory for the manufacture of his rifle, and the shortsighted verdict of the West Point board ruined him financially.[66]

Burnside deserves respect for his modesty and courageous self-analysis in twice refusing the command of the Army. It must also be admitted that, had he been allowed to conduct the explosion of the mine before Petersburg according to his own plan, he might have atoned to a large extent for his previous errors.

Among his brother officers Burnside was not popular, partly because of his attitude toward Fitz Porter[67] during and after the trial of the latter, partly on account of his ineptitude. Meade, who had fought under Burnside at Fredericksburg, was almost brutal in his contemptous criticism. "I feel sorry for Burnside," he wrote, "because I really believe that half the time he don't know what he is about, and he is hardly responsible for his acts."[68]

Nevertheless, Burnside was not without friends. As a cadet he had greatly impressed a saloonkeeper whose place of business was just outside the West Point limits. This man had prepared a special toast which he repeated every time he indulged in alcoholic refreshments. He invariably drank to the health of those he considered the two greatest men who ever lived—Saint Paul and Andrew Jackson. But he had taken such a fancy to Burnside that he added his name to the toast and ever thereafter, to the day of his death, he drank to Saint Paul, Andrew Jackson and Ambrose E. Burnside.[69]

Aside from the cut of his beard and a bridge commemorating one of his blunders, this is as close as Burnside came to immortality.

⫸ 15 ⫷

PROMINENT CONFEDERATE
GENERALS

A. NATHAN BEDFORD FORREST

WHEN still a colonel, Forrest once took fifty troopers on a scouting expedition. Turning a sharp bend in the road, they rode smack into an enemy camp where they were outnumbered twenty to one. A fight would have been hopeless, and it was too late to retreat. But Forrest thought of a way out. He motioned his troopers to do exactly as he did, then uttered a loud yell and pointed to the sky. His horsemen copied him, and the Federal soldiers did what Forrest had expected: they gaped to see at what the Confederates were pointing. Before they had recovered, Forrest and his men were out of range, leaving the campers behind, who cursed themselves for having fallen for such a simple ruse.[1]

This was Forrest, the man who always knew a way out.

When Gideon Welles wrote in his diary that "the best material for commanders in this civil strife may have never seen West Point," he may not have had Forrest in mind, but he could not have described him more accurately, especially when he added, "Courage and learning are essential, but something more is wanted for a good general—talent, intuition, magnetic power, which West Point cannot give."[2]

With the exception of learning, Old Bedford had all these qualities, and in addition possessed originality of thought, native shrewdness and a fighting heart. His highly unorthodox methods, often improvised while in action, time and again held greatly superior Union forces in check or forced them to surrender. He was full of wily tricks, against which his book-taught opponents were helpless. Though the stronger battalions were always on the other side, he lost only one battle, and this one because he fought it under orders from a West Pointer and against his own better judgment.

Due to the comparatively small number of men allotted to him, Forrest was compelled to limit most of his operations to guerrilla warfare, but it was not guerrilla warfare in the usual sense of the word. He never paid heed to minor objectives when major ones were in sight. He tried to co-ordinate his movements with the current Confederate strategy and, if executed at his own discretion, they were uniformly successful.

Forrest triumphed over some very capable Northern officers, who were bewildered by such stratagems as marching the same men and guns up and down in sight of the enemy so as to create the impression of overpowering strength. It was an expedient known to every stage manager, but against West-Point-trained soldiers it worked well. Even Colonel Abel D. Streight, an astute Federal officer, was deceived by it. Against him Forrest used also a rather childish prank, which would not have fooled a wide-awake schoolboy, but did deceive a man who had been taught to fight according to accepted rules and expected his opponent to do likewise. While Old Bedford conferred with the tired and hesitant Streight, who was still undecided whether to fight or give up, he had a colonel dash up and ask when his nonexistent brigade should attack. A few moments later another officer arrived and asked the same question. That did it. Streight's nerve crumpled, and he surrendered to a force one third as strong as his own.[3]

Forrest's brilliant military talent reached its climax in the battle of Brice's Cross Roads. It was a gem of clever leadership, in which home-grown psychology, eareful timing and lionhearted fighting all played their part. Forrest probably had never heard of the fight between the Horatians and Curiatians, but he shaped the battle into an almost perfect replica of that classic encounter. Like the one surviving Horatian, who ran away from three Curiatians and thereby separated them according to their remaining strength, Forrest split the Union army by making their cavalry and infantry rush at him piecemeal according to their degree of exhaustion. The result, as in the case of the surviving Roman, was a glorious victory.

Forrest's extraordinary gifts were not appreciated by the hidebound Confederate President, who believed in diplomas more than he did in ability. The untutored general's advice was never solicited, his potentialities were never fully utilized. Had he been allowed to continue a movement against a vital railroad instead of being ordered to stop an unimportant raid, he might have wrecked Sherman's Atlanta campaign and changed the course of events in the western theatre of the war.

After the return of peace, when the battle of Brice's Cross Roads was universally acclaimed as a military masterpiece, Davis offered a feeble excuse for his failure to give Forrest the recognition he had withheld from him. "That campaign," he declared, "was not understood at Richmond. The impression . . . was that Forrest had made another successful raid. . . . I saw it all after it was too late."[4]

Sherman considered Forrest his most dangerous adversary. On September 29, 1864, he wired Halleck about Hood, who was then preparing for the Tennessee campaign: "I can whip his infantry, but his cavalry is to be feared."[5] And this is what he said in his *Memoirs:* "On the 31st of October Forrest made his appearance on the Tennessee River opposite Johnsonville . . . and with his cavalry and field-pieces actually . . . captured two gunboats with five of our transports, a feat of arms which, I confess, excited my admiration."[6]

What Forrest might have accomplished in command of larger forces is a matter of conjecture. General Joseph Johnston, when asked after the war who had been its greatest general replied unhesitatingly, "Forrest, who, had he had the advantages of a military education and training, would have been the greatest central figure of the Civil War."[7] This assertion is debatable. He might have been either a sensational success or a complete failure. Hood did well as a brigade and division commander, but lost out as the head of an army, and Forrest may or may not have shared his fate. It is questionable also whether Forrest's unorthodox shrewdness would have been strengthened by having been chained to the rigid rules of standard textbooks.

All that can be said with assurance is that Forrest possessed all the prerequisites of a great military leader and had no apparent weaknesses to impede him. One distinguished Confederate officer declared that Forrest "had the eye and the nerve of a great commander. . . . He was full of strategy, energy, courage and common sense. . . . He never lost a wagon train, a regiment or a company; never was surprised by his enemy, and seemed able . . . to anticipate him on all occasions."" Even on the relatively small scale on which Forrest had to operate, his performances stamp him as the only Civil War general who approaches the stature of a military genius.

B. STONEWALL JACKSON

IT was Jackson's greatest merit that he was the only Confederate general who devised an effective countermeasure against McClellan's bulldozer-type war machine. He realized that the Confederacy could not afford to match force with force, and that a better way would have to be found to ward off defeat. As a former professor of natural sciences he made his military thinking conform to the well-known axiom of physics that energy equals mass times the square of velocity. Since the South could not equal the North in mass, compensation might be attained by superior velocity. The bulldozer was slow and clumsy; therefore he intended to match or overmatch it by speed and agility. The result of his cogitation was his famous foot cavalry.

The first testing ground for this novel method of warfare was the Shenandoah Valley. It was not more than a practice campaign, because the enemy troops Jackson fought there were scattered. Not until the Second Manassas campaign was the superiority of speed and agility over mass and clumsiness definitely demonstrated. There, with a much smaller force, Jackson ran rings around several Union army corps and drove Pope into confused and wrathful helplessness. He used his foot cavalry again at Chancellorsville and with it ruined Hooker's campaign. But there Jackson was killed, and his foot cavalry died with him.

The question arises why Jackson, so magnificent in the Valley, at Second Manassas and at Chancellorsville, turned in only indifferent performances at Gaines's Mill and Cedar Mountain, and failed miserably in the pursuit of McClellan on the Peninsula. The usual explanation is that he worked best as an independent commander, and to a certain extent this probably is true. The main reason, however, could have been that, wherever he was successful, he had an opportunity to use speed and agility. In the Valley he was confronted by a splintered bulldozer and slapped down all its pieces in turn, giving them no time to unite against him. At Antietam it was speed that enabled him to join Lee at a crucial hour; at Second Manassas he made it chase him and shatter itself against his defenses, and at Chancellorsville he stopped the bulldozer in its tracks. On the other hand, at Fredericksburg his defense was competent but not outstanding, while at Cedar Mountain, where speed was a matter of secondary importance, he became a mediocre commander. On the Peninsula, where speed was impossible, he turned in a lamentable performance.

Why Lee let the foot cavalry die at Chancellorsville is another speculation which arouses curiosity. Perhaps it was because no other general could have instilled into the troops the same fiery *élan* that inspired them under Jackson's leadership, or it may be that Lee did not have enough faith in another general to let him try. At any rate, foot cavalry would have lost much of its value in the last two war years, because its usefulness depended on open country. During the Wilderness campaign rapid movements were difficult, and became more so during the siege that followed.

Jackson's performance in battle ranged all the way from excellent to bad. Had all of them been equal to his actions when he was at his best, he would have outshone every army commander of his era. As it is, he still ranks very high and fully deserves the praise and admiration accorded him.

C. Joseph E. Johnston

"Allow me to introduce to you old Joe," wrote a private in Johnston's army. "Fancy a man about fifty years old, rather small . . . with an open and honest countenance and a keen . . . eye that seemed to read your very inmost thoughts. . . . |He is| the very picture of a general."[9]

But Johnston was not only a general by outward appearances, he was a general all the way through. Before throwing in his lot with the Confederacy, he had been quartermaster general in the United States Army and had demonstrated unusual ability in the Mexican War. General Scott was so anxious to keep him in the Northern ranks that, after being refused by Johnston himself, he pleaded with his wife, promising that her husband would never be disturbed. When she, too, turned a deaf ear to his arguments, Scott made one more attempt at persuasion. "Then let him leave our army," he sighed, "but do not let him join theirs."[10] It was as fine a compliment as anyone could wish for.

Scott's forebodings that Johnston was an opponent to be reckoned with, were borne out by future events. But the old general knew Johnston's weaknesses also, two of which were outstanding. One was his supersensitiveness, which contributed to his continuous conflict with President Davis, much to the detriment of their common goal; the other was his tendency to expose himself recklessly in battles. "He . . . has an unfortunate knack of getting himself shot in nearly every engagement," Scott commented.[11] Johnston was first wounded in the Seminole War,[12] then twice again in Mexico during the fighting at Cerro Gordo,[13] and received not less than three wounds in the attack at Chapultepec.[14]

This unfortunate knack of being hit followed him into the Civil War, and at Fair Oaks, early in 1862, where he is said to have already carried eleven wounds,[15] he was again so seriously hurt that he was not able to take the field for two years.

Johnston has often been pictured as a purely defensive fighter, but this contention does not stand up on close examination. He fought defensively whenever he faced superior forces, such as during the Atlanta campaign or in the Valley against Patterson, or when he occupied a strong defensive position like the one at Manassas. He was quite willing to take the offensive, however, when the odds were more favorable, as they were at Fair Oaks and in the concluding stages of the Vicksburg campaign. While Grant was transferring his army across the Mississippi at Bruinsburg, Johnston urged Pemberton to attack the Union army with his entire force before it could gain a firm foothold on the eastern shore. Pemberton disobeyed the order and thereby opened the path for Grant's victory.

On the Peninsula Johnston had shown his combativeness by proposing to pull in all the scattered detachments from the Carolinas and other places and meet the enemy in open battle. He believed that a victory near Richmond would leave McClellan in a precarious position, and was ready to risk the safety of the eastern seaports to gain this end. Davis and Lee vetoed his proposal; nevertheless, it showed that Johnston could think along aggressive lines, whenever he saw what looked to him like a promising opportunity.

The 1864 campaign showed Johnston's high talents at their best. Skillfully drawing Sherman toward Atlanta, he imposed on his opponent a long and vulnerable line of communications, while he himself had an almost impregnable fortress at his back. The Southern author Thomas Cooper De Leon was right when he observed that "[Johnston] was great enough to resist the opportunities for glorious battle, to offer himself to the condemnation of the unthinking masses, so as to insure the safety of Confederate life."[16] His valor, so most objective critics agree, was of a rare kind—unselfish and patriotic.[17]

Just when Johnston's carefully worked-out strategy was about to pay off, he was dimissed, but his military career was not at an end. During the last weeks of the war he was reinstated and required to defend a cause which already was lost. He accepted the command uncomplainingly and went on fighting. Stronger forces pushed him back, but did not defeat him. He was the one leading Confederate general who, handicapped though he was by Davis' unreasoning hostility, went through the entire war without losing a battle. Grant told Sherman that Johnston was "about the only general on the [Confederate] side whom he feared."[18] Sherman's undisguised relief when he heard of Johnston's discharge[19] shows that he shared Grant's belief. With less hard luck and greater facility to get along with Jefferson Davis, Johnston might have rivaled Lee in fame, if not in popularity, outside his army.

D. James Longstreet

LEE is reported to have said that it took three shots of canister to arouse Longstreet, but that once he was aroused, he was terrific. No better thumbnail sketch of Longstreet has ever been drawn.

The man who was to become Lee's "war horse" got off to a slow start. As a major he had been a paymaster in the United States Army, and he had aspired to the same position in the Confederacy. Being denied this request, he fought at First Manassas and on the Peninsula without distinguishing himself, although he discharged his duties satisfactorily.

His first opportunity came at Second Manassas, where he dared to disagree with Lee. The commanding general wanted to attack as soon as Longstreet had taken position beside Jackson, who up to this time had held out against a large portion of the Union army. Longstreet pointed out that Fitz John Porter's corps was on the Confederate right flank, and that another corps was coming up behind him; under these conditions it would be dangerous to advance and risk a full-fledged battle. Lee saw the point, and somewhat reluctantly postponed the attack till the next day.

Twenty-four hours later Longstreet was ordered by Lee to rush help to the hard-pressed Jackson, against whose weakening defenses Porter's regulars were being hurled. Longstreet, figuring correctly that it would take too long for his infantry to reach Jackson, ignored Lee's order; instead he let go with his artillery, which caught Porter in the flank, breaking up the attack. Then, with the quick eye of the gifted tactician that he was, Longstreet delivered his delayed counterstroke and forced Pope into an inglorious retreat.

Second Manassas was shortly followed by Antietam. More cautious than his chief, Longstreet had disapproved the Maryland campaign, convinced that it could never result in a decisive victory, while it might end in a catastrophe—which it almost did. Yet he fought with superb courage and held the center of the Confederate front against overpowering odds; he himself served a gun, after its crew had been killed. It was here that Lee conferred on him the title of "Old Warhorse," which probably was worth more to his lieutenant than a dozen citations. Here too he earned Taylor's encomium, that there never was any doubt about the security of a position if Longstreet held it.

Longstreet's role in the Gettysburg campaign has been the subject of heated debates. To an objective observer it would seem Longstreet was right in insisting that Lee should remain on the defensive, but wrong in giving him only sulking and halfhearted support after the battle had been joined.

The supreme chance for Longstreet came in the battle of Chickamauga. Again it was his quick eye that perceived the break in the Union front, and he drove into it with impetuosity, turning the fight into a Federal rout. It was his great misfortune that, because of Bragg's stubborn and shortsighted attitude, the Confederates were not allowed to reap the full fruits of their victory. To Longstreet it was a cruel premonition come true. It was he who had persuaded Lee to let him reinforce Bragg, and when he received permission to do so, he vowed that he would not risk the life of a single one of his soldiers unless he were allowed to exploit any victory to the point of destroying the enemy.[20] Now the very thing he had feared had happened. Disheartened and at loggerheads with his commander, Longstreet failed to protect the backdoor to Chattanooga, and thereby loosened the hold on the town, which the Confederates had gained at such a heavy cost.

The next months brought the hero of Chickamauga little honor. His pursuit of Burnside was languid, his attack on Knoxville ill-advised and poorly executed.

Seriously wounded in the Wilderness when victory appeared in sight, Longstreet did not resume his duties until late in 1864. He was then put in charge of the defenses north of the James, and was in time to save Richmond, outguessing the Federal General Godfrey Weitzel by blocking the Williamsburg road. It was a feat that deserves much greater emphasis than has usually been accorded it.

At Appomattox Longstreet still held his head up proudly, nor had his sense of humor left him. When General George Armstrong Custer demanded his surrender and threatened to renew hostilities while Lee and Grant were in conference, Longstreet calmly turned to his staff. "Colonel Manning," he said, "please order General |Bushrod R.| Johnson|'s| . . . division to the front and General Pickett's division . . . to . . . Gordon's left." Abashed, Custer withdrew. He had not thought that the Confederates still had such large forces at their command. As he passed out of hearing, Longstreet chuckled. The divisions of Johnson and Picket had been out of existence since the battle of Five Forks.[21]

This episode perhaps explains better than anything else the steadying influence Longstreet exerted on his troops, and why Lee always felt pleased and strengthened by his presence.

All that stood between Longstreet and a higher pedestal in the Hall of Fame was his commanding general's incompetence at Chickamauga and a misdirected bullet in the Wilderness.

E. P. G. T. BEAUREGARD

PIERRE G. T. BEAUREGARD was one of the most colorful figures of
the Civil War. His career as a general had its ups and downs, but
neither of the two was always due to his own doings.

His first up, the conquest of Fort Sumter, was cheaply bought;
his second, the victory of First Manassas, although well earned,
was no outstanding military achievement.

Then came his first down, the battle of Shiloh. Its loss was and
still is being blamed on Beauregard by many critics, who maintain
that he could have thrown Grant into Tennessee by a final thrust
at sundown. This accusation is unwarranted. By the time Beauregard had used up his reserves, many of his half-starved men were
feasting in Federal camps and completely out of hand. Moreover,
Lew Wallace with 5,000 Union troops had come close to the battlefield and menaced the rear of the Southern army. That he was going to be recalled before he could strike was something Beauregard
could not foresee. The adverse commentators also ignore a message
from a supposedly reliable source to the effect that Buell's relief
army was not marching toward Pittsburg Landing, but away from
it, so that a renewal of the battle on the following day would do as
well.[22] The blame for not trying that last thrust rests on hindsight
and therefore lacks validity.

What Beauregard should be blamed for was not that he failed
to make the attack, but that he wasted so much manpower and
time in assaulting the Hornet's Nest, into which Prentiss' division
had retreated in the early morning hours. Its capture was not
worth the sacrifices required, because this thicket, while forming

an impregnable natural fortress, also served as a prison for Prentiss' men, who could not break out without sustaining the same losses the Confederates suffered in storming against it over open fields. The spot that Beauregard should have tried to wrest from the Federals was not Prentiss' stronghold, but the Landing which, in Beauregard's hands, would have prevented Buell from crossing the river. Prentiss' surrender would have followed as a matter of course.

But not all the guilt for the Hornet's Nest blunder should be put on Beauregard's shoulders. The attack had been inaugurated by Albert Sidney Johnston, Beauregard's superior, who was killed at 2:30 P.M. Beauregard received the sad news soon after 3 P.M.[23] and it would have taken considerable time to disengage the troops and transfer them to the Landing. Furthermore, many of them were then out of ammunition.[24] Nevertheless, Beauregard should at least have made an effort to get larger forces to the Landing, which was the Achilles heel of the Federal position. Nothing in his writings indicate that this idea occurred to him, not even after he learned at 3 P.M. that David Stuart's Union brigade, which had been holding the outer defenses of the Landing, had finally been beaten back.[25] Now was the time to eliminate Stuart completely. Prentiss could have been contained where he was with just enough troops to neutralize him. But Beauregard probably still was enmeshed in the doctrine that an advancing army must destroy all obstacles in its rear, which was the principle on which Johnston had acted while in command.

After Shiloh poor health removed Beauregard from the picture for a time. In 1863 he conducted the defenses of Charleston creditably, but his great hour came in the spring of 1864, when he held Petersburg, the key to Richmond, with a handful of men against two Union corps of veterans. It was here that he rose to the greatest height he attained in his army career, displaying skill, boldness and shrewd tactics.

For three days the fate of the Confederacy lay with Beauregard, and he saved it from imminent ruin. This feat alone, even disregarding his other commendable services, entitles him to a place of honor among the leading generals of the war.

F. Braxton Bragg

When Bragg was a young lieutenant commanding a company, he once had to double as post quartermaster. As such he declined, day after day, to fill the requisitions that he had made on himself as commander, and as commander he insisted just as strongly that the requisitions be filled. "Mr. Bragg," exclaimed his superior officer, when he heard of these inter-ego squabbles, "you have quarreled with every officer of the army, and now you are [even] quarreling with yourself."[26]

Small wonder that no one in the Southern army liked Bragg. He had one champion, however—Jefferson Davis. Perhaps he saw in Bragg a replica of his own irritable disposition.

Bragg had the good fortune to gain the limelight at an early age, and without any special effort of his own. In the battle of Buena Vista his battery had played a prominent part, and the order of his superior officer, "A little more grapeshot, Captain Bragg,"[27] became a byword in military and journalistic circles. Nevertheless, Bragg's skill and courage on this occasion are undisputed, and caused him to be brevetted lieutenant colonel.

In the battle of Shiloh, on the sixth and seventh of April, 1862, Bragg was at least partially responsible for the one-day's delay that allowed Buell's Union army to rescue Grant in the nick of time. "Our troops were under arms at an early hour on the 3rd . . . , and preparations were of the slightest," wrote General Beauregard, who was second in command, "[but] Bragg's corps did not quit [their camp] until so late that afternoon that none of it reached Monterey, twelve miles away, until the next morning at 8:30, and one division . . . was not there until late on the 4th. . . . Hardee's corps ... could have easily reached its destination early enough ... had not General Bragg interposed his authority to check its advance."[28] Colonel Jordan, then adjutant general of the Confederate Army, complained that "the really inexplicable tardiness with which Bragg's corps was moved, ... caused the arrival of the army ... twenty-four hours later than was intended."[29] These twenty-four hours might well have spelled the difference between defeat and victory.

In the battle Bragg commanded the advance corps and almost mutinied—at least so he claimed later—against Beauregard's countermanding order to halt the last-hour attack against Grant, which already had begun. If this was true, his attitude did more honor to his combativeness than to his judgment. Being in the front line, far from headquarters, he should have surmised that Beauregard had weighty reasons to rescind his original order.

Shortly after the battle of Shiloh Bragg assumed command of the Army of Tennessee, and beat the Union General Buell in a race to Chattanooga. From there he started a campaign to free Tennessee and Kentucky from the Northern invaders. He might have achieved fame had he outrun Buell to Louisville, and not foolishly stopped to help install a new governor. Again his dilatoriness at a critical time ruined a campaign that had held promise of success.

Opposing Rosecrans at Murfreesboro a few weeks later, Bragg made a good start, but on the second day ordered his right corps to make a foredoomed assault, against which the corps commander had vehemently, but vainly, protested.[30] The resulting slaughter sickened even the victors and made Bragg an object of contempt among civilians. Shortly after the battle he met a countryman in a butternut suit. The general asked him if he belonged to Bragg's army. "Bragg's army?" was the reply. "He's got none; he shot half of them in Kentucky, and the other half got killed at Murfreesboro."[31]

Colonel D. Urquhart, a member of Bragg's staff, some twenty years later still recalled the retreat from Murfreesboro with angry disgust. "By this time," he wrote, "General Bragg's corps commanders, as well as their subordinates down to the regimented rank and file, scarcely concealed their want of confidence in him. ... He invited from his corps, division and brigade commanders an expression of their opinion on that point, and their replies, while affirming their admiration for his personal courage, devotion to duty and ability as an organizer, practically confessed that his army had lost confidence to such an extent in his capacity for chief commander as wholly to impair his further usefulness."[32]

It is doubtful that such politely worded contempt has any parallel in American history, and it passes understanding that a commander, after having been repudiated by both his officers and men, should not have immediately resigned.

Retiring beyond Chattanooga, Bragg found himself surrounded by scattered Union forces. Whether this situation had been brought about by his own shrewd reckoning or, as one of his corps commanders maintained, he was bewildered by it, is debatable.[33] Certain it is that he had several opportunities to deal Rosecrans a hard blow, and missed them all. He could have thrown his whole force on General Thomas L. Crittenden's corps and crushed it, or he could have lured General Thomas into MacLemore's Cove by offering a token resistance; he did neither, and then had to fight the reunited Union Army under much less favorable conditions.

If Bragg had profited from what he had witnessed at Shiloh, he could have atoned for bungling the Kentucky campaign. He was not responsible for Johnston's and Beauregard's poor tactics in wasting their strength by attacking the Hornet's Nest, but at Chickamauga it was he who committed the identical blunder. Foolishly he wore himself out against Thomas instead of pinning him down and trying to capture the fleeing Federals with the bulk of his army, as Longstreet and Forrest had begged him in vain to do.[34] "His vanguard," Oates wrote, "could have entered Chattanooga with Thomas's rearguard"; but nothing was done, and even on the next day, when Chattanooga still was a bedlam of confusion, the only order that came from Bragg was to gather up the arms on the battlefield.[35]

Bragg had some more bungling up his sleeve before he was relieved of his command. After the battle of Chickamauga he invested Chattanooga and had the garrison starving; if he had kept a tight ring around the city, it had to surrender. Yet, hard as it is to believe, he left one gate open, and one was as good as twenty. Neither he nor Longstreet, with whom he was scarcely on speaking terms, personally visited the vital Wauhatchie Valley and its gate, Brown's Ferry, where the valiant Colonel Oates with only 250 men was desperately crying for reinforcements.[36] Through this opening streamed masses of men in blue, and the siege was raised. Then, as a crowning piece of foolhardiness, Bragg sent Longstreet's corps away, and in his weakened position fell an easy prey to Grant.

While Chattanooga was still under siege, Jefferson Davis had asked all generals who were serving under Bragg for their opinion of him, and did so in his presence. Their opinion was what it had been before——that they would rather do without him. But Davis stood by his favorite, and as a reward for his mismanagement took him to Richmond and made him his chief of staff; even Lee had to report to him. In his new position he was no more useful than he had been in the field, but since all messages between Lee and Beauregard had to go through him, they were needlessly delayed, much to the detriment of the Southern cause.

If there is one commanding general who had a greater right than Bragg to be called the evil spirit of the Confederacy, his name has been withheld from the knowledge of later generations.

Acknowledgments,
List of Works Consulted,
and Notes

Acknowledgments

*

GRATEFUL acknowledgment is herewith made to the publishers and authors who gave me permission to quote from their copyrighted books. These are designated by an asterisk* in the list of works consulted.

I am also greatly indebted for help from:

Miss Mary Elizabeth Massey, who kindly acquainted me with the results of some of her recent research;

Joseph L. Eisendrath, for tracing and checking many obscure references;

Dr. Norman N. Franke, for helping me on some aspects of the medical embargo;

Dr. Bell Irvin Wiley, for advice on some facets of the Confederate Congress.

Many thanks for preparing the manuscript are extended to:

Mrs. Veronica Carroll

Mrs. Lucille Cherney

Mrs. Mel Holtz

Miss Eva Arlene Meng

Miss Christine Sarantakis

Mrs. William Wadenpohl

List of Works Consulted

*

Abbott, John S., *History of the Civil War in America*, 1863.

Alexander, E. P., *The American Civil War*, Siegler, Hill and Company, London, 1908.

Annals of the War, Philadelphia Weekly Times, 1879.

Badeau, Adam, *Military History of Ulysses S. Grant*, D. Appleton and Company, New York, 1867-1881.

*Ballad, Colin R., *The Military Genius of Abraham Lincoln*, Oxford University Press, Inc., New York, n.d.

Battles and Leaders of the Civil War, edited by R. U. Johnson and C. C. Buel, The Century Company, New York, 1887-1888.

*Beale, H. K., "The Diary of Edward Bates, 1839-1866," *Annual Report of the American Historical Association*, 1930.

Blaine, James Gillespie, *Twenty Years of Congress*, Henry Bill Publishing Company, Norwich, Conn., 1884.

Bradford, Gamaliel, *Union Portraits*, Houghton, Mifflin Company, Boston, 1916.

Brooks, Noah, *Washington in Lincoln's Time*, Rinehart and Company, Inc., New York, 1958.

Browne, Junius H., *Four Years in Secession*, O. D. Case and Co., Hartford, 1865.

*Bruce, Robert V., *Lincoln and the Tools of War*, Bobbs-Merrill Company, Inc., New York, 1956.

Campbell, James Havelock, *McClellan*, Neale Publishing Company, New York, 1916.

Chandler, Zachariah, *Life, The* (Detroit) *Post and Tribune*, 1880.

Chemical and Engineering News.

*Chesnut, Mary Boykin, *Diary from Dixie*, D. Appleton and Company, New York, 1905.

Chittenden, L. E., *Recollections of President Lincoln and His Administration*, Harper and Brothers, New York, 1891.

Civil War History Magazine, State University of Iowa.

Confederate States Medical and Surgical Journal.

*Cunningham, H. H., *Doctors in Gray*, Louisiana State University Press, Baton Rouge, 1958.

Cutting, Elizabeth, *Jefferson Davis, Political Soldier*, Dodd, Mead & Co., New York, 1930.

Davis, Jefferson, *Rise and Fall of the Confederate Government*, D. Appleton & Co., New York, 1912.

Davis, Varina J., *A Memoir*, by his wife, Bedford Co., 1890.

*Dennett, Tyler, editor, "Lincoln and the Civil War." In *Diaries and Letters of John Hay*, Dodd, Mead and Company, New York, 1939.

*Donald, David, editor, *Inside Lincoln's Cabinet: The Civil War Diaries of Salmon P. Chase*, Longmans, Green and Company, Inc., New York, 1954.

Doubleday, Abner, *Forts Sumter and Moultrie*, Harper & Bros., New York, 1875.

Eisenschiml, Otto, *Why the Civil War*, The Bobbs-Merrill Company, Inc., Indianapolis, 1958.

———, *Why Was Lincoln Murdered?* Grosset and Dunlap, New York, 1957.

———, *The Story of Shiloh*, The Civil War Round Table, Chicago, 1946.

*———, *The Celebrated Case of Fitz John Porter*, The Bobbs-Merrill Company, Inc., Indianapolis, 1950.

*———, editor, *Vermont General*, Devin-Adair Company, New York, 1960.

*——— and E. B. Long, *As Luck Would Have It*, The Bobbs-Merrill Company, Inc., Indianapolis, 1948.

*——— and Ralph Newman, *Eyewitness* [*The American Iliad*], Grosset and Dunlap, Inc., New York, 1956.

Encyclopedia of American History.

Fish, Carl R., *The American Civil War*, Longmans, Green and Company, New York, 1937.

Fiske, John, *The Mississippi Valley in the Civil War*, Houghton, Mifflin Company, Boston, 1901.

*Fletcher, R. S., *The History of Oberlin College*, Oberlin College, Oberlin, Ohio, 1943.

Franke, Norman H., *Pharmaceutical Conditions and Drug Supply in the Confederacy*, American Institute of the History of Pharmacy, University of Wisconsin.

*Freeman, Douglas Southall, *Robert E. Lee*, 4 vols., Charles Scribner's Sons, New York, 1935.

*———, *Lee's Lieutenants*, 3 vols., Charles Scribner's Sons, New York, 1942-1944.

*——— and Grady McWhiney, editors, *Lee's Confidential Dispatches to Jefferson Davis*, G. P. Putnam's Sons, New York, 1957.

*Govan, Gilbert and James Livingood, *A Different Valor*, Bobbs-Merrill Company, Inc., New York, 1956.

Grant, Ulysses S., *Personal Memoirs*, Longmans, Green and Company, New York, 1954.

Greenbie, Marjorie Barstow, *My Dear Lady*, Wittlesey House, New York, 1940.

*———, Sydney and Marjorie Barstow, *Anna Ella Carroll and Abraham Lincoln*, Traversity Press, Penobscot, Me., 1959.

Gresham, Otto, *The Greenbacks*, The Book Press Company, Chicago, 1927.

Hassler, Warren W., Jr., *General George B. McClellan*, Louisiana State University Press, Baton Rouge, 1957.

*Henry, Robert Selph, *"First with the Most" Forrest*, The Bobbs-Merrill Company, Inc., Indianapolis, 1944.

Herndon, William, *Lincoln*, 3 vols., Bedford Co., Chicago, 1889.

Holtzman, Robert S., *Stormy Ben Butler*, Macmillan Company, New York, 1954.

*Horan, James D., *Confederate Agent*, Crown Publishers, Inc., New York, 1954.

Johnston, Joseph E., *Narrative of Military Operations*, D. Appleton and Company, New York, 1874.

*Jones, Katharine M., *Heroines of Dixie*, Bobbs-Merrill Company, Inc., New York, 1935.

*Jones, Virgil Carrington, *Gray Ghosts and Rebel Raiders*, Henry Holt and Company, Inc., New York, 1956.

Journal of the Illinois Historical Society.

Lee, Fitzhugh, *General Lee*, Chapman and Hill, Ltd., London, 1895.

*Lincoln, Abraham, *The Collected Works*, 9 vols., Rutgers University Press, New Brunswick, N. J., 1953.

Long, A. L., *Memoirs of Robert E. Lee*, J. M. Stoddard and Company, 1886.

Longstreet, James, *From Manassas to Appomattox*, J. P. Lippincott Company, Philadelphia, 1895.

*Lonn, Ella, *Salt as a Factor in the Confederacy*, Neale Publishing Company, New York, 1933.

Lossing, B. J., *Pictorial History of the Civil War*, T. Belknap, Hartford, 1868.

Mahan, A., *A Critical History of the Late American War*, A. S. Barnes & Co., New York, 1877.

*Massey, Mary Elizabeth, *Ersatz in the Confederacy*, University of South Carolina Press, 1952.

*McCartney, Clarence E., *Little Mac*, Dorrance and Company, Philadelphia, 1940.

McClellan, George B., *McClellan's Own Story*, Charles L. Webster Company, New York, 1887.

McCulloch, Hugh, *Men and Measures of Half a Century*, Charles Scribner's Sons, New York, 1888.

Medical Life.

*Monaghan, Jay, *Diplomat in Carpet Slippers*, Bobbs-Merrill Company, Inc., New York, 1945.

Morse, John T., *Abraham Lincoln*. In *American Statesmen* Series, 2 vols., Houghton, Mifflin Co., New York, 1893.

New York Tribune.

Nicolay, John George, *Outbreak of the Rebellion*, Charles Scribner's Sons, New York, 1881.

—— and John Hay, *Abraham Lincoln, A History,* The Century Co., New York, 1890.

Oates, William C., *The War between the Union and the Confederacy,* Neale Publishing Company, New York, 1905.

Official Records.

*Owsley, Frank L. and Harriet C., *King Cotton Diplomacy*, University of Chicago Press, 1931.

*Pease, T. C. and J. G. Randall, editors, *The Diary of Orville Hickman Browning, 1850-1864,* Illinois State Historical Library, 1925.

Philadelphia *Weekly Times.*

Photographic History of the Civil War, Review of Reviews Company, 1912.

Pollard, Edward A., *The Lost Cause,* 1866.

Poore, Ben P., *The Life and Public Services of Ambrose E. Burnside,* J. A. and R. A. Reid, Providence, R. I., 1882.

Randall, James G., *Lincoln, the President*, Dodd, Mead and Company, New York, 1945.

——, *Constitutional Problems under Lincoln*, University of Illinois Press, Urbana, Ill., 1951.

*Rhodes, James Ford, *History of the United States, 1850-1896*, 8 vols., Macmillan Company, New York, 1920.

Rice, Allen Thorndike, editor, *Reminiscences of Abraham Lincoln by Distinguished Men of His Time*, North American Publishing Company, New York, 1886.

Riddle, Albert Gallatin, *Recollections of War Times*, 1895.

Russell, William H., *My Diary—North and South,* T. O. H. P. Burnham, 1863.

*Sandburg, Carl, *Abraham Lincoln: The War Years*, Harcourt, Brace and Company, Inc., 1939.

Schiller, Friedrich von, *Wallenstein.*

*Schurz, Carl, *Reminiscences*, Doubleday and Company, Inc., New York, 1917.

Seward, Frederick W., *Reminiscences of a War-Time Statesman and Diplomat*, J. P. Putnam's Sons, New York, 1916.

Sheridan, Philip H., *Personal Memoirs*, Charles L. Webster, New York, 1888.

Sherman, W. T., *Personal Memoirs*, Charles L. Webster Company, New York, 1891.

Strode, Hudson, *Jefferson Davis, Confederate President*, Harcourt, Brace and Company, New York, 1959.

*Tate, Allan, *Jefferson Davis, His Rise and Fall*, G. P. Putnam's Sons, New York, 1929.

Taylor, Richard, *Destruction and Reconstruction*, D. Appleton and Company, New York, 1879.

Townsend, E. D., *Anecdotes of the Civil War*, D. Appleton and Company, New York, 1883.

*Turner, George Edgar, *Victory Rides the Rails*, Bobbs-Merrill Company, Inc., New York, 1953.

*Vandiver, Frank E., *Mighty Stonewall*, McGraw-Hill Book Company, Inc., New York, 1957.

*———, *Ploughshares into Swords: Josiah Gorgas and Confederate Ordnance*, University of Texas Press, Austin, Tex., 1952.

*Welles, Gideon, *Diary*, Houghton, Mifflin Company, Boston, 1911.

*Wiley, Bell Irvin, *The Life of Johnny Reb,* The Bobbs-Merrill Company, Inc., Indianapolis, 1943.

Williams, Kenneth P., *Lincoln Finds a General*, Macmillan Company, New York, 1949.

Wise, Jennings C., *The Long Arm of Lee*, J. B. Bell Company, Inc., Lynchburg, Va., 1915.

*Younger, Edward, editor, *The Diary of Robert Garlick Kean*, Oxford University Press, Inc., New York, 1957.

*

INVITATION

[1] Sherman, *Memoirs*, I, 204.
[2] Bradford, *Union Portraits*, 94.
[3] Chandler, *Life*, 187-188, 218.
[4] Riddle, *Recollections*, 308.
[5] Rice, *Reminiscences*, 478.

BOOK 1

CHAPTER 1

[1] Abbott, *History of the Civil War*.
[2] Schurz, *Reminiscences*, II, 229.
[3] Beale, *Bates Diary*, IV, 182.
[4] Nicolay and Hay, *Abraham Lincoln*, IV, 368.
[5] Owsley, *King Cotton Diplomacy*, 251.
[6] *Encyclopedia of American History*.
[7] Owsley, 252.
[8] *Ibid.*, 285.
[9] Beale, *Bates Diary*, IV, 427.
[10] Welles, *Dairy*, I, 174.
[11] Owsley, 59.
[12] Monaghan, *Diplomat in Carpet Slippers*, 81-82.
[13] *Ibid.*, 118.
[14] Davis, *Rise and Fall*, II, 10.
[15] Eisenschiml and Long, *As Luck Would Have It*, chapter VI.
[16] Owsley, 575.
[17] Seward, *Reminiscences*, 213.
[18] Younger, *Inside the Confederate Government*, 51.
[19] Monaghan, 22.

[20] Russell, *Diary*, 40.

[21] *Ibid.*, 43.

[22] *Ibid.*, 60-61.

[23] *Ibid.*, 62.

[24] *Ibid.*, 381.

[25] *Ibid.*, 381-382.

[26] Monaghan, 230-231.

[27] *Battles and Leaders of the Civil War*, II, 705.

[28] Ernest E. East in *Journal of the Illinois Historical Society*, Spring, 1959; p. 116.

[29] Monaghan, 229, 233.

[30] *Ibid.*, 155-157.

[31] *Ibid.*, 288.

[32] *Ibid.*, 155.

[33] *Ibid.*, 289.

[34] Owsley, 307.

[35] *Ibid.*, 309-312.

[36] Monaghan, 223.

[37] Seward, *Reminiscences*, 218.

[38] Owsley, 574.

CHAPTER 2

[1] Dennett, *Diaries and Letters of John Hay*, 11.

[2] Nicolay and Hay, IV, 369.

[3] *Ibid.*, 368-369.

[4] *Ibid.*, 301.

[5] *Ibid.*, 302.

[6] *Ibid.*, 301-303.

[7] Taylor, *Destruction and Reconstruction*, 118.

[8] Sherman, *Memoirs*, I, 416.

[9] Townsend, *Anecdotes*, 55.

[10] *Ibid.*, 262.

[11] Beale, *Bates Diary*, 183-184.

[12] *Ibid.*, 184.

[13] *Ibid.*, 296.

[14] McClellan's *Own Story*, 101.

[15] *Ibid.*, 489.

[16] Nicolay and Hay, IV, 164-165. Quoted in Eisenschiml, *Why the Civil War?*, 130.

[17] Russell, *Diary*, 432.

[18] Letter from McClellan to Halleck, Sept. 11, 1862. *Official Records,* vol. XIX, part 2, 280.

[19] Letter from Halleck to McClellan, Sept. 13, 1862. *Ibid.,* 280.

[20] Beale, *Bates Diary,* IV, 183.

[21] Donald, *Inside Lincoln's Cabinet,* 125.

[22] Mahan, *Critical History,* 188. Statement by Heintzelman to Dr. Mahan.

[23] *Battles and Leaders,* II, 603. Lee had less than 40,000 effectives at that time, and his army was short of equipment and ammunition.

[24] Welles, *Diary,* I, 439.

[25] *Ibid.,* 439.

[26] Lincoln, *Works.* Lincoln to McClellan, June 28, 1862.

CHAPTER 3

[1] Fletcher, *History of Oberlin College,* 472. "There never was any doubt about Mahan's high moral principles, his sincerity, his devotion to truth . . . [but] he was egotistical, overbearing, would brook no opposition or criticism."

[2] Mahan, 122.

[3] *Ibid.,* 122.

[4] *Ibid.,* 122.

[5] Sherman, II, 162.

[6] Mahan, 125.

[7] *Ibid.,* 12-13.

[8] *Ibid.,* 4.

[9] *Ibid.,* 4.

[10] *Ibid.,* 19-20.

[11] *Ibid.,* 24.

[12] *Ibid.,* 25-26.

[13] *Ibid.,* 25.

[14] *Ibid.,* 26.

[15] *Battles and Leaders,* I, 182.

[16] *Ibid.,* 130.

[17] Mahan, 27-28.

[18] McClellan's *Own Story,* 53.

[19] *Battles and Leaders,* I, 172.

[20] Mahan, 33.

[21] *Ibid.,* 85.

[22] *Ibid.,* 80.

[23] *Ibid.,* 81.

[24] *Ibid.,* 81.

[25] *Ibid.,* 100.

[26] *Ibid.*, 231.
[27] *Ibid.*, 230.
[28] *Ibid.*, 233.
[29] *Ibid.*, 239-240.
[30] *Ibid.*, 240-241.
[31] *Ibid.*, 241.
[32] *Ibid.*, 242-243.
[33] *Ibid.*, 233.
[34] *Ibid.*, 233.
[35] *Ibid.*, 5, 234.
[36] *Ibid.*, 234.
[37] *Ibid.*, 234.
[38] *Ibid.*, 235.
[39] *Ibid.*, 235.
[40] *Ibid.*, 235.
[41] *Ibid.*, 236.
[42] *Official Records*, XVIII, 819. Quoted in Freeman's *Lee's Lieutenants*, II, 467.
[43] Freeman, *R. E. Lee*, II, 439.
[44] *Ibid.*, 478.
[45] Oates, *War between the Union and the Confederacy*, 175.
[46] Mahan, 236.
[47] *Ibid.*, 237.
[48] *Ibid.*, 237.
[49] *Ibid.*, 239.
[50] *Ibid.*, 258.
[51] *Ibid.*, 259. Also Freeman's *R. E. Lee*, II, 502.
[52] Lossing, *Pictorial History*, III, 127.
[53] Mahan, 259.
[54] *Ibid.*, 259-260.
[55] Chandler, *Life*, 219.
[56] Mahan, 253.
[57] *Battles and Leaders*, III, 444, 458.
[58] *Ibid.*, III, 456.
[59] Taylor, *Destruction and Reconstruction*, 153.
[60] *Ibid*, 205.
[61] *Ibid.*, 192.
[62] Mahan, 254.
[63] *Ibid.*, 255.
[64] *Ibid.*, 340.
[65] *Ibid.*, 341.
[66] *Battles and Leaders*, IV, 2 ff.
[67] Freeman, *R. E. Lee*, I, 609-611.

[68] Long, *Lee Memoirs,* 139-140.

[69] *Ibid.,* 144.

[70] Mahan, 354.

[71] *Ibid.,* 355.

[72] *Ibid.,* 355.

[73] *Ibid.,* 360.

[74] *Official Records,* XXXIII, 1282. Also Freeman and McWhiney, *Lee's Dispatches,* 159-160.

[75] *Lee's Dispatches,* 174.

[76] *Battles and Leaders,* IV, 195-196.

[77] *Ibid.,* IV, 103.

[78] Mahan, 361-362.

[79] *Ibid.,* 362.

[80] A good map to illustrate Mahan's plan may be found in Freeman, *R. E. Lee,* III, 299.

[81] *Lee's Dispatches,* 7.

[82] Mahan, 382-383.

[83] *Battles and Leaders,* IV, 281.

[84] *Mahan,* 413.

[85] Sherman, II, 164. Also Grant *Memoirs,* II, 359.

[86] Mahan, 440 ff.

[87] *Ibid.,* 440.

[88] *Ibid.,* 443.

[89] *Ibid.,* 446-447.

[90] *Ibid.,* 447.

[91] *Battles and Leaders,* IV, 259.

[92] *Ibid.,* 698.

[93] Govan and Livingood, *A Different Valor,* 359.

[94] Mahan, 451.

[95] Fitzhugh Lee, *General Lee,* 372.

[96] Mahan, 440.

[97] Johnston, *Narrative,* 372.

[98] Govan and Livingood, 347.

[99] Mahan, 350.

[100] Fletcher, *History of Oberlin College,* 472.

[101] Greenbie, *Anna Ella Carroll and Abraham Lincoln,* 278-279.

[102] *Ibid.,* 303-304.

[103] *Ibid.,* 290.

[104] *Ibid.,* 367.

[105] *Battles and Leaders,* I, 399.

[106] Greenbie, 324.

[107] *Ibid.,* 304.

[108] *Battles and Leaders*, IV, 255.

[109] *Ibid.*, III, 39.

[110] Riddle, *Recollections*, 189-191.

[111] Greenbie, *My Dear Lady*, the entire book.

[112] Eisenschiml, *Why the Civil War?*, 140 ff.

[113] Riddle, *Recollections*, 191.

[114] Greenbie, *Anna Ella Carroll and Abraham Lincoln*, 242-243.

[115] *Ibid.*, 243.

[116] Eisenschiml and Long, *As Luck Would Have It*, 199 ff.

CHAPTER 4

[1] Herndon's *Lincoln*, II, 334 ff.

[2] Beale, *Bates Diary*, 218.

[3] *New York Tribune*, Feb. 20, 1862. Quoted in Eisenschiml, *Why Was Lincoln Murdered?* 475-476.

[4] Lincoln, *Works*, Lincoln to McClellan, April 9, 1862.

[5] Morse, *Abraham Lincoln*, II, 55.

[6] Lincoln, *Works*, Lincoln to McClellan, June 1, 1862.

[7] *Ibid.*, June 18, 1862.

[8] McClellan's *Own Story*, 634.

[9] *Ibid.*, 634. The fact was that the horses were suffering from hoof-and-mouth disease, though apparently the sickness was not diagnosed as such.

[10] Welles, *Diary*, I, 183.

[11] *Battles and Leaders*, III, 85.

[12] Rice, *Reminiscences*, 278.

[13] Poore, *Life of Burnside*, 183. Burnside's plan was not approved until November 14.

[14] Herndon's *Lincoln*, III, 512.

[15] Rhodes, *History of the United States*, IV, 294.

[16] *Ibid.*

[17] *Ibid.*

[18] *Annals of the War*, Philadelphia *Weekly Times*, 1879, p. 455.

[19] Welles, *Diary*, I, 367.

[20] *Ibid.*, 368.

[21] *Ibid.*, 364, 368.

[22] *Annals of the War*, 455. Quoted in Eisenschiml and Newman, *Eyewitness* [*The American Iliad*], 505-506.

[23] *Battles and Leaders*, III, 379.

[24] Eisenschiml and Newman, 505.

[25] Sandburg, II, 344.

[26] Eisenschiml, *Vermont General*, 138.

[27] Welles, *Diary*, I, 368.

[28] Nicolay and Hay, VII, 280.

[29] Hay, *Diary*, 67.

[30] *Ibid.*

[31] *Ibid.*

[32] Welles, *Diary*, I, 364.

[33] Grant, *Memoirs*, I, 384.

[34] Donald, *Inside Lincoln's Cabinet*, 100.

[35] *Ibid.*, 107.

[36] *Battles and Leaders*, II, 704.

[37] *Ibid.*, III, 443.

[38] *Ibid.*, III, 453.

[39] Badeau, *Military History of U. S. Grant*, I, 126.

[40] *Ibid.*, 135.

[41] Grant, *Memoirs*, I, 424.

[42] *Ibid.*, 435.

[43] Badeau, I, 140.

[44] Sherman, I, 345.

[45] Badeau, I, 128-129.

[46] Sherman, I, 332.

[47] Badeau, I, 130.

[48] *Ibid.*, I, 183.

[49] *Battles and Leaders*, IV, 93-96.

[50] Welles, *Diary*, I, 531-532.

[51] Sandburg, II, 548.

[52] Lincoln, *Works*, Lincoln to Grant, April 30, 1864.

[53] Grant, *Memoirs*, II, 139.

[54] Lincoln, *Works*, Lincoln to Grant, August 3, 1864.

[55] *Ibid.*, April 30, 1864.

[56] *Ibid.*, June 15, 1864.

[57] *Ibid.*, April 7, 1865.

[58] *Ibid.*, August 3, 1864.

[59] Sherman, II, 166.

CHAPTER 5

[1] Sandburg, II, 60.

[2] Butler was dismissed shortly after the 1864 election.

[3] Welles, *Diary*, 39.

[4] Nicolay, *Outbreak of the Rebellion*, 12.

[5] Lincoln, *Works*, Message to Congress, July 4, 1861.

[6] Welles, *Diary*, I, 85.

[7] *Ibid.*, 86.

[8] *Ibid.*, 84.

[9] *Ibid.*, 84-85.

[10] *Ibid.*, 86.

[11] Blaine, 374.

[12] Donald, *Inside Lincoln's Cabinet*, 105-106.

[13] Welles, *Diary*, II, 190.

[14] *Civil War History Magazine*, June 1958; p. 184.

[15] *Ibid.*, 185.

[16] *Ibid.*, 191.

[17] Oates, 428.

[18] Younger, *Inside the Confederate Government*, 64.

[19] *Ibid.*, 73.

[20] *Ibid.*, 103, 160, 180.

[21] Tate, *Jefferson Davis*, 238.

[22] Pease and Randall, *Diary of Orville Hickman Browning* in *Illinois Historical Collections*, vol. XX, p. 578.

[23] *Ibid.*, 585-586.

[24] Sherman, I, 294.

[25] Pease and Randall, *Browning Diary*, 659.

[26] Welles, *Diary, II*, 139-140.

[27] *Ibid.*, II, 84-85.

[28] Sherman, I, 365.

[29] Lincoln, *Works*, Message to Congress, December 3, 1861.

[30] Davis, *A Memoir*, 550.

[31] Wiley, *Life of Johnnie Reb*, 268.

[32] Lincoln, *Works*, Proclamation, Aug. 16, 1861.

[33] Jones, *Gray Ghosts and Rebel Raiders*, 52.

[34] Sherman, I, 312.

[35] Lossing, III, 40.

[36] Sheridan, *Personal Memoirs*, I, 375.

[37] Davis, *Rise and Fall*, II, 602.

[38] The first reference to this meeting I found in Mary Elizabeth Massey's excellent book, *Ersatz in the Confederacy*, 115.

[39] *Confederate States Medical and Surgical Journal*, 1864; p. 106.

[40] Welles, *Diary*, II, 21.

[41] Jones, *Heroines of Dixie*, 54.

[42] Franke, *Pharmaceutical Conditions and Drug Supply in the Confederacy*, 22.

[43] Massey, *Ersatz*, 116.

Notes

[44] Davis, *A Memoir*, 550.

[45] Jones, *Heroines of Dixie*, 285.

[46] Davis, *Rise and Fall*, II, 5-6.

[47] Franke, *supra*.

[48] Cunningham, *Doctors in Gray*, the whole book.

[49] Massey, *Ersatz*, 115.

[50] Holtzman, *Stormy Ben Butler*, 94.

[51] A brilliant and extensive presentation of this subject will be found in Ella Lonn's *Salt as a Factor in the Confederacy*. For this incident, see p. 13.

[52] *Ibid.*, 226.

[53] Sherman, I, 295.

[54] *Official Records*, Series I, vol. XVII, part 2, 140-141.

[55] *Ibid.*, vol. XV, 898-899.

[56] *Ibid.*, vol. XXXI, 735-736.

[57] Lonn, 148.

[58] *Battles and Leaders*, IV, 423.

[59] *Ibid.*, 478-479.

[60] Taylor, 114.

[61] Lonn, 71, 193.

[62] Massey, *Ersatz*, 63-64.

[63] Lonn, 43-44.

[64] *Ibid.*, 42.

[65] Henry, *First with the Most Forrest*, 368.

Chapter 6

[1] Alexander, *American Civil War*, 53.

[2] Bruce, *Lincoln and the Tools of War*, 101.

[3] *Ibid.*, 112.

[4] *Ibid.*, 212.

[5] Welles, *Diary*, I, 239-240.

[6] *Battles and Leaders*, I, 617.

[7] Bruce, 71.

[8] Welles, I, 506.

[9] McCulloch, *Men and Measures of Half a Century*, 261 ff.

[10] Chittenden, *Recollections*, 239 ff.

[11] Bruce, 224.

[12] *Ibid.*, 216.

[13] *Ibid.*, 224.

[14] *Ibid.*, 224.

[15] *Ibid.*
[16] Lossing, III, 329.
[17] *Battles and Leaders,* IV, 25.
[18] *Ibid.,* II, 6.
[19] *Ibid.,* IV, 628.
[20] Badeau, II, 483.
[21] Welles, I, 397.
[22] Poore, *Life of Burnside,* 238, 240.
[23] Holtzman, 45.
[24] *Ibid.,* 147.
[25] Bruce, 73.

CHAPTER 7

[1] Chittendem, 296.
[2] Fish, *American Civil War,* 430.
[3] Blaine, *Twenty Years in Congress,* 412.
[4] Donald, *Inside Lincoln's Cabinet,* 43.
[5] Chittenden, 308.
[6] *Ibid.,* 307-308.
[7] Welles, II, 63-65.
[8] McCulloch, 187-188.
[9] Rhodes, *History,* IV, 509.
[10] Chittenden, 314.
[11] *Ibid.,* 315.

BOOK II

CHAPTER 8

[1] Davis, *Rise and Fall,* I, 230.
[2] Davis, *A Memoir,* 392.
[3] Welles, I, 376.
[4] *Ibid.*
[5] Chesnut, *Diary from Dixie,* 11.
[6] Lossing, II, 21-22.
[7] *Ibid.* Also *Battles and Leaders,* I, 239.
[8] Govan and Livingood, *A Different Valor,* 98, 101.
[9] Younger, *Diary of R. G. Kean,* 72.

Notes

[10] *Ibid.*

[11] *Ibid.*, 28-29.

[12] *Ibid.*, 31.

[13] *Battles and Leaders*, III, 456.

[14] Long, *Memoirs of Robert E. Lee*, 102.

[15] Pollard, *The Lost Cause*, 133.

[16] Long, *Memoirs*, 103.

[17] Oates, 530.

[18] *Ibid.*, 503 ff.

[19] Otto Gresham, *The Greenbacks*, 158.

[20] Chesnut, *Diary*, July 8, 1863, p. 224.

[21] Oates, 504.

[22] Henry, *First with the Most Forrest*, 44.

[23] Pollard, 659-660.

[24] *Ibid.*, 660.

[25] Oates, 504.

[26] Johnston, *Narrative*, 275.

[27] Davis, *Rise and Fall*, I, 340.

[28] Chesnut, *Diary*, 79.

[29] Freeman and McWhiney, *Lee's Dispatches*, 7.

[30] Hood, *Advance and Retreat*, 153-155.

[31] *Ibid.*, 6.

[32] Vandiver, *Ploughshares into Swords*, 206.

[33] Freeman and McWhiney, *Lee's Dispatches*, 144-145.

[34] *Ibid.*, 192.

[35] Long, 266.

[36] *Ibid.*, 403.

[37] Gresham, *The Greenbacks*, 158.

CHAPTER 9

[1] Davis, *A Memoir*, 160.

[2] *Photographic History of the Civil War*, vol. VI, p. 28.

[3] Davis, *A Memoir*, 160.

[4] Johnston, *Narrative*, 422.

[5] Davis, *A Memoir*, 344.

[6] Owsley, 39.

[7] *Photographic History of the Civil War*, VI, 30.

[8] Owsley, 146.

[9] *Ibid.*, 150.

[10] Tate, *Rise and Fall*, 93.

[11] Strode, *Jefferson Davis*, 14.

[12] Cutting, *Jefferson Davis*, 239.

[13] Tate, *Rise and Fall*, 160.

[14] Lincoln, *Works*, Proclamation, April 19, 1861.

[15] Randall, *Constitutional Problems*, 92.

[16] Donald, *Inside Lincoln's Cabinet*, 49.

[17] Davis, *Rise and Fall*, II, 11.

[18] Eisenschiml and Long, chapter 6.

[19] Owsley, 149.

[20] *Ibid.*, 234.

[21] *Ibid.*, 244.

[22] *Ibid.*, 367.

[23] *Ibid.*, 168, 172.

CHAPTER 10

[1] Eisenschiml and Long, *As Luck Would Have It*, 202-203.

[2] Johnston, *Narrative*, 372.

[3] Horan, *Confederate Agent*, 16. This book gives a good insight into Confederate activities in the North.

[4] Lossing, III, 17-18.

[5] *Ibid.*, 19.

[6] Badeau, III, 11.

[7] *Ibid.*, 12.

[8] *Ibid.*, 15.

[9] Horan, 18.

[10] McCulloch, 182.

[11] Eisenschiml in *Chemical and Engineering News*, Jan. 8, 1951, pp. 110-111. Also Vandiver, 192.

[12] *Chemical and Engineering News*, op. cit.

[13] Vandiver, 146.

[14] Davis, *Rise and Fall*, II, 208.

[15] *Battles and Leaders*, I, 364.

[16] Browne, *Four Years in Secession*, 72.

[17] *Battles and Leaders*, IV, 5; I, 530.

[18] Tate, *Rise and Fall*, II, 209.

[19] *Battles and Leaders*, II, 5.

[20] Welles, I, 247.

[21] *Battles and Leaders*, IV, 67-68.

22 *Ibid.*, 27.

23 *Ibid.*, 383, (Footnote).

24 *Ibid.*, 412.

25 *Ibid.*, I, 630.

26 Nicolay and Hay, IV, 20. Also Doubleday, *Forts Sumter and Moultrie,* 40.

27 *Ibid.*, 76.

28 Sherman, II, 194.

29 Davis, *Rise and Fall*, II, 97.

30 Wise, *Long Arm of Lee*, 181.

31 *Ibid.*, 178 ff.

32 Davis, *Rise and Fall*, II, 424-425.

33 *Ibid.*, 98.

34 *Battles and Leaders*, IV, 63.

35 *Ibid.*, IV, 643.

36 Sherman, II, 199.

37 Vandiver, 250.

38 *Battles and Leaders*, IV, 391.

39 *Medical Life*, 1935, p. 493.

40 Cunningham, *Doctors in Gray*, 137.

41 *Photographic History of the Civil War*, VII, 246.

42 *Ibid.*

43 Owsley, 553. The dispatch was dated December 27, 1864.

CHAPTER 11

1 Davis, *Rise and Fall*, II, 35.

2 *Battles and Leaders*, III, 452. Most likely it was Sherman who suggested the expedition. (Sherman, I, 324).

3 *Battles and Leaders*, IV, 418.

4 *Ibid.*, 627.

5 Lossing, III, 142.

6 Welles, I, 376-377.

7 Johnston, *Narrative*, 265.

8 *Ibid.*, 266-272.

9 *Ibid.*, 267-268.

10 *Ibid.*, 274.

11 Sherman, II, 72.

12 Tate, *Rise and Fall*, 89.

13 Davis, *A Memoir*, 579.

14 *Ibid.*, 587.

BOOK III

Chapter 12

[1] Fiske, *Mississippi Valley*, 147.

[2] Taylor, 149.

[3] Lee, Fitzhugh, *General Lee*, 327.

[4] *Battles and Leaders*, III, 564-565.

[5] Morse, II, 279.

[6] Rice, *Reminiscences*, pp. XLII-XLIII.

[7] Dennett, *Hay Diary*, 176.

[8] Welles, II, 242.

[9] Rice, *Reminiscences*, p. XXVIII.

[10] Sandburg, II, 538.

[11] Grant, II, 105.

[12] Sheridan, *Personal Memoirs*, I, 316.

[13] Grant, II, 90.

[14] *Ibid.*, 99.

[15] Freeman, *R. E. Lee*, III, 459.

[16] Grant, I, 306.

[17] *Ibid.*, I, 340.

[18] *Ibid.*, 347.

Chapter 13

[1] Freeman and McWhiney, *Lee's Dispatches*, 246-247.

[2] *Ibid.*, 282.

[3] *Ibid.*, 283-284.

[4] Freeman, *Lee's Lieutenants*, I, 135.

[5] *Ibid.*, 143.

[6] Davis, *A Memoir*, 316-317. The italics are Mrs. Davis'.

[7] Davis, *Rise and Fall*, II, 122.

[8] See reproduction of map in Freeman, *R. E. Lee*, II, 138 opposite.

[9] Taylor, 86-87.

[10] *Battles and Leaders*, II, 352.

[11] Freeman, *R. E. Lee*, II, 205.

[12] *Ibid.*, 249.

[13] Taylor, 86.

[14] Freeman, *Lee's Lieutenants*, I, 589.

[15] Long, 179-180.

[16] *Ibid.*, 180.

[17] Oates, 127.

[18] Long, map opposite p. 171.

[19] Vandiver, *Mighty Stonewall*, 274.

[20] *Ibid.*, 345.

[21] *Ibid.*, 377.

[22] *Ibid.*, 458, 464.

[23] Long, 194.

[24] Eisenschiml and Newman, 388.

[25] Long, 256.

[26] Freeman, *R. E. Lee*, III, 196.

[27] Lee, Fitzhugh, 330-331.

[28] Freeman, *R. E. Lee*, III, 291.

[29] Vandiver, 460.

[30] Freeman, *R. E. Lee*, III, 382.

[31] Freeman, *Lee's Lieutenants*, III, 693.

[32] Longstreet, *From Manassas to Appomattox*, 384.

[33] Alexander estimated the number as "fully 90,000." *American Civil War*, 357.

[34] *Ibid.*, 358.

[35] *Ibid.*

[36] *Battles and Leaders*, III, 247.

[37] *Ibid.*

[38] Davis, *Rise and Fall*, II, 152.

[39] *Battles and Leaders*, III, 246. Also *Annals of the Civil War*, 417.

[40] *Ibid.*, III, 293. Also *Annals*, 422.

[41] *Annals*, 417.

[42] *Battles and Leaders*, III, 293.

[43] Lee, Fitzhugh, 289.

[44] Davis, *Rise and Fall*, II, 447.

[45] *Annals*, 421.

[46] Freeman, *R. E. Lee*, III, 81.

[47] Long, 269.

[48] *Ibid.*, 278-279.

Chapter 14

[1] Eisenschiml and Newman, 303. (This quotation is not verbatim.)

[2] McCulloch, 275.

[3] Chittenden, 364.

[4] Sherman, II, 117.

[5] Chandler, *Life*, 246.

[6] Eisenschiml and Newman, 302.

[7] *Ibid.*, 531.

[8] McCartney, *Little Mac*, 222.

[9] Eisenschiml, *Celebrated Case of Fitz John Porter*, 24.

[10] Told to the writer by Porter's daughter.

[11] Eisenschiml, *Celebrated Case*.

[12] Schiller, *Wallenstein*, "Von der Parteien Gunst und Hass verwirrt, schwankt sein Characterbild in der Geschichte."

[13] McClellan's *Own Story*, 488.

[14] *Battles and Leaders*, II, 114.

[15] Johnston, *Narrative*, 31.

[16] *Journal of the Illinois State Historical Society*, Autumn 1957, p. 326.

[17] Donald, *Inside Lincoln's Cabinet*, 133-134.

[18] Randall, *Lincoln, the President*, II, 92.

[19] Donald, 240.

[20] Hassler, *General George B. McClellan*, 238-239.

[21] Campbell, *McClellan*, 142.

[22] McClellan's *Own Story*, 424-425.

[23] *Ibid.*, 335, 346.

[24] Williams, *Lincoln Finds A General*, II, 214.

[25] Mahan, 104.

[26] McClellan's *Own Story*, 562.

[27] *Ibid.*, 618.

[28] *Ibid.*, 601.

[29] Freeman, *R. E. Lee*, II, 427.

[30] Turner, *Victory Rides the Rails*, 85.

[31] Randall, *supra*, II, 276-277.

[32] McClellan's *Own Story*, 137.

[33] Welles, I, 120.

[34] Mahan, 144-145.

[35] Lincoln, *Works*, July 14, 1862.

[36] Welles, I, 108-109.

[37] *Ibid.*, XXIX.

[38] *Ibid.*, 180.

[39] Dennett, *Hay Diary*, 166.

[40] Beale, *Bates Diary*, 303-304.

[41] *Ibid.*, 468.

[42] *Battles and Leaders*, II, 281.

[43] Nicolay and Hay, V, 102-103.

[44] Lincoln, *Works*, Lincoln to Halleck, January 1, 1863.

[45] Brooks, *Washington in Lincoln's Time*, 139-140.

[46] *Ibid.*, 140.

[47] Sandburg, II, 430.

[48] Poore, *Life of Burnside*, 44.

[49] *Ibid.*, 119.

[50] *Battles and Leaders*, I, 640-670.

[51] *Ibid.*, 660.

[52] Poore, 154.

[53] *Ibid.*, 155.

[54] *Ibid.*, 162.

[55] James I. Robertson, Jr. in *Civil War History Magazine*, June, 1960.

[56] McClellan's *Own Story*, 604.

[57] *Ibid.*

[58] Poore, *Life of Burnside*, 174.

[59] *Ibid.*, 179-180.

[60] *Ibid.*, 180.

[61] *Ibid.*, 214-215.

[62] Sherman, I, 383.

[63] Dennett, *Hay Diary*, 92.

[64] Poore, *Life of Burnside*, 252-253.

[65] *Ibid.*, 261.

[66] *Ibid.*, 76-88.

[67] Eisenschiml, *Celebrated Case of Fitz John Porter*.

[68] Sandburg, III, 155.

[69] Lee, Fitzhugh, *General Lee*, 221.

CHAPTER 15

[1] Told this writer by one of Forrest's veterans.

[2] Welles, I, 85.

[3] Told to the author by Dr. John Ware of Rome, Georgia.

[4] Oates, 479-480.

[5] Sherman, II, 144.

[6] *Ibid.*, 164.

[7] Oates, 478.

[8] *Ibid.*, 480.

[9] Eisenschiml and Newman, 607.

[10] Govan and Livingood, *A Different Valor*, 27. Also *Mrs. Chestnut's Diary*, 133.

[11] Govan and Livingood, 20.

[12] *Ibid.*, 17.

[13] *Ibid.*, 19.

[14] *Ibid.*, 20.

[15] *Ibid.*, 184.

[16] Eisenschiml and Newman, 618.

[17] *A Different Valor* (Title).

[18] Sherman, I, 356.

[19] *Ibid.*, II, 72.

[20] *Battles and Leaders*, III, 652.

[21] Eisenschiml and Newman, 683-684.

[22] Eisenschiml, *Story of Shiloh*, 43, 46-47.

[23] *Battles and Leaders*, I, 590.

[24] *Ibid.*, 591.

[25] *Ibid.*, 589.

[26] Grant, *Memoirs*, II, 86-87.

[27] Oates, 315. Bragg denied that these were the exact words used (*Battles and Leaders*, III, 604-605).

[28] *Battles and Leaders*, I, 582.

[29] *Ibid.*, I, 596.

[30] Eisenschiml and Newman, 308.

[31] *Battles and Leaders*, III, 609.

[32] *Ibid.*, III, 608.

[33] *Ibid.*, III, 644.

[34] Eisenschiml in *Civil War History Magazine*, March, 1955, p. 208.

[35] Oates, 264. See also Eisenschiml in *Civil War History Magazine*, March, 1955.

[36] Oates, 281.

Index

Index

Index

Index

Index

Index